BATTERSEA AND CLAPHAM IN 50 BUILDINGS

LUCY McMURDO

AMBERLEY

For Monty, who brings such joy into our lives

First published 2025

Amberley Publishing, The Hill, Stroud
Gloucestershire GL5 4EP

www.amberley-books.com

British Library Cataloguing in Publication Data.
A catalogue record for this book is available from the British Library.

ISBN 978 1 3981 2095 2 (print)
ISBN 978 1 3981 2096 9 (ebook)

Typesetting by SJmagic DESIGN SERVICES, India.
Printed in Great Britain.

Appointed GPSR EU Representative: Easy
Access System Europe Oü, 16879218
Address: Mustamäe tee 50, 10621, Tallinn, Estonia
Contact Details: gpsr.requests@easproject.com,
+358 40 500 3575

Contents

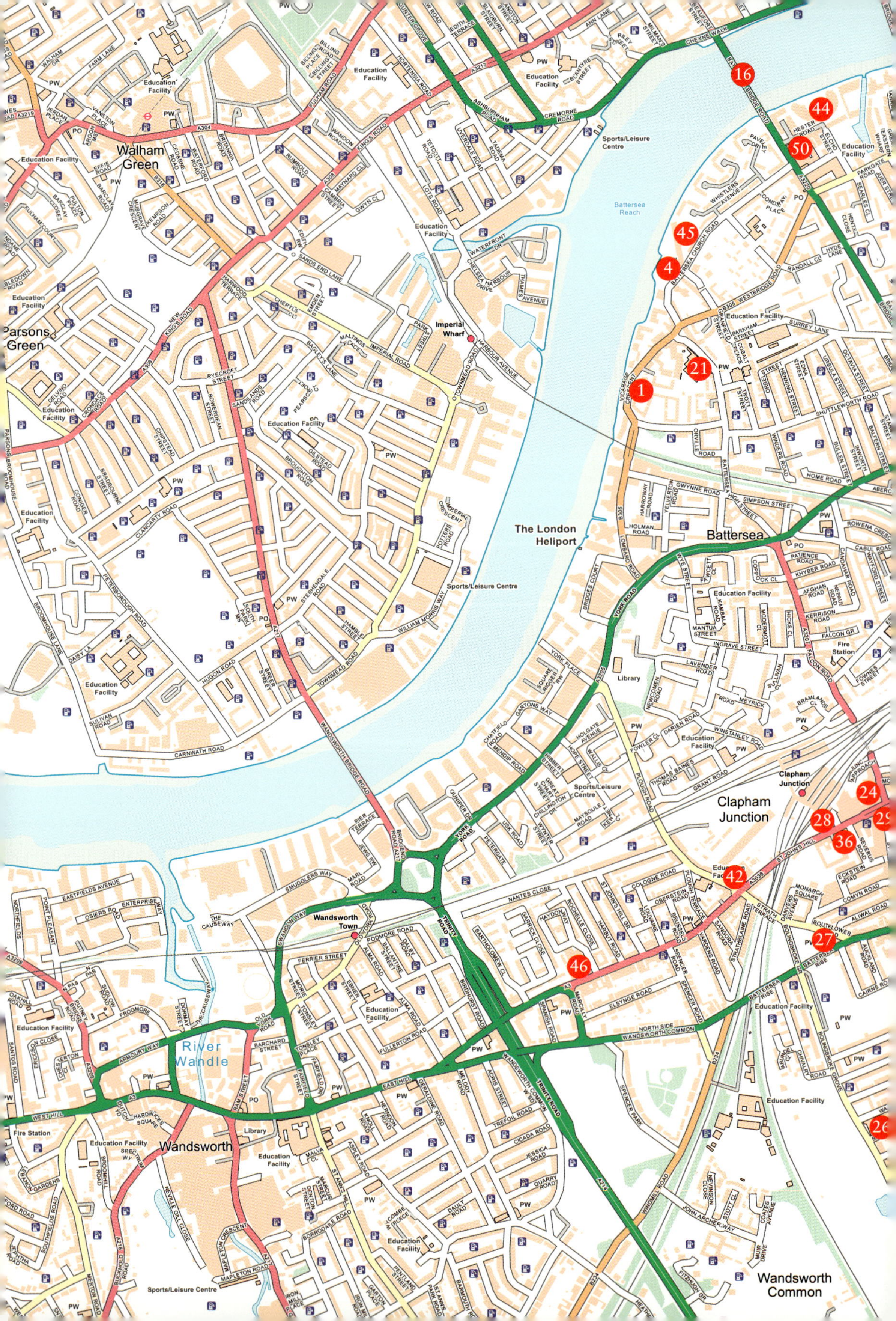

Walham Green
Parsons Green
Imperial Wharf
Battersea Reach
The London Heliport
Battersea
Clapham Junction
Wandsworth Town
River Wandle
Wandsworth
Wandsworth Common
Sports/Leisure Centre
Education Facility
Library
Fire Station
16
44
50
45
4
21
1
24
28
29
36
42
27
46
26

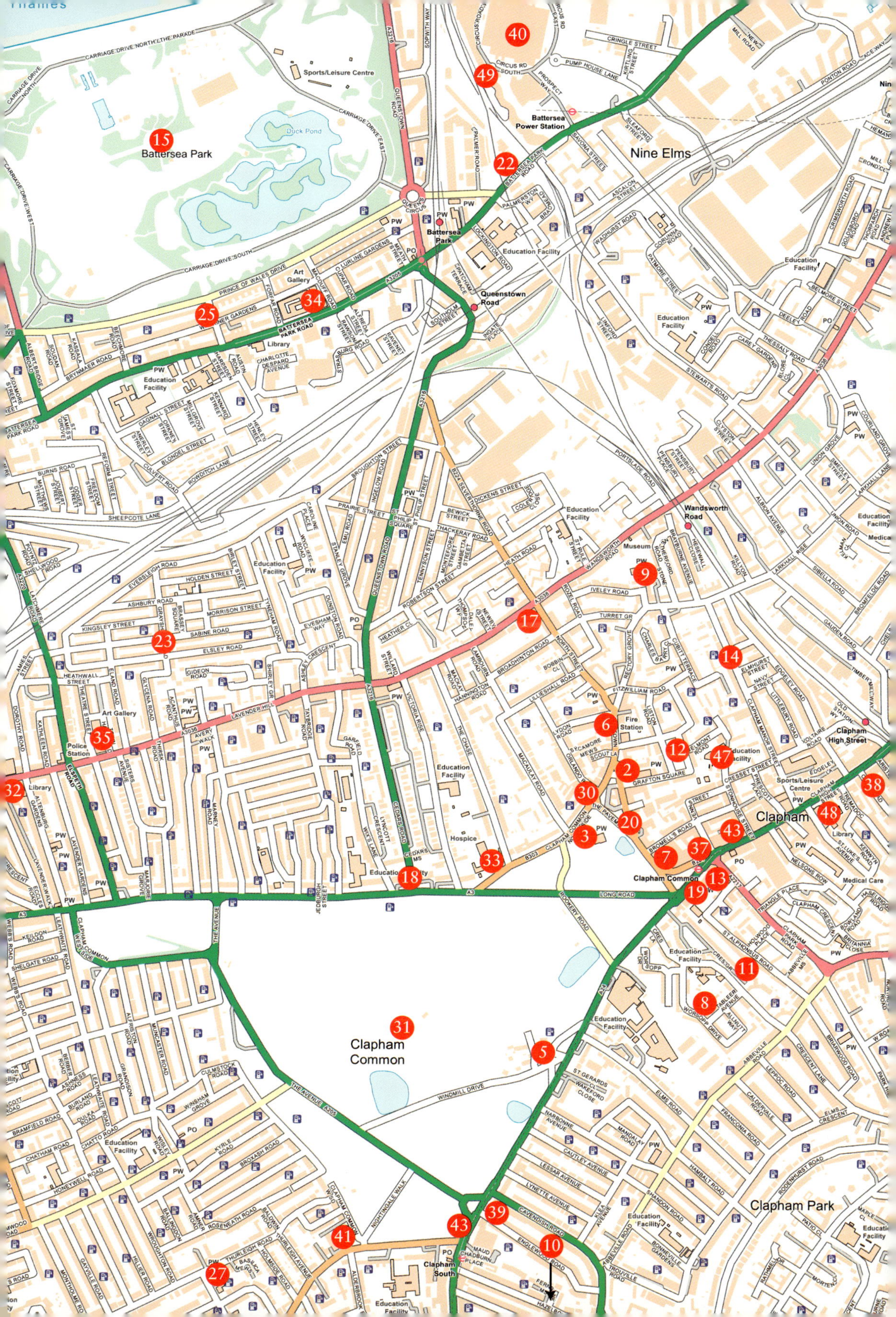

Thames
Battersea Park
15
Duck Pond
Sports/Leisure Centre
Carriage Drive North
Carriage Drive East
Carriage Drive South
Carriage Drive West
Queens Circus
Battersea Park
Battersea Power Station
40
49
22
Nine Elms
Queenstown Road
Prince of Wales Drive
Art Gallery
34
25
Battersea Park Road
Library
Education Facility
Queenstown Road
Wandsworth Road
Lavender Hill
Museum
9
17
14
23
35
Police Station
32
Library
Art Gallery
Fire Station
6
2
12
47
30
20
3
7
37
43
48
38
Clapham
Clapham High Street
Sports/Leisure Centre
Clapham Common
13
19
33
18
Hospice
Long Road
Rookery Road
11
8
31
Clapham Common
5
Windmill Drive
The Avenue
Nightingale Walk
39
43
41
27
10
Clapham South
Clapham Park
Cavendish Road
Medical Care

Key

1. Old Battersea House, No. 30 Vicarage Crescent, SW11
2. Nos 39–43 Old Town, Clapham, SW4
3. Holy Trinity Church, Clapham Common, SW4
4. St Mary's Battersea, Battersea Church Road, SW11
5. The Windmill Inn and Hotel, Clapham Common, South Side, SW4
6. Sycamore House, No. 4 Old Town, SW4
7. The Pavement, Old Town, SW4
8. The Orangery, Worsopp Drive, SW4
9. St Paul's Church, Rectory Grove, SW4
10. Clapham Park, SW4 and SW12
11. Crescent Lane and the Former Headquarters of the Post Office Workers, SW4
12. Grafton Square, SW4
13. St Mary's Church (Our Lady of Victories), Clapham Park Road, SW4
14. Former Clapham General and Provident Dispensary, No. 42 Clapham Manor Street, SW4
15. Battersea Park, Battersea, SW11
16. Battersea Bridge, SW11
17. The Hibbert Almshouses, Nos 715–729 Wandsworth Road, SW8
18. Nos 43-47 and 48–52 Cedars Terrace, Clapham Common North Side, SW4
19. The Alexandra Hotel, Nos 12–16 Clapham Common South Side, SW4
20. Old Fire Station, No. 33 The Pavement, SW4
21. Former Sir Walter St John's Grammar School, Nos 28–40 Battersea High Street, SW11
22. Battersea Dogs and Cats Home, No. 4 Battersea Park Road, SW8
23. The Shaftesbury Park Estate, Battersea, SW11
24. The Falcon, No. 2 St John's Hill, Battersea, SW11
25. No. 7 Alexandra Avenue and Prince of Wales Road, Battersea, SW11
26. Bolingbroke Academy (Former Hospital), Wakehurst Road, Battersea, SW11
27. Victorian Churches: St Mark's and St Luke's
28. Clapham Junction Station, Battersea, SW11
29. Former Arding and Hobbs Department Store, Lavender Hill and St John's Road, SW11
30. The Omnibus Theatre (Former Clapham Library), Clapham Common North Side, SW4
31. Clapham Common Bandstand, SW4
32. Battersea Library and Reference Library, No. 265 Lavender Hill and Altenburg Gardens, SW11
33. Trinity Hospice, Nos 29–32 Clapham Common North Side, SW4
34. Former Battersea Polytechnic Institute, Battersea Park Road, SW11
35. Battersea Arts Centre (Former Battersea Town Hall), Lavender Hill, SW11
36. The Clapham Grand, Nos 21–25 St John's Hill, Battersea, SW11
37. Clapham Common Station and Clock Tower, The Pavement, SW4
38. Former Temperance Billiard Halls, No. 47 Clapham High Street, SW4 and No. 66. Battersea Rise, SW11
39. Former South London Hospital for Women and Children, Clapham Common South Side, SW4
40. Battersea Power Station, Circus Road West, SW11
41. Hightrees House, Nightingale Lane, Clapham Common South Side, SW4
42. Former Granada Cinema, No. 58 St John's Hill, Battersea, SW11
43. Deep Shelters, Clapham Common, SW4
44. Albion Riverside, No. 22 Hester Road, Battersea, SW11
45. The Montevetro Building, No. 112 Battersea Church Road, SW11
46. St John's Therapy Centre, No. 162 St John's Hill, Battersea, SW11
47. Clapham Manor School, Belmont Road, Clapham, SW4
48. Mary Seacole House and The Library Building, Clapham High Street, SW4
49. Battersea Power Station Village: Circus West Village, Prospect Place and Battersea Roof Gardens, SW11
50. The Royal College of Arts Campus, No. 1 Hester Road, Battersea, SW11

Introduction

Battersea and Clapham are two much-loved and popular south-west London suburbs, largely due to their excellent range of facilities, transport, good housing stock and proximity to central London. Both areas have been in existence for hundreds of years but grew dramatically in the nineteenth century as London became a major global industrial centre and its population increased so significantly. They have a lot of similarities: large green and leafy open spaces, Georgian and Victorian terraced housing, centres of entertainment, impressive civic buildings, pubs, and the railway. However, each has its own very distinct personality and history.

Battersea is the older of the two villages. Originally a farming settlement beside the River Thames, it was built around marshland and where river trades were practised. Initially it was centred around the parish church of St Mary (the area leading to Battersea High Street and Battersea Square today) surrounded by fields, but by the late eighteenth century this was changing, and with the rapid rise of manufacturing in London during the 1800s the riverside village was taken over by chemical works, potteries, lime kilns, factories, mills, power stations, wharves and, later, the railway. Almost overnight Battersea's market gardens vanished and its main products – asparagus (sold as Battersea Bundles) and lavender – and its pig-breeding enterprises died out, as did its supply of fruit, vegetables and flowers to the London markets. As farmland disappeared, many new manufacturing jobs were created and the population swelled from a mere 6,600 in 1841 to almost 170,000 by 1901. The newly built industrial sites were soon surrounded by row upon row of terraced houses accommodating the increased workforce and Battersea began to expand southwards towards Clapham. By the end of the 1800s it had become a thriving London suburb renowned throughout the world for its enormous railway intersection, misleadingly called Clapham Junction despite being based in Battersea. The coming of the railway allowed Battersea's residents to travel cheaply and easily into central London. Unfortunately, as the district became ever more popular it became incredibly overcrowded and many of its homes were deemed to be unsanitary and turned into slums. This led to the introduction of new affordable homes by philanthropists such as Peabody and Guinness and resulted in the construction of housing estates like Shaftesbury Park, built between the river and Lavender Hill, to provide reasonably priced and solid housing for the working classes.

Battersea Vestry, the forerunner of Battersea Borough Council (formed in 1900), took great pride in its neighbourhood and commissioned the top architects of the age to build its civic and academic establishments. E. W. Mountford, James Gibson, John Oldrid Scott, William Butterfield, Robert Austin and Joseph Bazalgette all contributed to the wonderful assortment of architecture that survives today in Battersea's streets and is a tribute to the Victorian age. Many religious buildings were designed by local and famous architects and Battersea's department store, Arding and Hobbs, opened at Clapham Junction in 1888.

In 1871 the Temporary Home for Lost and Starving Dogs moved south of the river from Holloway and changed its name to Battersea Dogs Home. Nowadays, the animal rescue centre is renowned throughout the world for its care of dogs and cats and its site close to Battersea Power Station has grown significantly to include a veterinary hospital, an assessment wing and a kennel centre.

Battersea established itself as a major centre for recreation and entertainment when Queen Victoria opened Battersea Park in 1858. This 200-acre green space (formerly Battersea Fields, which had long been an established meeting place for duels) provided both locals and Londoners with wonderful parkland away from the capital's industry and polluted streets where they could attend concerts at the bandstand, enjoy nature and take part in sport and recreation. Almost a century later, in 1951, the park hosted the Festival Pleasure Gardens during the Festival of Britain, and visitors to the park today still enjoy the Fountain Lake and Flower Gardens that were created at that time. The 1930s saw the arrival of cinema in Battersea with films shown in a most opulent building on St John's Hill. The Granada Theatre was a 'super cinema' run by the Granada chain and films were played to packed audiences for many years until competition from television finally brought about its demise.

Nowadays, Battersea is the most vibrant of London's suburbs and the area continues to grow. Most recently, after years of closure, Battersea Power Station has been resurrected as a shopping mall and the land around it is being established as a brand-new 'mini-city', with its own Underground station and some striking housing and office developments designed by top international architects. The power station has been one of the capital's most globally recognised buildings since the 1970s when the English rock band Pink Floyd used it as a backdrop on its album cover *Animals* which featured an image of an inflatable pig flying between its chimneys. Londoners were astonished to see the pig unexpectedly let loose from its moorings, drifting down the Thames towards Heathrow Airport!

Since the end of the twentieth century Battersea's waterfront and skyline have changed out of all recognition, and little remains today to remind us of its industrial past. Rank Hovis McDougall's prominent waterfront flour mill has been replaced by luxurious modern apartments, railway arches are now occupied by bars, cafés

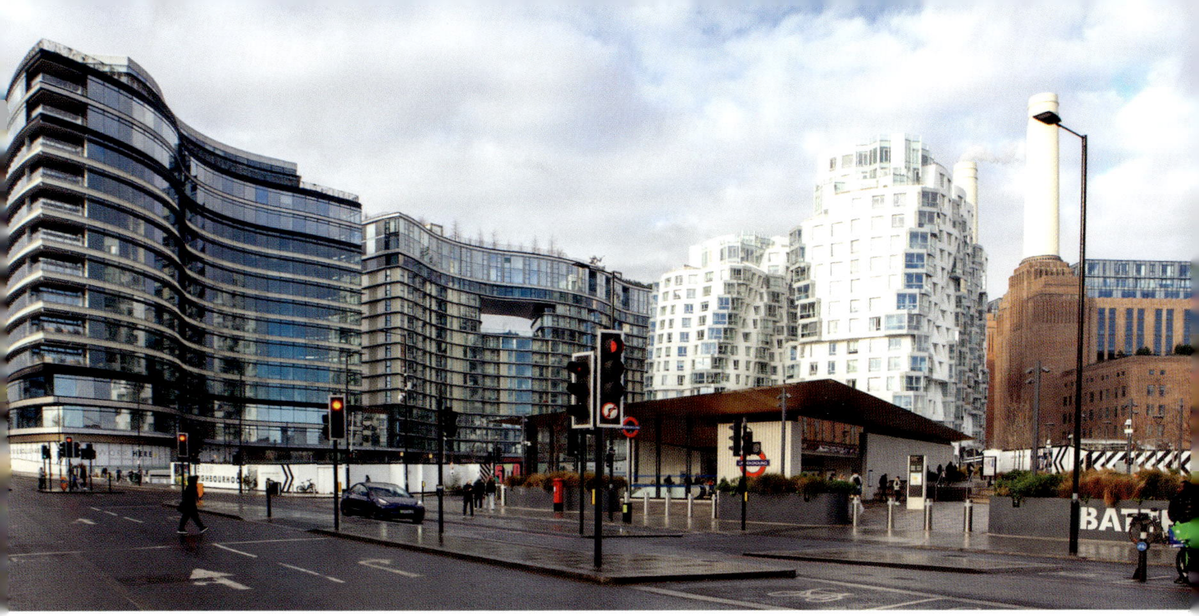

Battersea Roof Gardens, Prospect Place, and Battersea Power Station.

and restaurants, and the Royal College of Art has established a large campus for itself near Battersea Bridge overlooking the river. The architectural practice of Norman Foster, Baron Foster of Thames Bank, was built on the waterside in 1990, and he subsequently developed Albion Riverside next to his premises in the early 2000s. So, in a matter of only a few decades the land on either side of Battersea Bridge has been filled with offices, apartments, health centres and shops, adapting to twenty-first-century urban living.

Clapham lies south of Battersea and really came to prominence in the late seventeenth and eighteenth centuries when affluent merchants, politicians and the gentry built their country houses here because of its clean air away from the noise, bustle and pollution of the City of London. These new residents built enormous villas and mansions for their families around Clapham Common, moving the heart of Clapham away from its roots in Old Town and its parish church of Holy Trinity in Rectory Grove. By the late 1700s it was obvious that the village needed a larger church and one near to the common. This led to the opening in 1776 of a new and much larger Holy Trinity Church (the earlier Rectory Grove Church changed its name to St Paul's) facing Clapham Common North Side. Parishioners included a group of campaigning men who became known as the Clapham Sect, famous for their efforts to abolish slavery. Today, a plaque with many of their names inscribed sits on the church façade commemorating them and their endeavours.

Nearly all of Clapham's early mansions have disappeared, some divided up into smaller residences whilst others have been replaced by apartment blocks or demolished. However, it is possible to get a feeling for how grand the housing once was when you walk past Royal Trinity Hospice or Cedars Terraces on Clapham Common North Side and see the size of the properties and their grounds. Cedars Terraces, consisting of two blocks of highly ornate terraced housing built in the French Renaissance style, continue to be perhaps Clapham's most iconic buildings.

Throughout the 1800s, streets were laid out and new accommodation built to meet Clapham's expanding population (having increased from 5,000 in 1801 to 54,000 by 1901) designed by eminent architects of the day such as l'Anson, Knowles Sr and Knowles Jr. Initially, the housing was decidedly upmarket (as seen in Thomas Cubitt's development of Clapham Park), but as the century progressed smaller properties appeared, many of them built in rows of red-brick terraces. The nature of the housing changed as thousands of people moved from rural areas to take up employment in the capital, so that by the end of the century many Clapham residents were living in modest two-storey houses and the newly

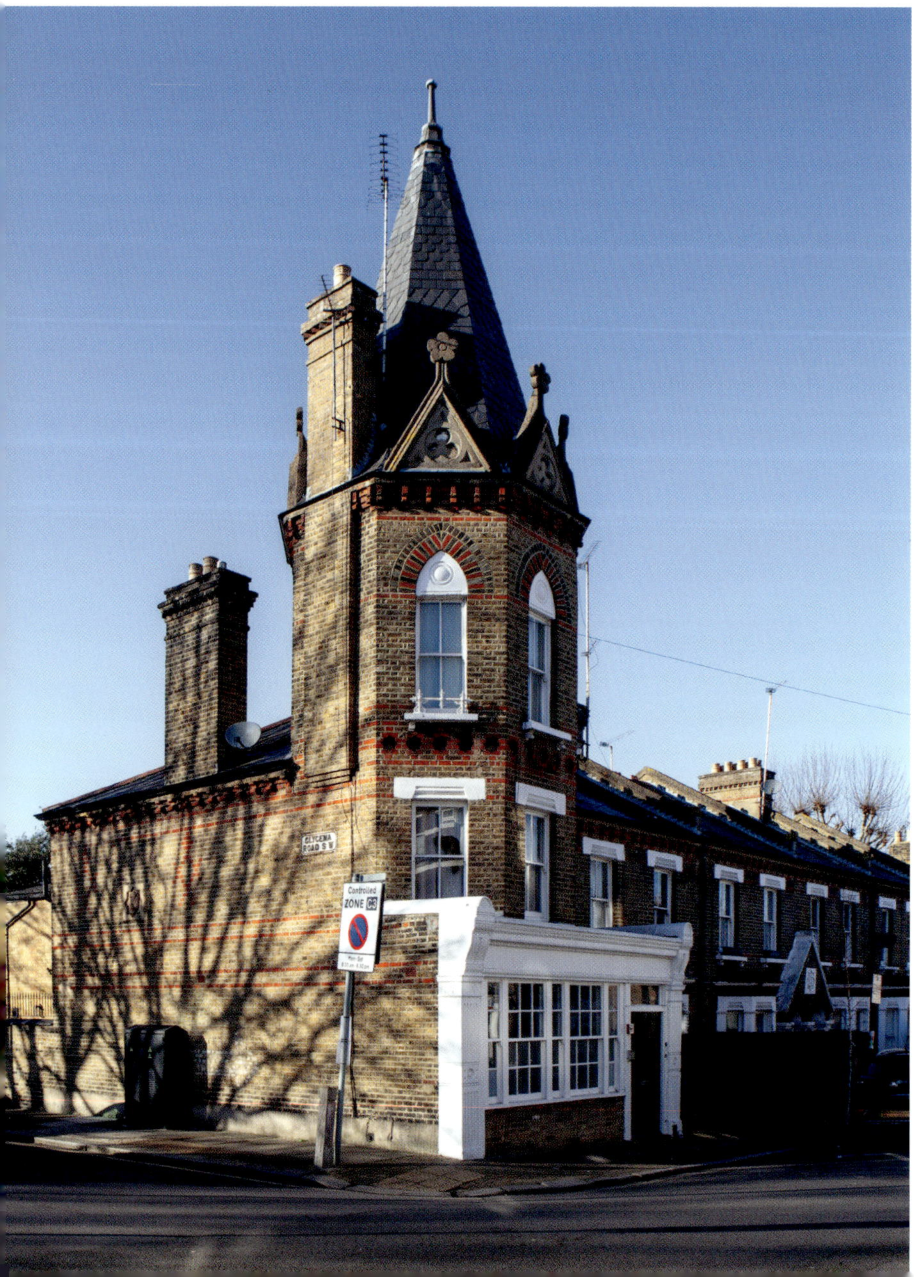

Entrance to Shaftesbury Park Estate.

introduced purpose-built flats and maisonettes. Like much of London, Clapham was damaged by enemy bombing during the Second World War which led to restoration or rebuilding in the 1950s and 1960s and the rise of local authority housing. Development still continues today, but much of the Victorian housing stock remains and is popular with young families who can take advantage of the area's great amenities, its excellent schools, shops, libraries, its theatre and, of course, Clapham Common. With the construction of a new library on Clapham High Street in 2012 (itself a landmark building boasting curves, blocks and terraces), the area has continued to evolve. The former library, now the Omnibus Theatre, is a thriving arts centre and attracts people from far and wide.

Clapham today is well served by its three Northern Line Underground stations as well as the Mildmay Line and National Railway at Clapham High Street. Although not immediately obvious at street level, the circular cement structures next to Clapham's Underground stations lead to tunnels which were built specifically to provide refuge during wartime bombing raids. The tunnels have had several uses since their creation: the provision of accommodation to Britain's first Caribbean immigrants in the 1940s, as archive stores and most recently the setting for a subterranean hydroponic farm.

Unsurprisingly, Clapham has been – and is still – home to many well-known people. Julia Barfield, the designer of the London Eye, is a current resident while Dame Vivienne Westwood lived in Old Town for many years before her death in 2022. In the late seventeenth century the diarist Samuel Pepys lived and died in the home of his colleague and friend William Hewer on Clapham Common. Today the area is awash with Historic England blue plaques, highlighting how many famous names have lived here over the years.

It is obvious that Battersea and Clapham have great and interesting histories and are filled with wonderful architecture. Walking around the streets is always an exhilarating experience with so much to see and architecture to admire. It is no wonder that people choose to live here, inspired by the streetscape, the open spaces and the area's great entertainment, dining and shopping facilities.

How to Use This Book

In accordance with the 50 Buildings series, the buildings appear in chronological order according to the time of their original construction.

Many of the buildings within the book appear on English Heritage's Register of Listed Buildings, a designation that recognises historic and/or architectural significance. This 'listed status' (ranging from the top Grade I, through II* to II) necessitates strict planning rules which helps to prevent essential features of the buildings from being lost, preserving them for future generations.

The map provides identification of each of the buildings by a number that corresponds to the numbers used in the text.

The 50 Buildings

1. Old Battersea House, No. 30 Vicarage Crescent, SW11

One of Battersea's oldest buildings, the house is a substantial mansion facing the River Thames and was originally surrounded by lavender fields and watercress beds. Constructed between 1669 and 1699, the house was allegedly built for Samuel Pett, a naval administrator – and was possibly the work of Christopher Wren, but this is unverified. If Pett was the original owner, it might explain the mathematical instruments and the globe found on the west entrance frieze of Old Battersea House, items often associated with shipbuilding and navigation.

From the 1840s until the early 1920s the house was occupied by an educational establishment but in 1930 Battersea Council bought Old Battersea House and then used some of its spacious grounds to build the St John's housing estate. The council had intended to demolish the building as it had become neglected and was now in need of costly repair.

However, Terrace House, as it was then known, was given a reprieve when art collectors Colonel Charles Stirling and his wife, Wilhelmina, showed interest in renting it and filling the property with their splendid collection of Victorian art. In return for a peppercorn rent they agreed to open the house, thus allowing the public to view their magnificent collection. The collection included not only works of the Pre-Raphaelite artists, but also contained many artworks of husband and wife William and Evelyn de Morgan. Wilhelmina was Evelyn's younger sister and an avid enthusiast of her sibling's drawings and paintings as well as William's pottery and ceramics. Following Charles's death, she liked nothing better than giving tours around the house, some of which were said to have lasted five hours! After Wilhelmina's passing in 1965, the collection was housed in a local library and is now displayed at the De Morgan Foundation in Barnsley.

Old Battersea House was acquired and restored in the 1970s by Michael Forbes, the publishing magnate and founder of the Forbes List. Here he displayed his family's own fine collection of art and frequently entertained members of the

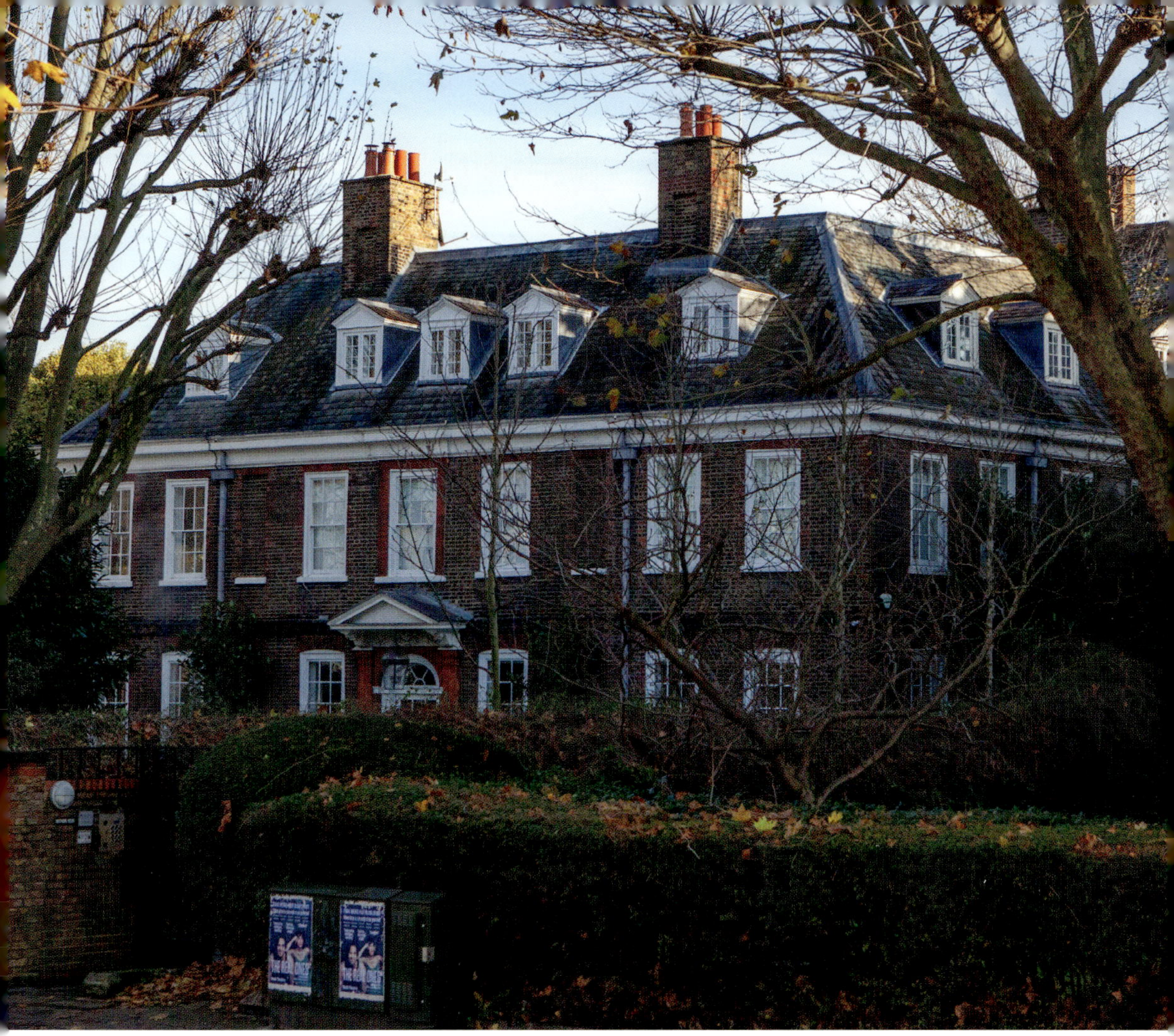

Old Battersea House.

royal family, American presidents and Hollywood stars. Since Forbes sold the property in 2011 the house has remained in private hands.

2. Nos 39–43 Old Town, Clapham, SW4

Old Town became established from the seventeenth century, appealing to affluent City of London residents who wanted more spacious homes and clean air away from the capital. At this time Clapham was quite isolated, being little more than a village in the countryside, and was centred around St Paul's Church on Rectory Grove (see Building 9). Although many of the early houses have long since disappeared, a row of three very fine Queen Anne houses still exist at Nos 39–43 Old Town that date to 1706, built to the designs of Daniel Clarke. These two-storey yellow stock brick houses are sizeable properties with an attic and basement

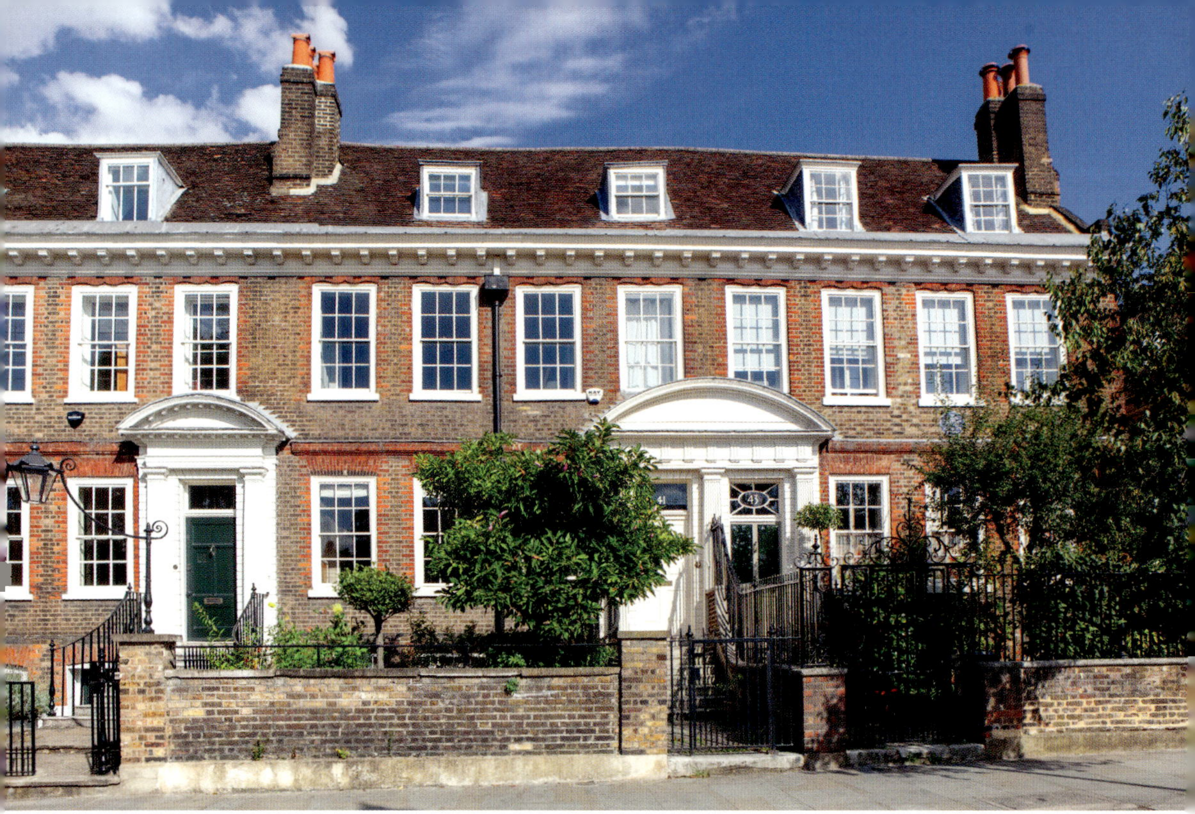

Above: Nos 39–43 Old Town.

Below: Nos 41–43 Old Town.

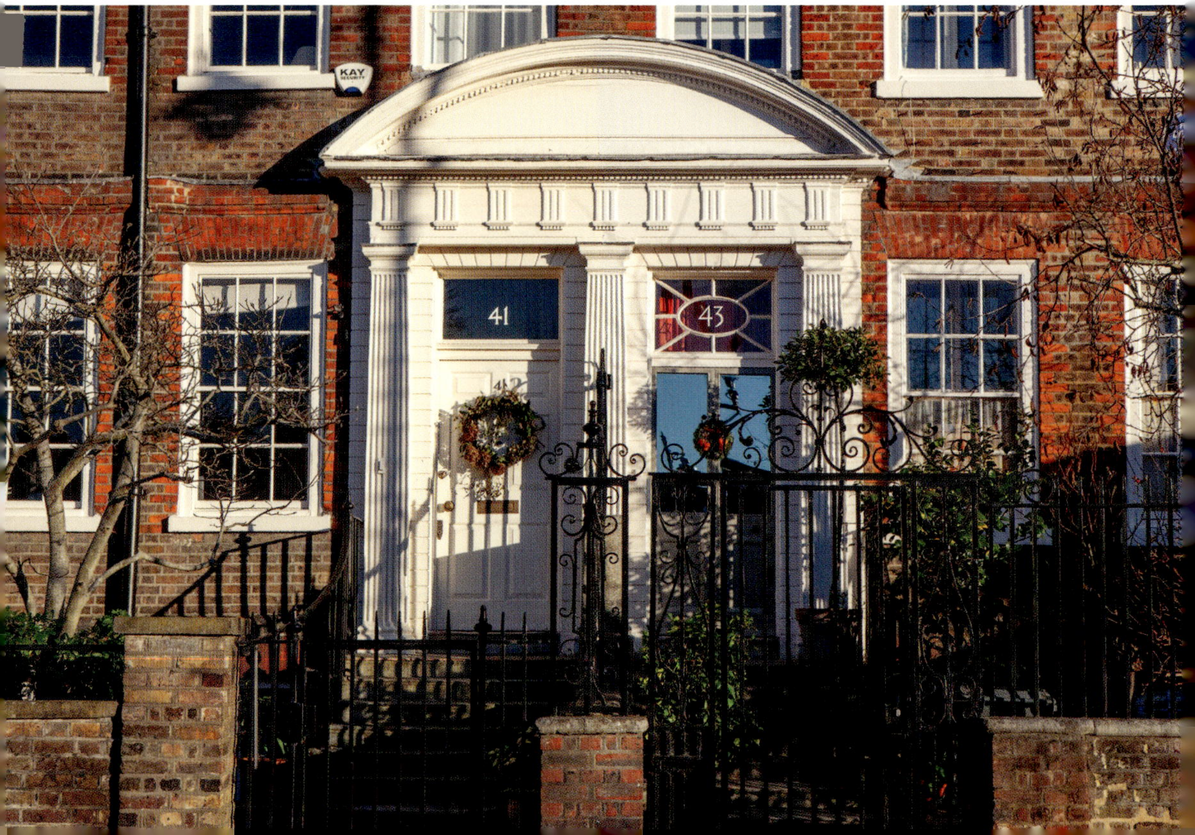

and are easily recognised by their striking doorways which have Doric pilasters and curved wooden pediments.

Between 1876 and 1896 No. 43 was occupied by the Yorkshire architect J. F. Bentley (1839–1902) who had moved to London in the 1850s and set up his own architectural business in 1868. A most successful draughtsman, he was famous not only for his attention to detail but also his ability to ensure that his buildings and contents were designed in total harmony. Bentley was responsible for many church commissions but probably his best-known design was for the magnificent Byzantine-style Roman Catholic Cathedral in Westminster.

3. Holy Trinity Church, Clapham Common, SW4

Located on the north side of Clapham Common close to the Underground station, Holy Trinity Church is one of Clapham's key landmarks. Occupying a large plot, it is surrounded by high trees and is an imposing building in its surroundings despite its simple style. The church opened in 1776 and was designed by Kenton Couse, an architect who worked for the Office of Works. Built as a replacement for the old parish church in Rectory Grove (now too small for the area's growing population), Holy Trinity is a sizeable rectangular building embellished externally by a prominent clock, small tower and portico – the latter was added in 1812 to give shelter to prosperous parishioners alighting from their carriages. Although the church interior has been altered several times during its lifetime, its shape has remained largely unchanged. Holy Trinity is remarkably light inside which contrasts well with its dark wooden Doric columns and galleries. The church is Grade II* listed and Historic England gives as reasons for the designation that it is a 'plain classical church of 1774–6, exemplifying the characteristics of the "preaching box" with original galleries', and for its 'Strong connection with the Clapham Sect, a group active in campaigning for the abolition of the slave trade'.

The Clapham Sect was comprised of an evangelical group of mainly wealthy industrialists, MPs, bankers, government officials, clergymen and writers who held similar moral and religious beliefs. The majority lived around Clapham Common and were worshippers at the church. Determined to abolish slavery and the slave trade, the group worked tirelessly to bring this about, and their efforts were finally rewarded by the passing of the Abolition of Slave Trade Act 1807. Outside the church there are several wall plaques commemorating the sect's members and for its role in the abolition of slavery.

Perhaps the group's best-known member was William Wilberforce who became the face of the Clapham Sect in Parliament, but the campaign's success was as much due to the Thornton family, Charles Grant, Granville Sharp, Henry and John Venn, Zachary Macaulay, Thomas Clarkson, Thomas Babington, James Stephen, John Shore and Mrs Hannah More.

www.holytrinityclapham.org

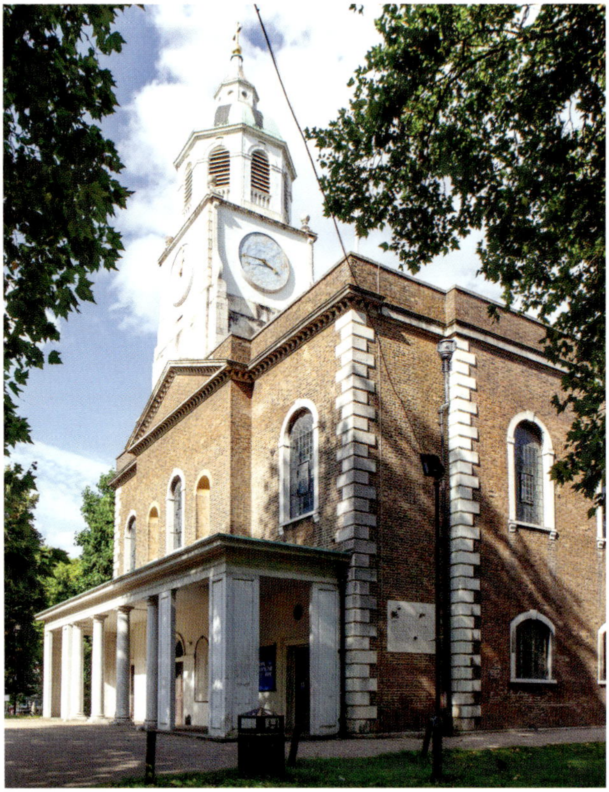

Left: Holy Trinity Church.

Below: Wall plaque commemorating the Clapham Sect's members.

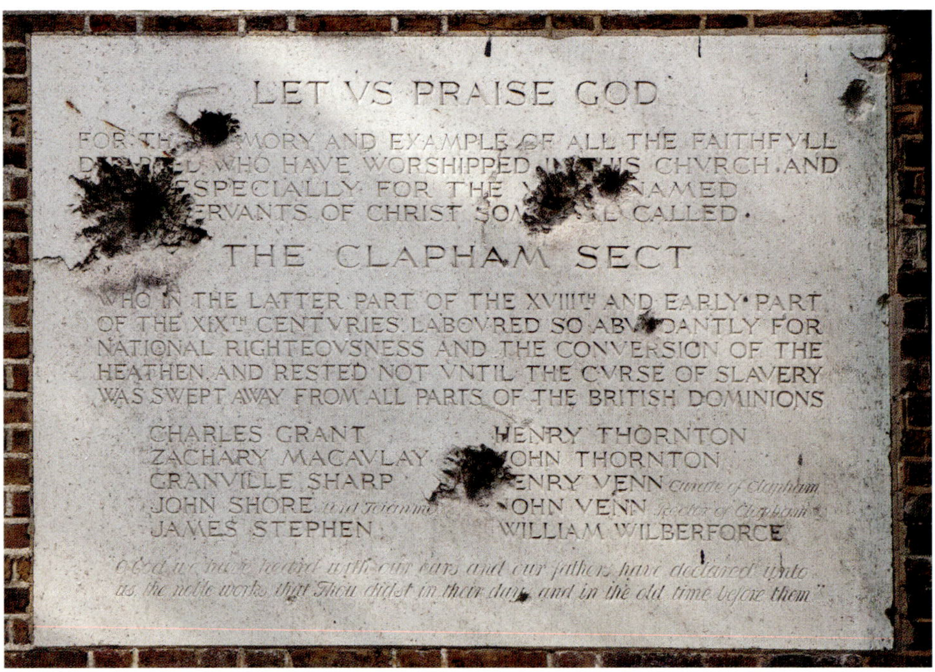

4. St Mary's Battersea, Battersea Church Road, SW11

St Mary's Church has a fabulous location beside the River Thames, directly opposite Chelsea Creek and the former Lots Road Power Station. The present church, designed by local architect Joseph Dixon, dates to 1777 but it is believed that worship took place here from at least AD 800. The church is made of brown brick and stone and has a particularly attractive entrance porch supported by Tuscan columns and a pediment, above which sits a tower, a clock and small spire. It is the oldest of Battersea's churches and is Grade I listed for its historical and architectural merit.

The rectangular interior is light and airy, with a simple flat ceiling from which an elegant chandelier hangs. Upstairs the three galleries are surprisingly large and surrounded by memorial wall plaques. The window at the East end of the church (preserved from an earlier fourteenth-century church on the site) is lit by magnificent medieval painted glass donated to St Mary's in 1631 when Sir John St John became lord of the manor of Battersea. It displays portraits of

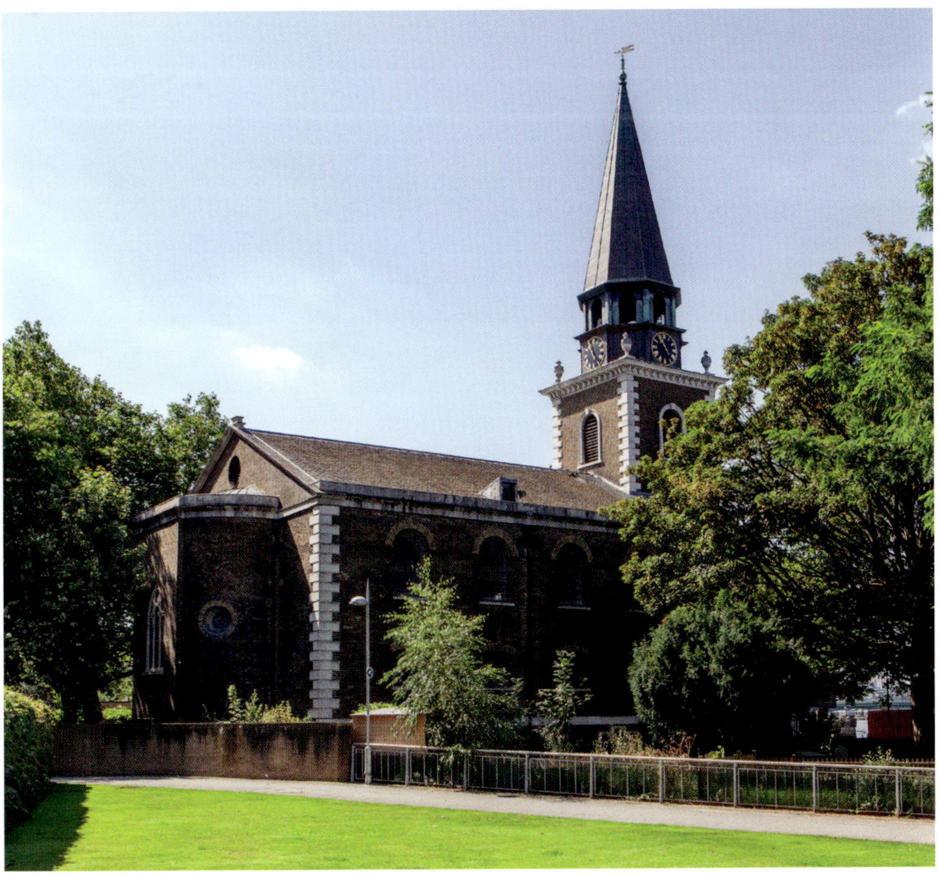

Above and overleaf pages: St Mary's, Battersea.

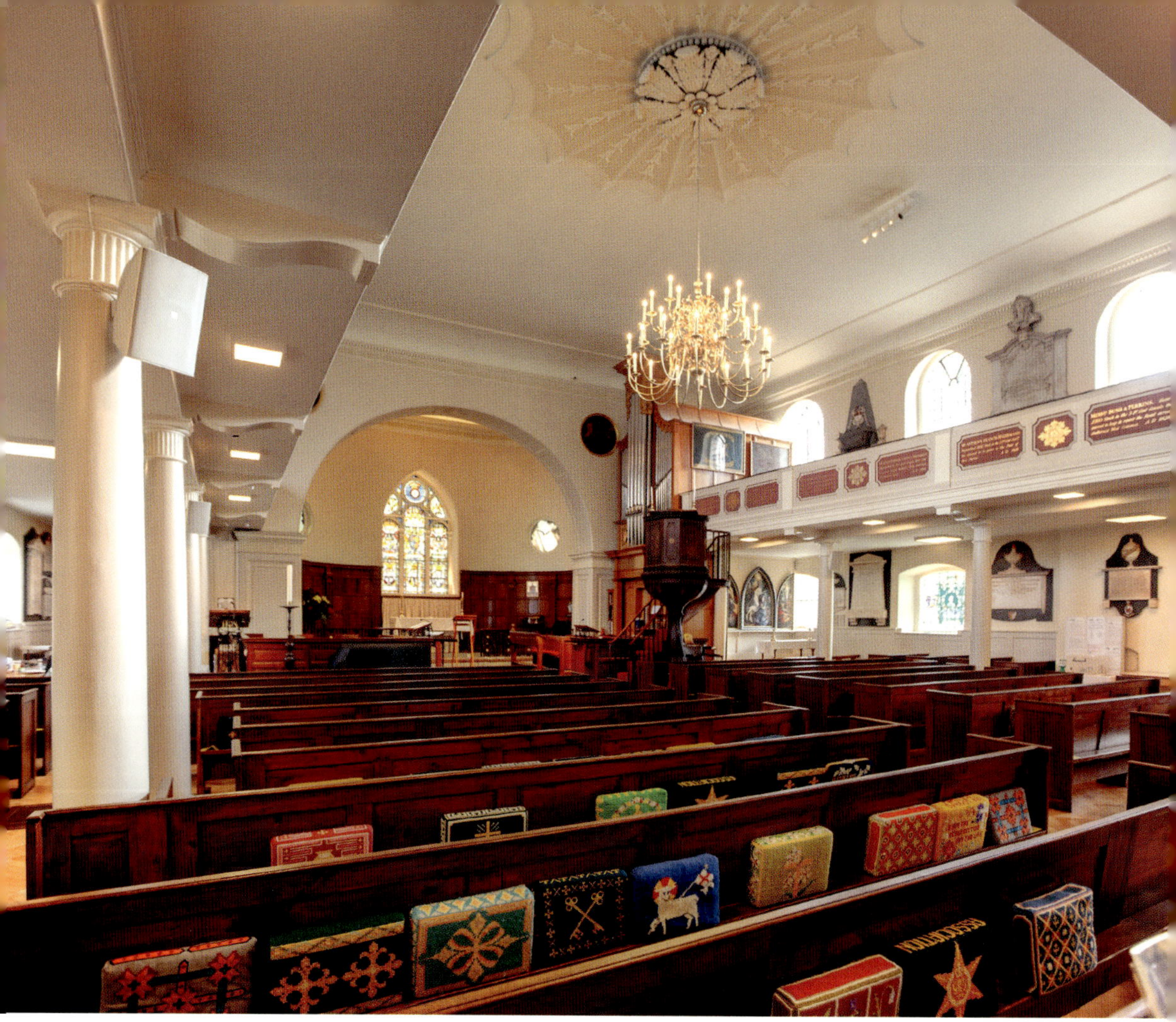

Henry VII, his grandmother Margaret Beauchamp and Elizabeth I, with whose families St John was linked by marriage. There are also some good examples of modern stained glass on the ground floor commemorating people associated with St Mary's, including the artist J. M. W. Turner, who visited the church regularly and made sketches of the Thames whilst seated at the upper vestry window, and the engraver, poet and artist William Blake, who married Catherine Boucher at the church in 1782. It is interesting to note that, being illiterate, she was only able to sign her name with an 'x' on the marriage certificate.

Other windows remember the botanist William Curtis, founder of the Linnean Society, and the soldier General Benedict, who defected to the British Army during the American War of Independence – both of whom are buried here.

Few major alterations have occurred since the church opened 250 years ago; however, a new organ, bearing the symbolic 'ram' of Young's Brewery (its main contributor) on its case, was added in 1991.

www.stmarysbattersea.org.uk

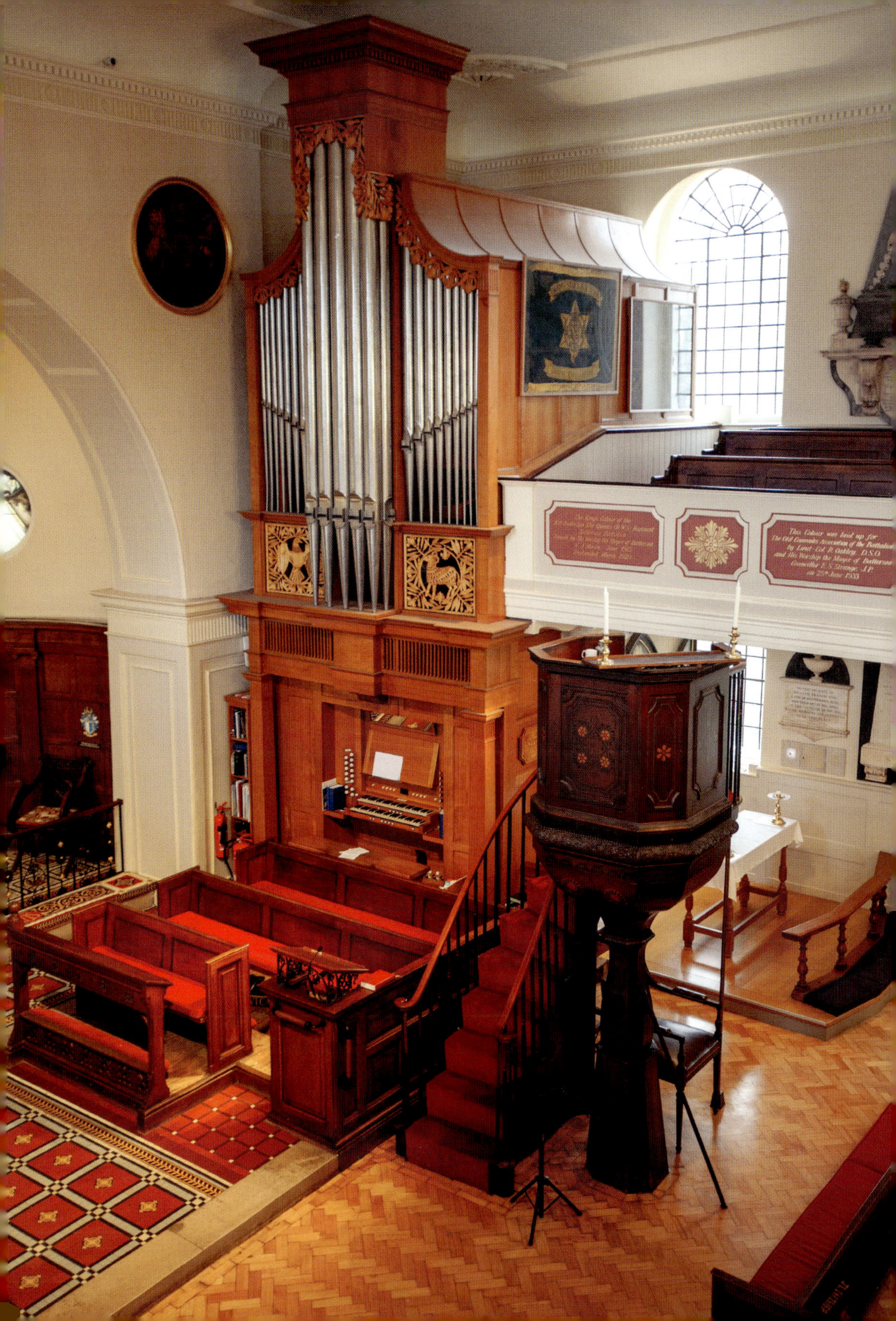
This Colour was laid up for
The Old Comrades Association of the Battalion
by Lieut-Col R. Oakley, D.S.O.
and His Worship the Mayor of Battersea
Councillor F. S. Strange, J.P.
on 25th June 1933

5. The Windmill Inn and Hotel, Clapham Common, South Side, SW4

Today's Windmill Inn is a very popular venue, both as a pub and a boutique hotel. It is named after a much earlier windmill that occupied this site beside Clapham Common in 1665. Located at the end of Windmill Lane, it is an imposing building that has seen many changes since it was built in the 1790s. In recent times several new extensions and a spacious conservatory have been added, as well as a new section containing forty-two distinctive hotel rooms. The Windmill is built on two floors and is filled with luxurious furnishings and a warm fire greets visitors on entering the building in the winter months. Customers have a choice of eating areas: at tables beside the bar, in the wildlife-themed decorated restaurant or in the light and sunny conservatory. Two further food stalls open outside during the summertime. It offers a wide range of menus and markets itself as a 'haven for the hungry, the weary and those with a powerful thirst'.

During the nineteenth century there was a dairy farm and grand house close to the inn, the latter being the home of the Young family, famous for founding Young's Brewery in nearby Wandsworth. Even though the house was demolished in the 1880s the association of the Young family with Windmill Inn has continued; the brewery purchased the inn's freehold in 1848 and has remained its proprietor ever since.

From the early 1800s the Windmill was a successful and renowned coaching inn, a place where stagecoaches paused on their journeys in and out of London.

The Windmill Inn and Hotel.

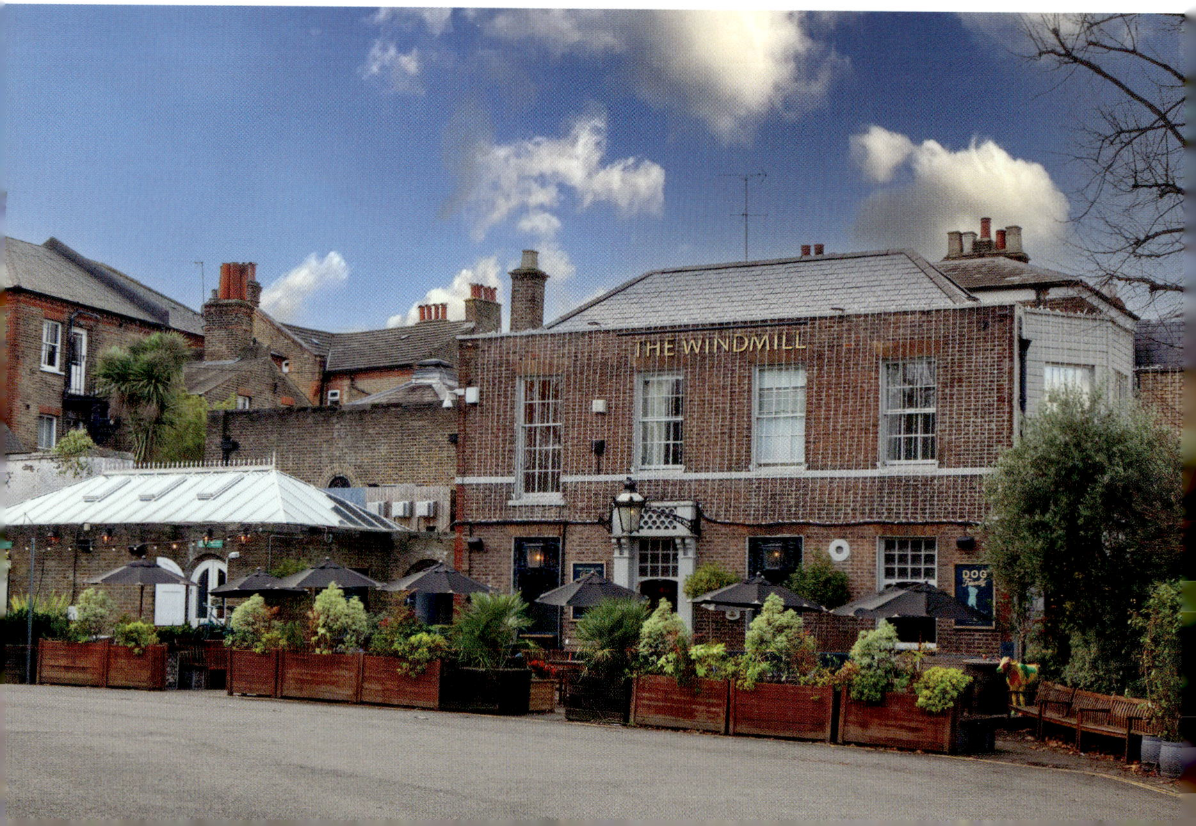

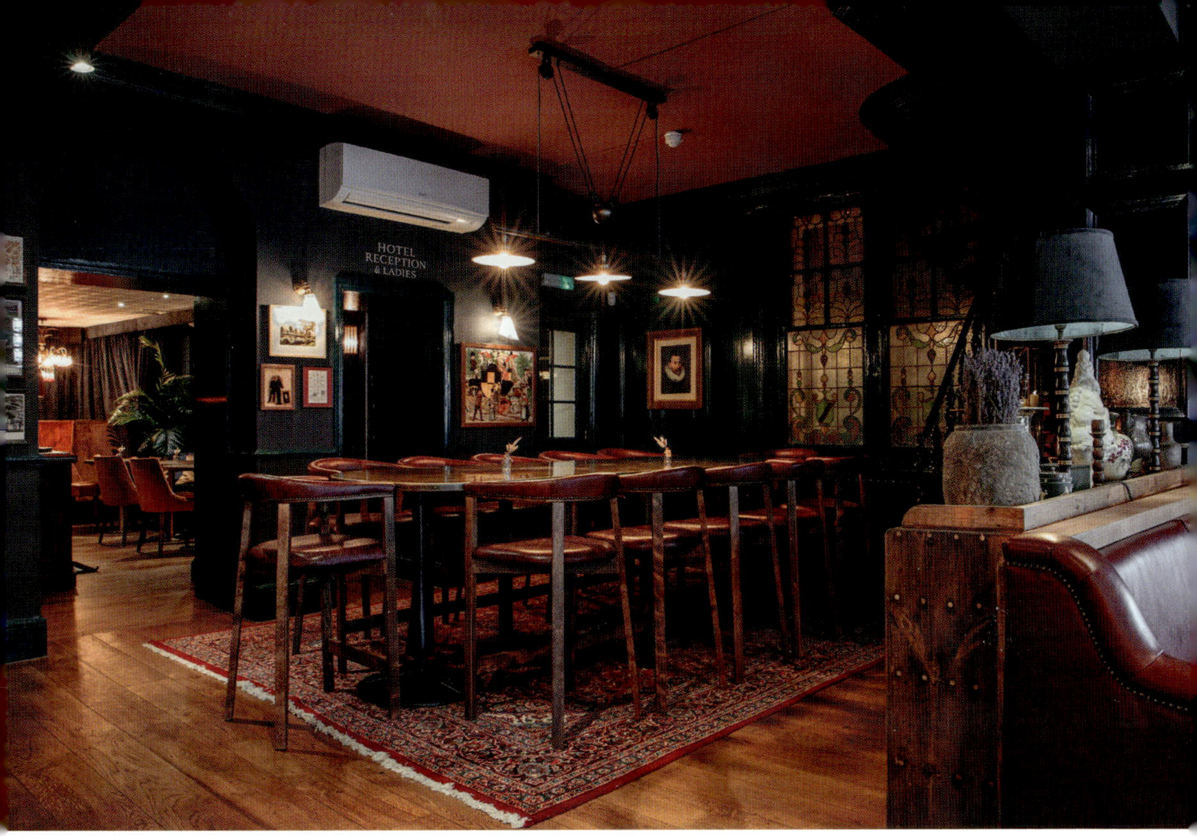

Above: The Windmill Inn and Hotel bar. (Courtesy of Young's)

Below: Dining room, the Windmill Inn and Hotel.

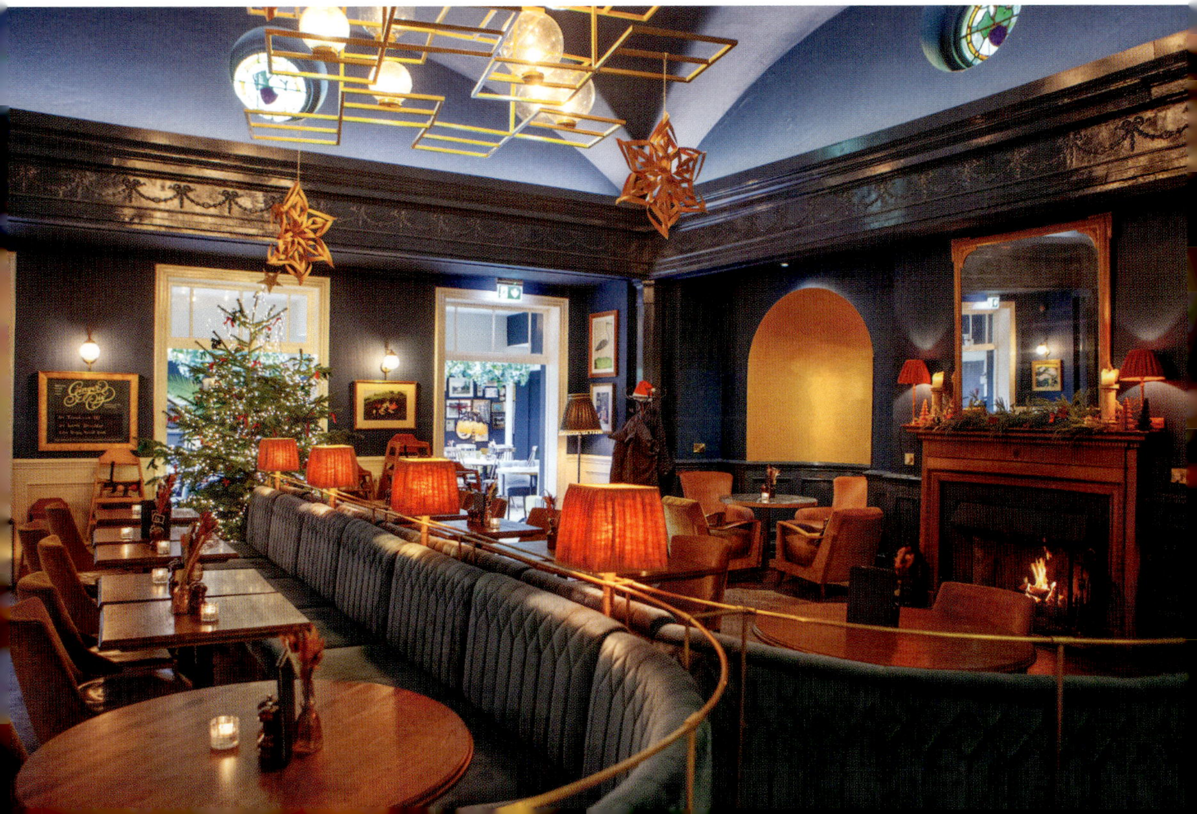

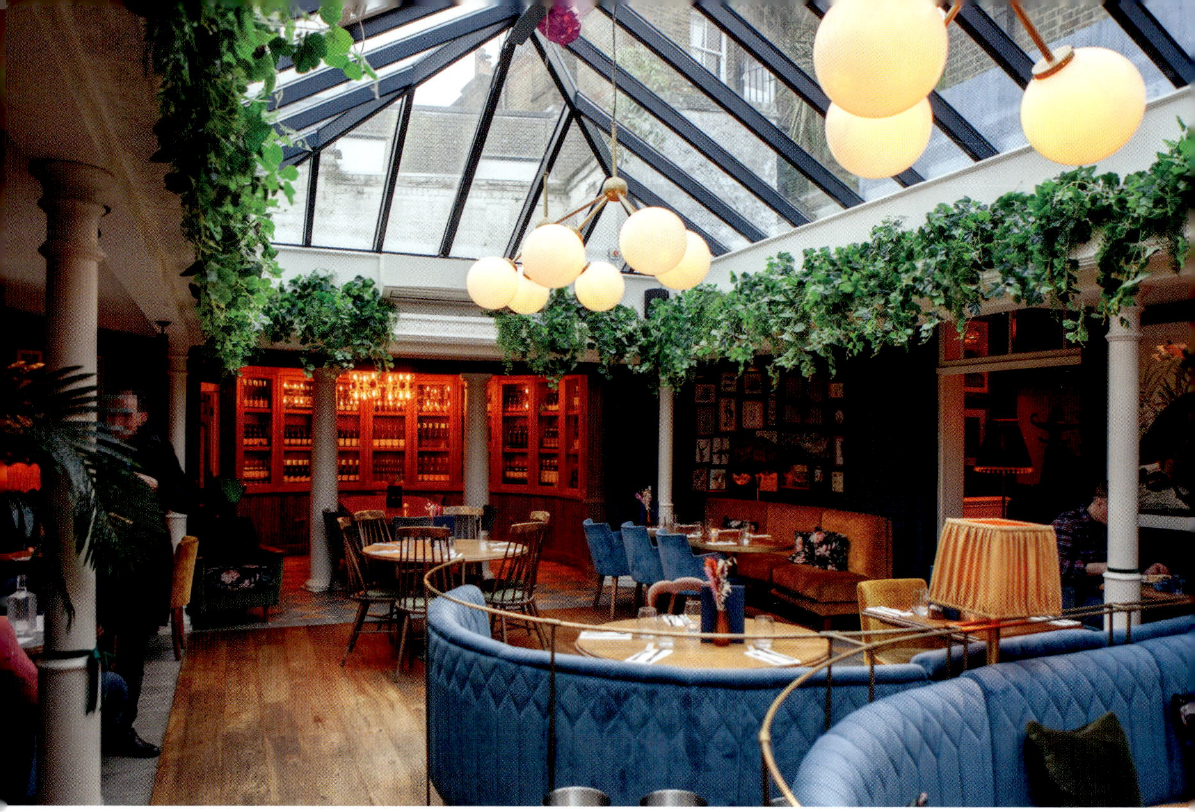

Conservatory, the Windmill Inn and Hotel.

The inn welcomed passengers providing them with commodious and comfortable rooms, a place to relax, eat, drink, and perhaps stay, before continuing with their journey. The horses were equally well looked after, being given food and water and placed in stables where they could rest.

The Windmill Inn is clearly visible in the background of a painting by the artist John Frederick Herring Sr (1795–1865), famous for his paintings of horses and rural scenes. The painting entitled *The Return from the Derby* depicts the crowds watching coaches passing through Clapham on Derby Day on the way to Epsom.

www.windmillclapham.co.uk

6. Sycamore House, No. 4 Old Town, SW4

For more than 100 years this elegant late eighteenth-century house was the centre of a most successful enterprise, the Sycamore Laundry. Begun in 1865 by Mrs Buckland, a local laundress, the business moved into Old Clapham in the 1880s. The laundry industry was thriving in London at this time, possibly due to the male fashion of wearing stiff collars, and laundry workers would often be seen on the street wheeling barrows filled with clothing to be washed and ironed at home. The Sycamore Laundry flourished after it was taken over by Mrs Buckland's son-in-law, Alexander Leman, and he moved the business into the house at No. 4 Old Town around 1898. The laundry was collected from customers by the company's own horse-drawn van and initially washing was hung out to dry in the back garden of the house. However, as the business grew the garden disappeared to be replaced by an array of laundry buildings and equipment.

Sycamore Laundry was to earn itself four royal warrants during its lifetime – from Queen Elizabeth II, the Duke of Edinburgh, Elizabeth the Queen Mother and Charles, Prince of Wales (our present King Charles III). The firm was extremely highly regarded and particularly famous for its laundering of delicate and historic pieces such as Queen Victoria's christening gown. Generation after generation of the Leman family ran the business until 1994 when the company merged with a larger firm and moved elsewhere. At this time the laundry buildings behind the house were demolished and a housing development, Sycamore Mews, was built on the land. The main house, with its Robert Adam features, was then restored and divided up into apartments. One of these was purchased by the celebrated furniture designer Tim Gosling whose career has been spent in the world of design, the arts, architecture

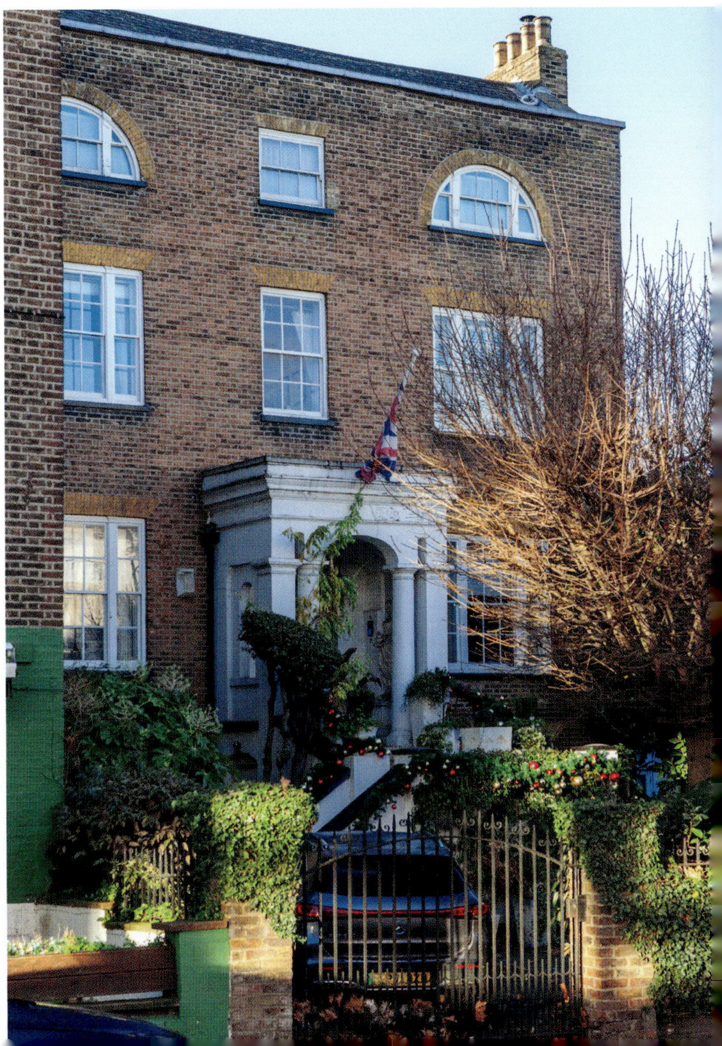

Sycamore House.

and interiors. Within ten years Gosling had acquired two further apartments and transformed them all into one large grand home reflecting his passion for the classical style of 1787 when the house was first built. Today, apart from being Gosling's own residence, No. 4 Old Town is also where his studio is based.

7. The Pavement, Old Town, SW4

The Pavement lies in the very heart of Old Clapham opposite the common and beside Clapham Common Underground station. It is the most attractive curved Georgian terrace, characterised by its non-uniformity and made up three- and four-storey houses with shops at ground level. The buildings were constructed over the course of about 100 years (roughly between the mid-1700s and mid-1800s), several of which are Grade II listed on account of their features and architecture.

The shops and businesses here have always attracted customers due to their proximity to the main transport hubs. No. 17 The Pavement, a substantial and four-storey-high building erected in the early 1800s has retained its early shop front, looking much as it did when it opened. Initially, it traded as a grocer's shop but in 1837 Henry Deane set up his pharmacy here. Some of his apothecary

Below left and below right: Former Deane's Chemist, The Pavement.

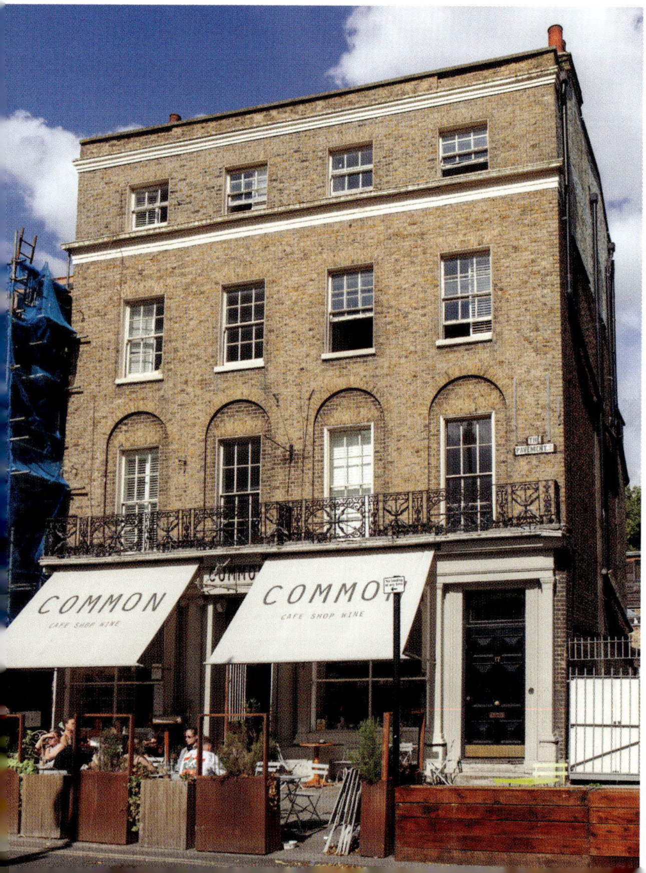

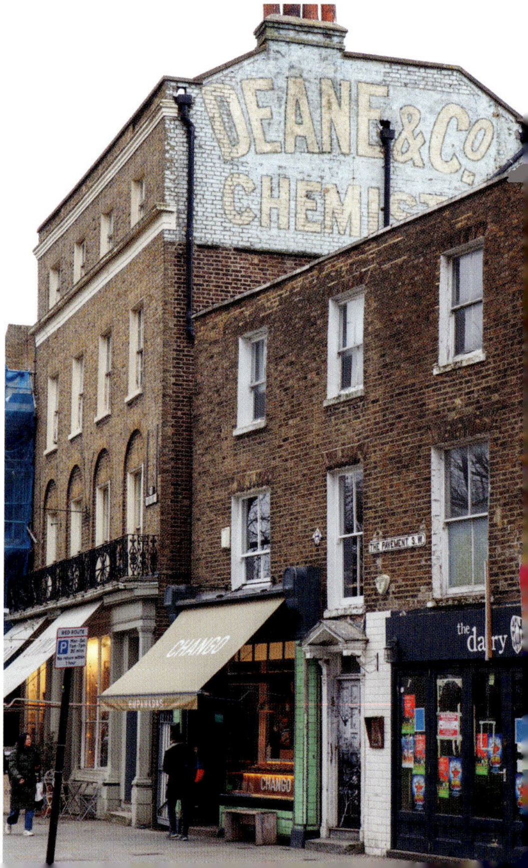

furniture – wooden drawers and glass display cases – can still be seen today within the premises, now the COMMON Café and Shop. Deane was a renowned pharmacist who became president of the Pharmaceutical Society in 1853. When he died the shop was taken over by his son, and subsequently by other chemists. Towards the end of the nineteenth century the pharmacy was run by two women who not only managed the shop but also set up a pharmaceutical school where they trained and hired only female chemists. The shop remained as a pharmacy until 1986, by then known as Deane & Co. Today if you approach the shop from Clapham High Street a large painted sign bearing this name can be seen on the upper wall of the building, an enduring reminder of the shop's former use.

The houses next door at Nos 18–19 have been boarded up since a fire in 1999. At the time of writing they are sadly still in this condition, but the good news is that planning permission has finally been approved for their restoration. The appointed architects, Marks Barfield, have stated they will 'create a distinctive high quality contemporary infill that completes the terrace while respecting its heritage context'.

8. The Orangery, Worsopp Drive, SW4

Just behind Clapham Common South Side is one of the area's most unusual and hidden curiosities: a late eighteenth-century greenhouse known as the Orangery. Built in a classical style, its façade consists of Portland stone columns above which is a decorated pediment bearing high reliefs of fruits and flowers. Beneath this is

The Orangery.

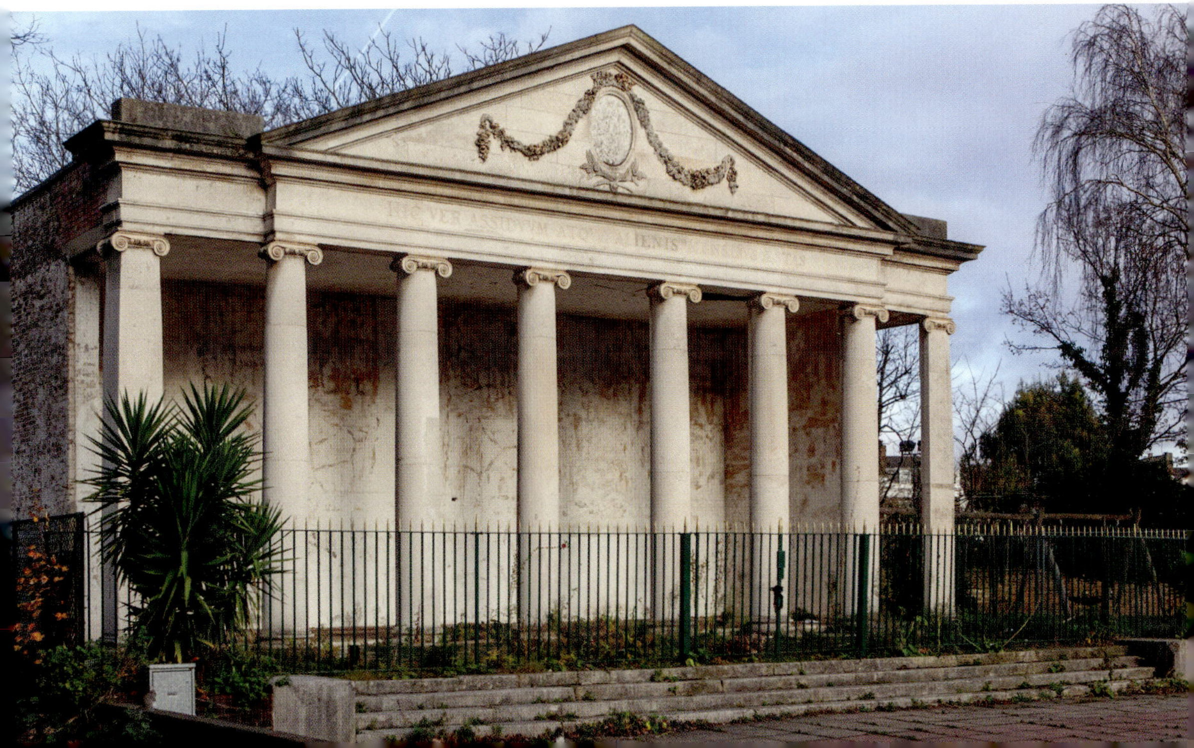

a carving of a quotation from the Roman poet Virgil which translates as 'Here is eternal spring and summer in months not her own'.

Unfortunately, today the structure has an air of neglect as it stands fenced in and isolated in the middle of the Notre Dame housing estate. It was once part of a magnificent house owned by Robert Thornton (1757–1826) which boasted an ornamental park with a lake and extensive lawns. A magnificent greenhouse was added in 1792–93, which, apart from housing plants, was where Thornton entertained high-ranking guests such as Queen Charlotte and her two daughters. The house and grounds were replaced by the Notre Dame convent school when Thornton became bankrupt and fled oversea. After the school was closed in 1939 the local council covered the land with housing but left the Orangery in situ – perhaps acting as a reminder of the area's former incarnation.

9. St Paul's Church, Rectory Grove, SW4

Until the 1770s the village of Clapham had been concentrated around the medieval parish church, known then as Holy Trinity, but as new roads and houses were constructed around Clapham Common the focus of the village changed. There was now a need to build a much larger church for Clapham's growing community, and in 1776 a new Holy Trinity Church was erected on Clapham Common (see Building 3) and was assigned parish church status. The former church at Rectory Grove was demolished and in 1815 a new chapel of ease, built to relieve pressure on the overcrowded Holy Trinity and now called St Paul's, replaced it on the site. Built by the architect Christopher Edmonds, the church is a simple rectangle constructed from stock brick in the classical style and has a west pediment. The church was extended at the east end in the late 1800s by the renowned architect Sir Arthur Blomfield, but, following damage in the Second World War, it was completely restored and then designated a Grade II* listed building. The church today is characterised by its wide nave and aisles and is renowned for its many monuments and memorials. One important monument to seek out is that of the former lord of the manor Sir Richard Atkins (d. 1689), his wife and three children. There is also a tablet to Samuel Pepys's friend and colleague Willliam Hewer, who had lived in a house beside Clapham Common (and was where Pepys died), a monument of the Lord Mayor of London, Bartholomew Clerke (d. 1589) and a wall plaque to Henry Thornton, a key member of the Clapham Sect.

Outside in the churchyard you will discover the tombs of two other important Clapham families, namely the Hibberts and Thorntons, as well as some ancient gravestones. The churchyard has superb views over the Thames and London and is a truly peaceful spot. Together with the adjacent Eden Nature Garden it has received Green Flag awards for providing locals with a place to enjoy nature, to rest and relax, or to participate in activities such as bird watching and pond dipping.

www.stpaulsclapham.org

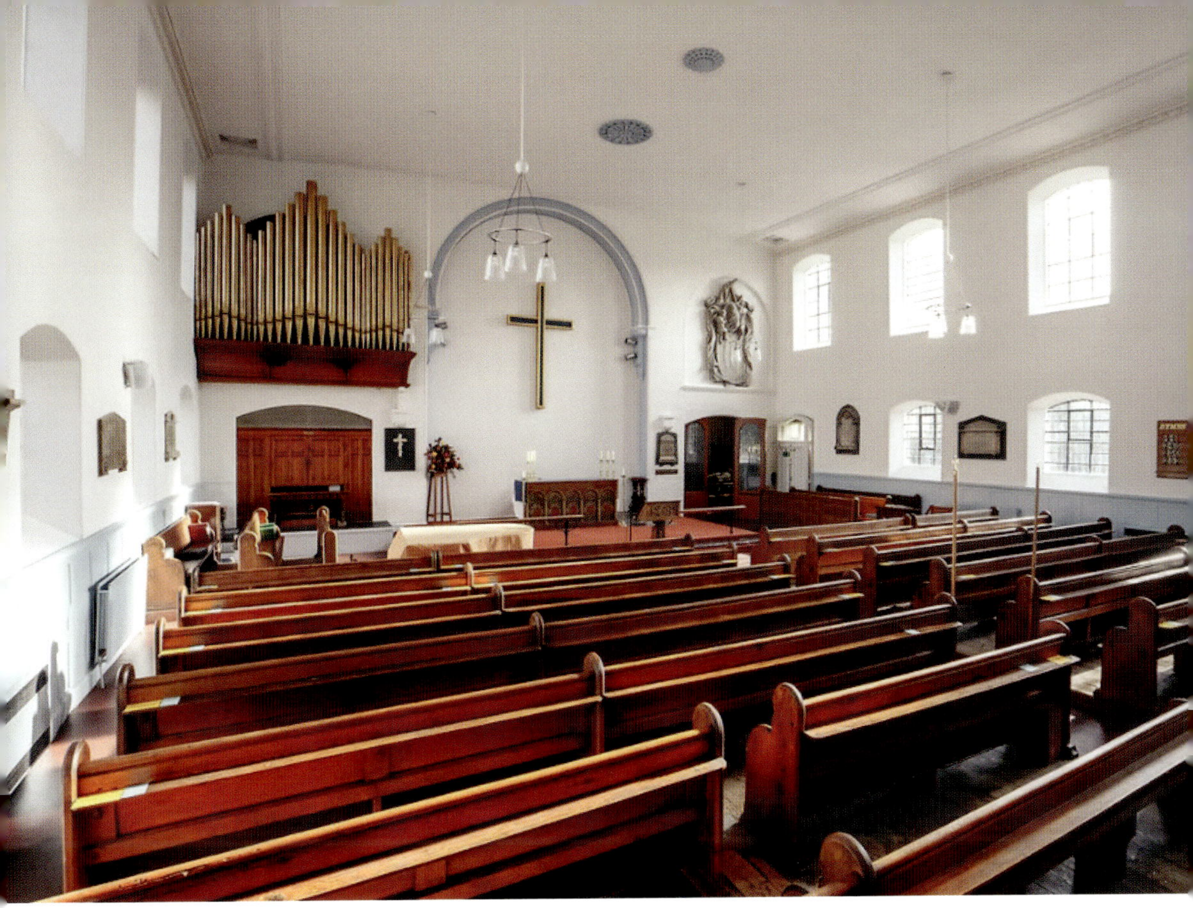

Above and below: St Paul's Church. (Courtesy of St Paul's Church)

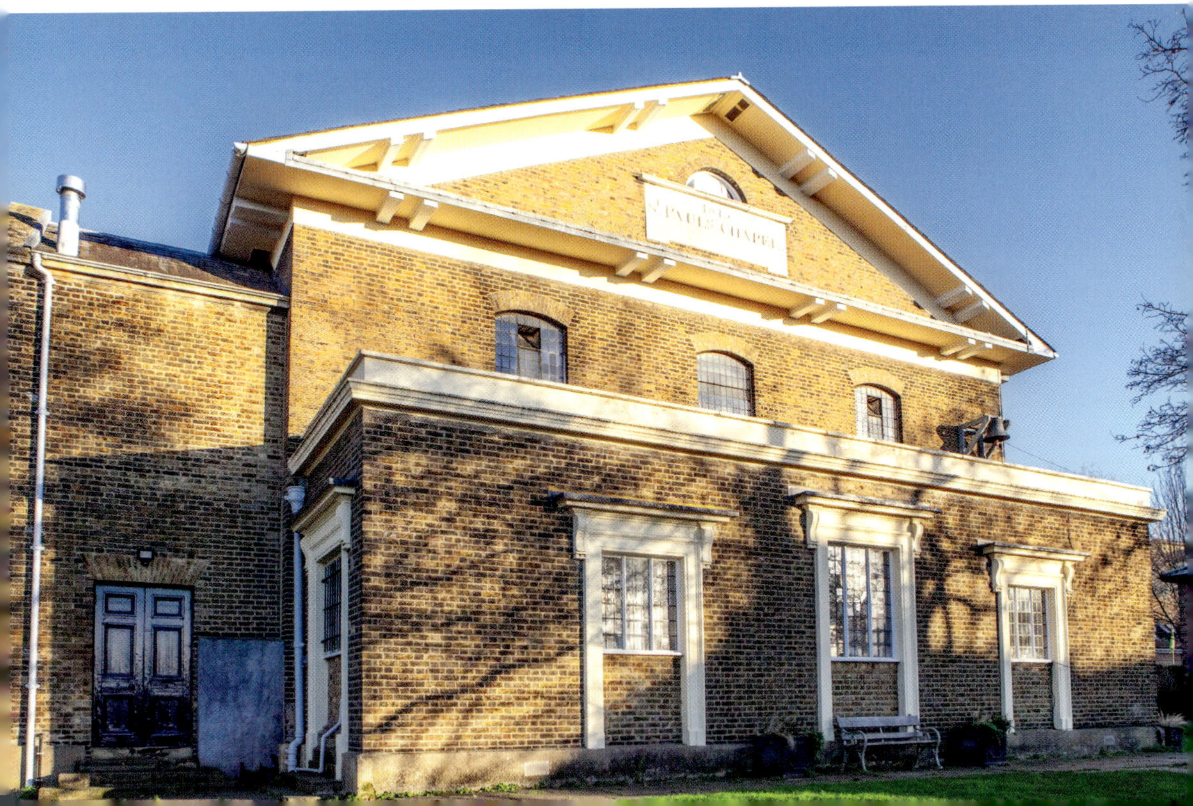

10. Clapham Park, SW4 and SW12

This was initially a speculative development by the master builder-cum-entrepreneur Thomas Cubitt (1788–1855), known for his work in Belgravia, Pimlico and Bloomsbury. On arriving in London, Cubitt set up his own building company where he employed a team of tradesmen skilled in every type of building work. This way of working was entirely new and he became somewhat of a living legend.

In Clapham, Cubitt seized the opportunity to create a new high-class neighbourhood on what had previously been an area of barren land behind Clapham Common South Side. He established a network of streets, a sewage system and lined his wide avenues with trees and greenery. The plots for his houses were large and each consisted of a detached Italianate villa, a grand carriage entrance and gardens, and some even had their own stables and greenhouses. Not all the houses in Clapham Park are attributed to Cubitt, but his buildings were the template for other developers to follow. Unfortunately, a mix of factors in the 1830s led to the decline of upmarket status of the new estate; problems existed in the economy and this together with the introduction of rail travel making it quicker and easier to reach the outer parts of London resulted in Clapham Park becoming less desirable. By the 1870s greater numbers of people could travel cheaply on the new horse-drawn tram transport and this meant that the area, but not the large properties, became increasingly attractive to the working classes. Consequently, many of the grand houses were either demolished or divided up into smaller plots to meet the increased population's housing requirements. Today, only a few original Cubitt houses survive in King's Avenue and Thornton Road. Many of the villas that have disappeared have been replaced by rows of Victorian terraced housing, as can be seen along Abbeville Road and Crescent Lane.

Having suffered severe war damage, much new housing was built in Clapham Park in the post-war period. Lambeth Council is currently carrying out a major regeneration of the estate and aims to provide 2,400 more homes and to establish a range of new community facilities for its residents.

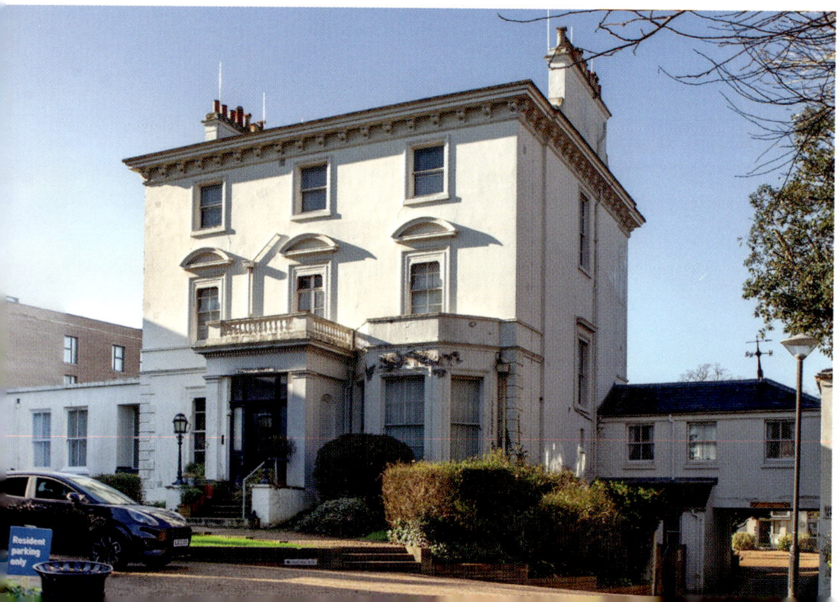

An original estate mansion, Clapham Park.

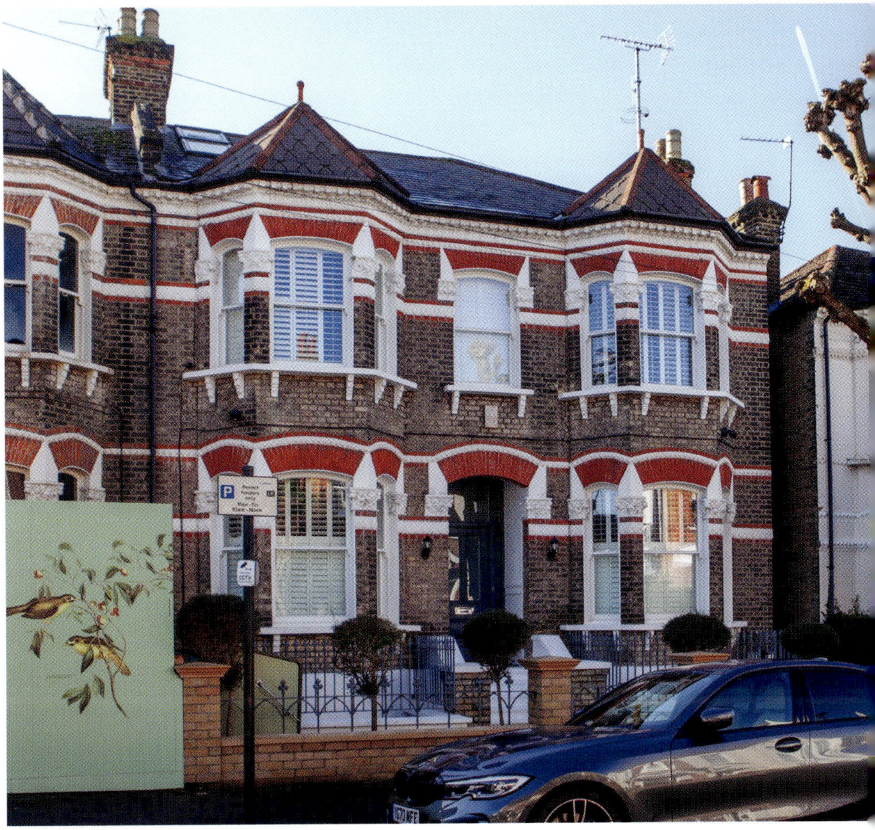

Right: Victorian terraced houses, Clapham Park.

Below: Recent regeneration at Clapham Park.

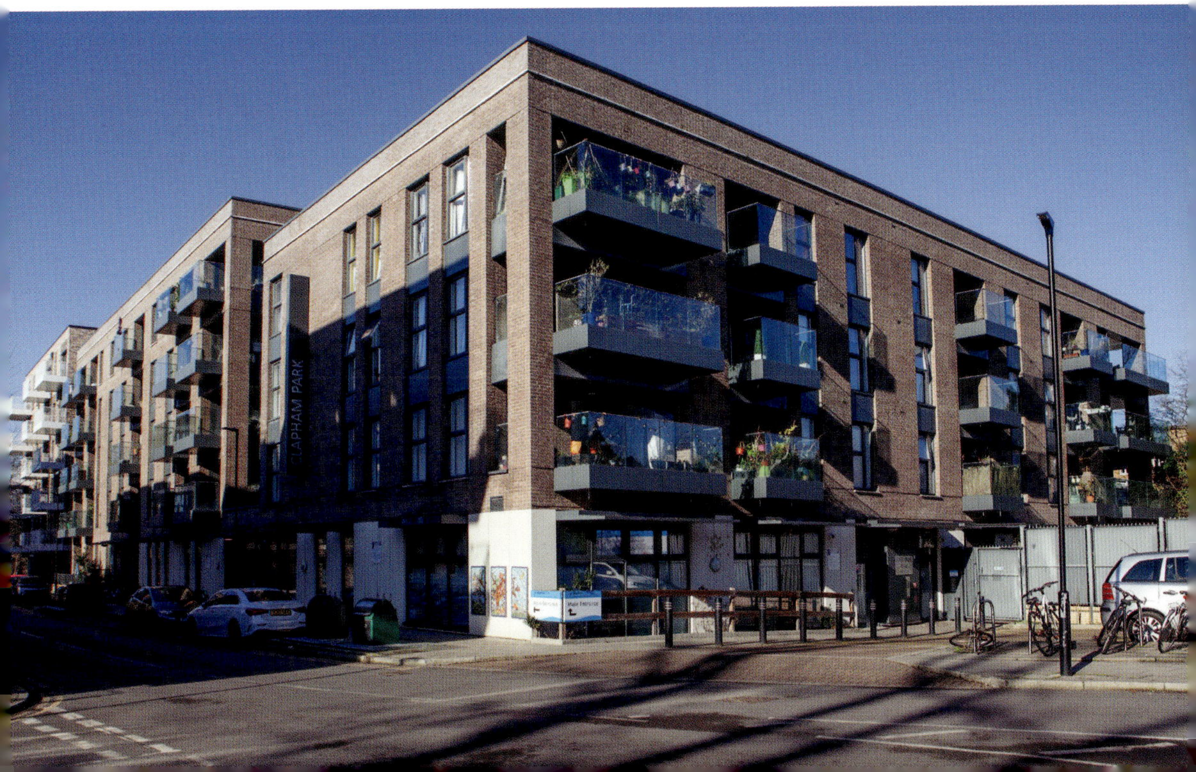

11. Crescent Lane and the Former Headquarters of the Post Office Workers, SW4

A large mansion previously occupied this site. It was called Grove Lodge and built for Francis Child, the developer of the Crescent Grove private estate. Erected in the mid-1820s, it was an imposing house with substantial grounds and was the only detached property on the estate. Child developed the land as an investment and many of its original residents were members of his family. Crescent Grove Estate is still privately owned and is now one of Clapham's most select addresses. As its name suggests it consists of a crescent of Georgian terraced houses which face a straight row of semi-detached houses linked by coach houses, and the two sides are separated by a pretty central garden.

In the early twentieth century Grove Lodge was put on the market and bought by the Amalgamated Union of Building Trade Workers to use as their headquarters. Within a decade the building had changed hands again, this time sold to the Union of Post Office Workers (UPW). The UPW immediately demolished the house and divided up its grounds, building themselves a brand-new headquarters, approximately where the original Grove Lodge had stood. A separate building facing Abbeville Road was commissioned in 1935 for the Builders Union and the architect L. A. Culliford was responsible for the design of both buildings.

The new UPW head office was built in the shape of a crescent and fronted by a circular drive. An impressive-looking building it was embellished by a grand entrance set in a stone doorway with wide oak doors and an oriel window above. The main interior rooms were opulent: wood-panelled in walnut, limed oak and Oregon pine. As the union grew it needed more office space, so a new floor

The former headquarters of the Post Office workers in Crescent Lane.

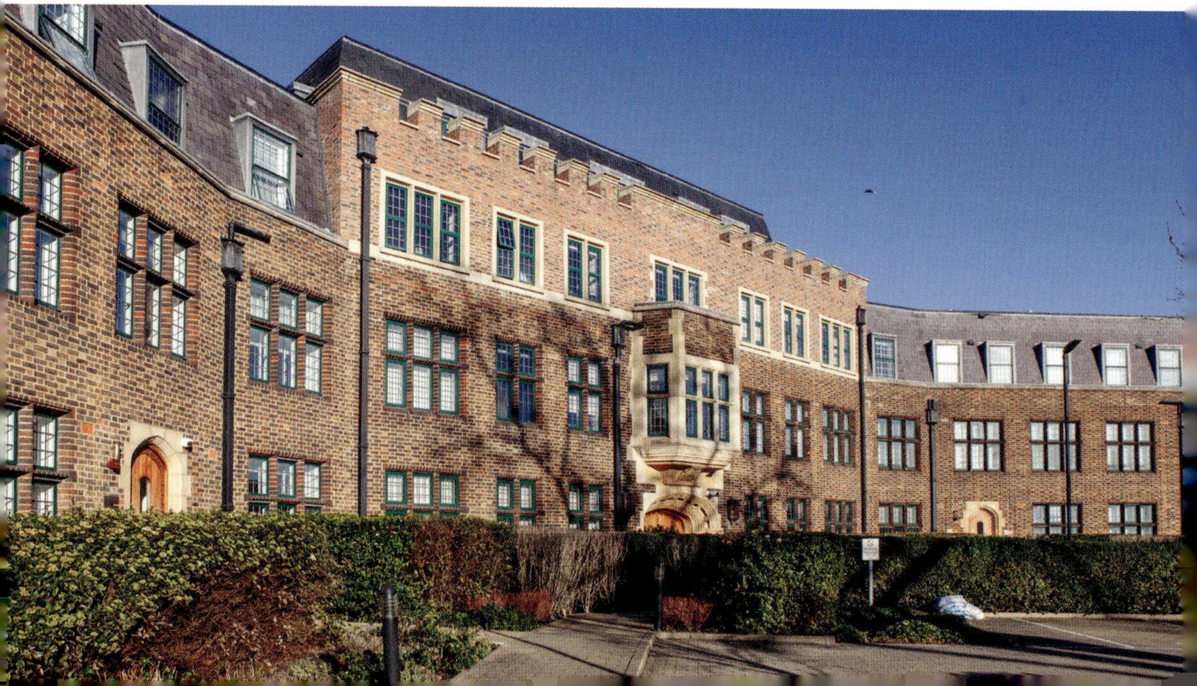

was added in 1976. Twenty years on the union vacated the building and it was taken over by the Metropolitan Housing Trust. Galliard Homes subsequently redeveloped the site in 2016 and converted the former offices into luxurious apartments at which point the development was renamed Metropolitan Crescent.

Two famous ex-residents of Grove Lodge in the 1800s were the publisher Henry Butterworth and Henry Twining (of Twinings tea).

12. Grafton Square, SW4

Grafton Square was laid out only twenty-five years after the Crescent Lane union headquarters (see Building 11), yet it is striking to see the contrast in architecture between the two. The square and its central garden was developed by Irish Militia Captain Thomas Ross, who established some fine Georgian stuccoed terraces (three to four storeys high with basements) on two sides of the square, while a third side was made up of smaller houses. At the time the fourth side remained unbuilt after a fire had interrupted work. Although such squares were a familiar sight north of the river (for example, St James's Square, Bloomsbury Square, Bedford Square), they were far less common in South London in this period and thus appeared particularly grand. In the late 1840s when the square was developed Clapham mainly attracted the affluent, which accounted for the quality of the terraces and their ornate and unusual, if not unique, exterior decorations. Within only a few years, however, once new affordable transport links with London were established, the profile of Clapham's resident population took a downward turn

Grafton Square houses.

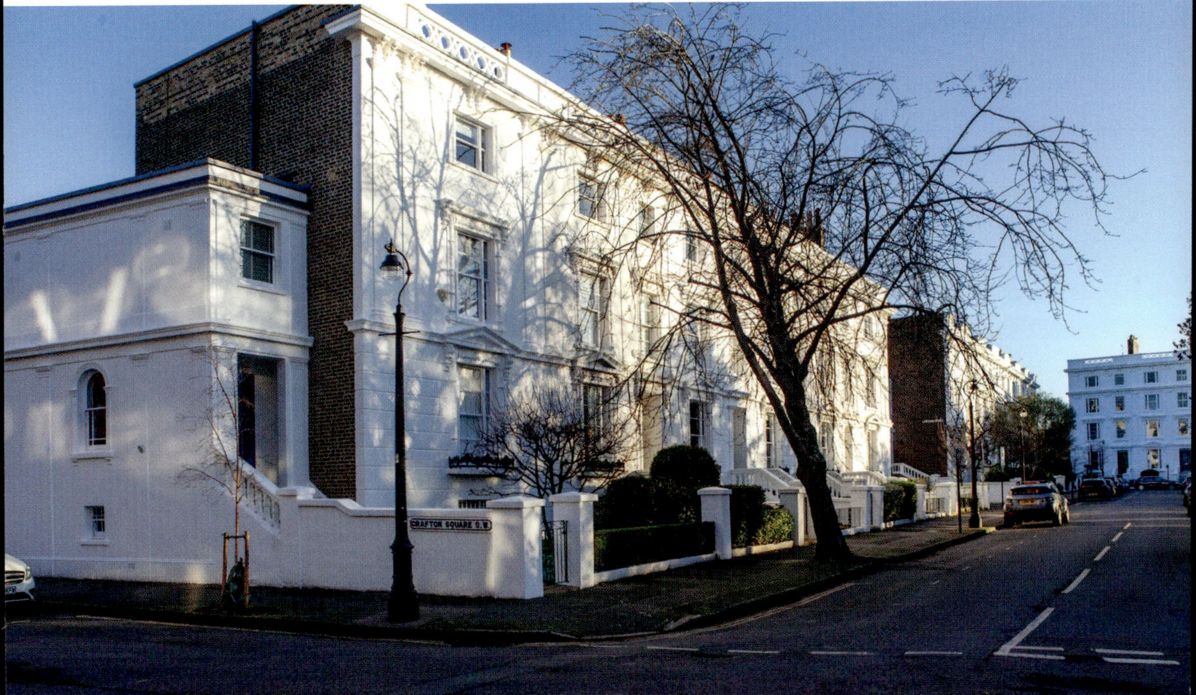

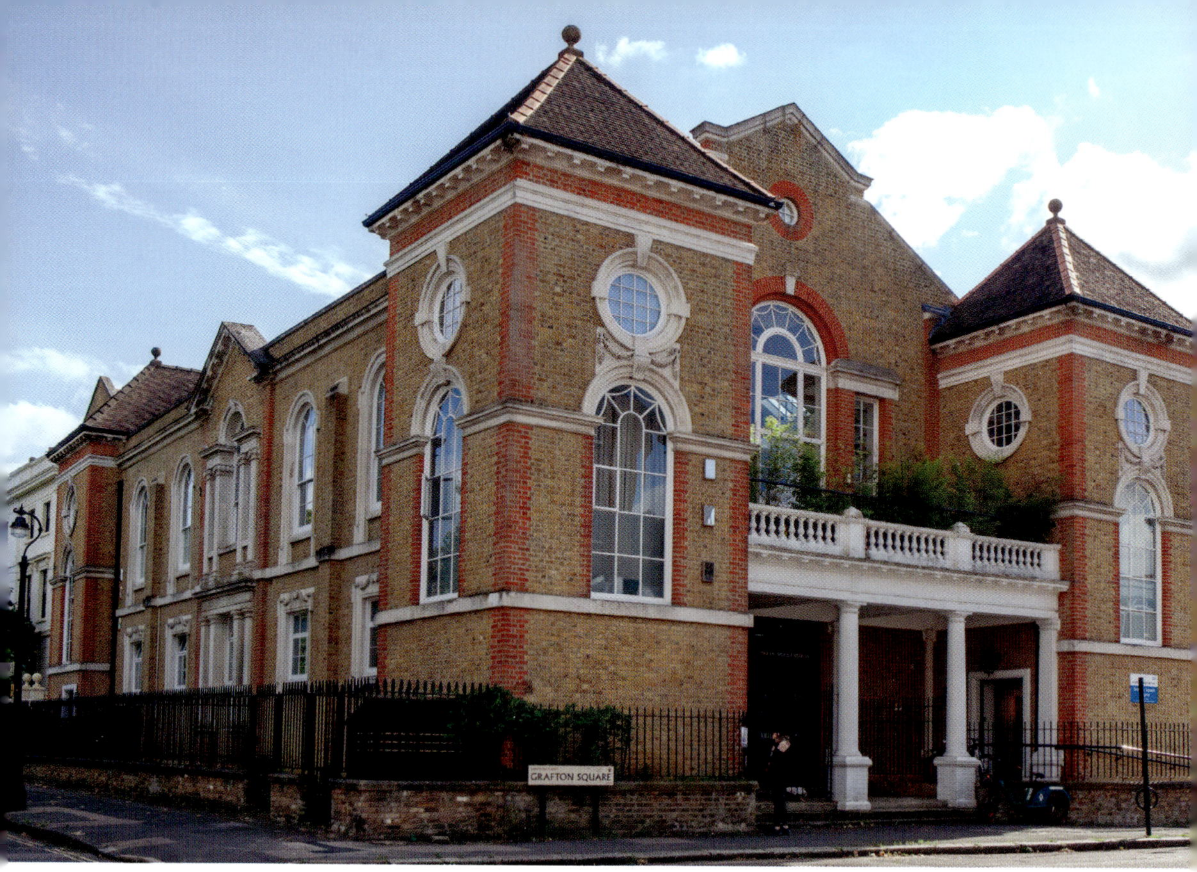

The former People's Church in Grafton Square.

and developers were forced to erect much more modest housing to accommodate 'the man on the Clapham Omnibus'.

In addition to the housing the square also became home to two churches: a large Congregational Church in its south-west corner was the first to be built in 1851. This church was so badly damaged during the war that it was replaced in the 1960s by a new church of the United Reformed Church – nowadays, the Maranatha Ministries International Christian Centre (MMICC). A Baptist Chapel was built on the north-west corner of the square in the 1880s. This imposing building still survives and is characterised by its portico, colonnade and by the two towers flanking them. It was designed by William Nevin and became known as the People's Church. The Baptists continued to use the building until the early 2000s but ultimately sold the church due to its poor state of repair at which time it was converted for private residential use.

13. St Mary's Church (Our Lady of Victories), Clapham Park Road, SW4

It is impossible to pass by this church and not appreciate its style and quality of craftsmanship. With its elegant and towering 170-foot stone spire, St Mary's can be seen from far and wide and has a real presence in the area. It was one of the

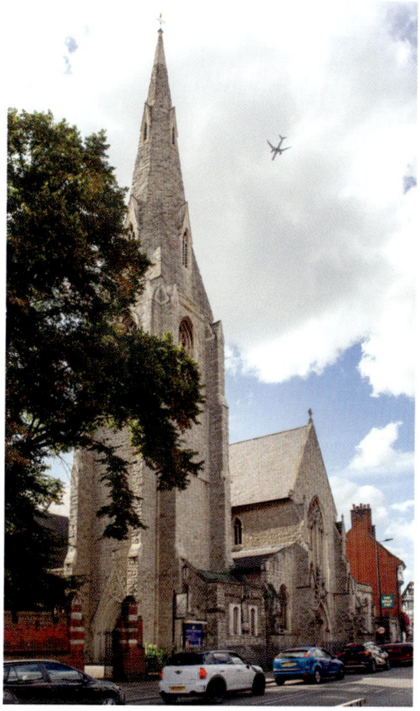

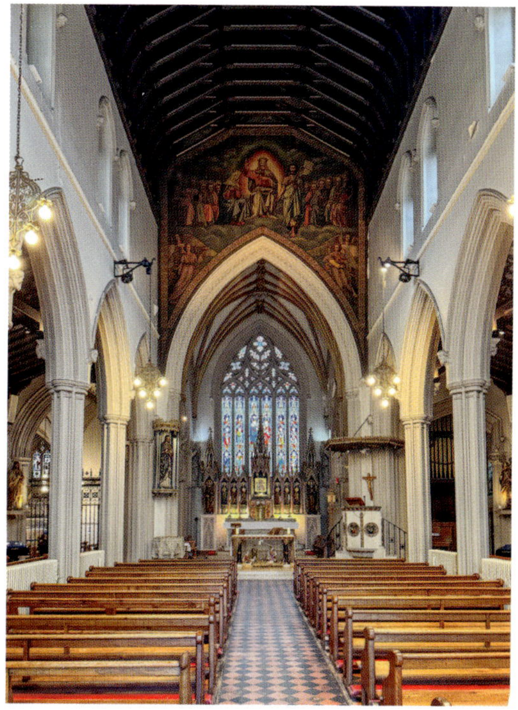

Above left, above right and below: St Mary's Church.

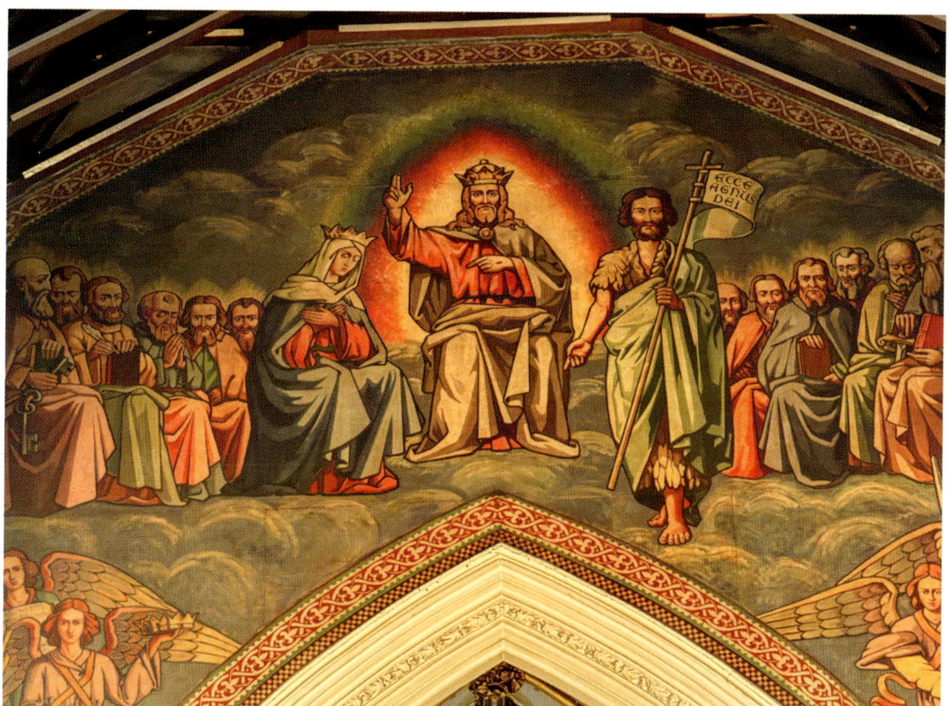

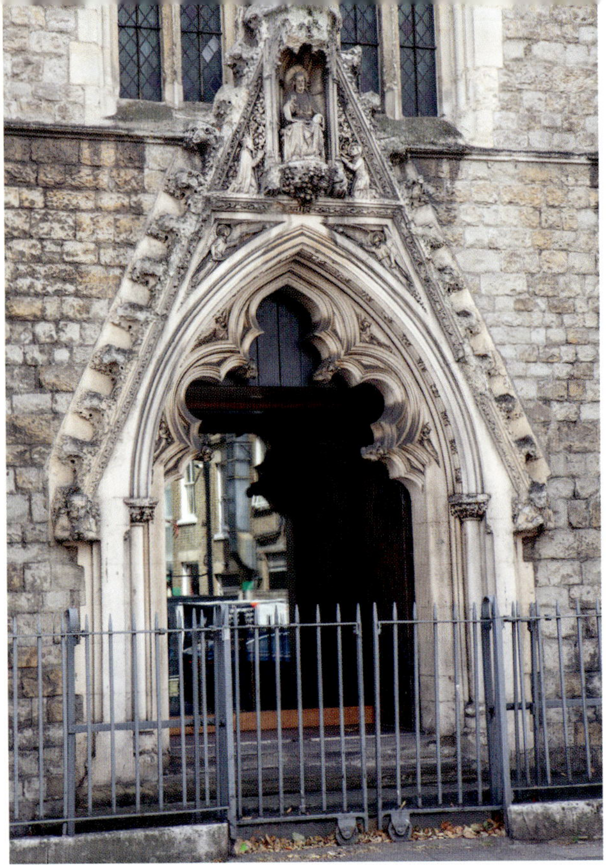

Main entrance, St Mary's Church.

first Catholic churches to have been constructed following the 1829 Catholic Emancipation Act and has been designated a Grade II* listed building on account of its historic and architectural significance. Designed by the architect William Wardell, who was a pupil of A. W. N. Pugin (renowned for his Gothic Revival style of architecture and for his work on the Houses of Parliament), the church was opened in the mid-1800s, and many believe that it is one of south London's finest ecclesiastical buildings. The local architect J. F. Bentley (see Building 2) was also associated with St Mary's, responsible for the design of both the Lady Chapel and Transept Chapel and for the fittings and stained glass in the Lady Chapel. After Bentley's death his work inside the church was undertaken by his son Osmund.

The interior of St Mary's is quite splendid and has many beautiful features including stone figure corbels holding up the aisle roofs, a wonderful painting over the chancel arch of the Last Judgement by J. Linthout and a six-bay arcade of quatrefoil piers.

About forty years after the church opened J. F. Bentley designed St Mary's Redemptorist Monastery on the grounds beside the church. Built in warm red brick in the Arts and Craft Gothic style, the monastery connects to the church and is also Grade II* listed by Historic England. It is easily recognised by its high-pitched roof, low cupola and gabled dormers and its castellated wall along the neighbouring St Alphonsus Road. The land was formerly part of Samuel

Thornton's eighteenth-century house, and a part of that garden remains today. In the early 1900s St Mary's Boys' School was set up at the end of the garden but since merging with the girl's school in Crescent Lane the site has been used by Ace of Clubs as a day centre for the homeless.

www.stmarys-clapham.org.uk

14. Former Clapham General and Provident Dispensary, No. 42 Clapham Manor Street, SW4

Not only is it astonishing to find this most ornate Italian-looking 'palazzo' in the middle of a residential street, but also to learn that the building was first built as a dispensary. As London's population grew rapidly in the late eighteenth century there was increasing concern over the plight of the poor especially in respect to accessing affordable medical care. Enlightened philanthropists and charitable organisations were keen to address this problem and established a system whereby free healthcare was made available for the poor at purpose-built dispensaries. However, in the early 1800s a change in societal thinking resulted

Former Clapham General and Provident Dispensary.

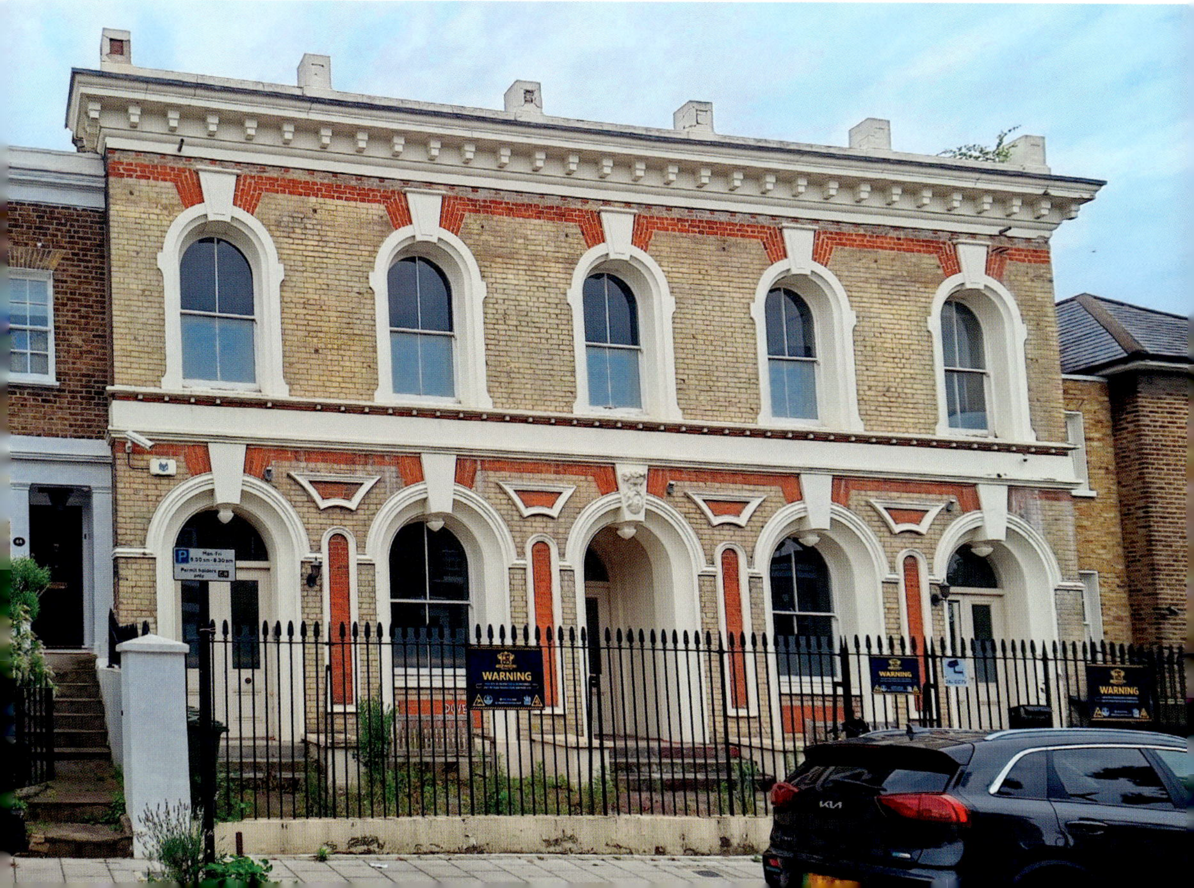

in the introduction of a new approach to free healthcare provision. This was 'providence', which introduced the idea of the poor paying a subscription to receive 'free' medical treatment. In practice this meant that those in work and mainly able to provide for their families had to pay a weekly subscription while those who were either seasonal workers or paupers would have their subscriptions paid for by charitable donations and parish subscriptions, respectively.

Forty-six provident dispensaries appeared all over London between 1833 and 1898 and the Clapham General and Provident Dispensary, set up in 1849, moved into its premises here in 1854. Now, it is one of the capital's earliest dispensary's to have survived and for both this reason and due to its design by the famous architect James Thomas Knowles Sr (1806–84) the building carries Grade II listed status. Knowles designed the dispensary free of charge and in his favourite Italianate style which is so eye-catching. The building itself was paid for by public subscription. Two storeys high, its warm yellow and red brick façade is full of interesting features including an attractive keystone above the main entrance containing a mask and a very fine block modillion cornice.

The dispensary finally closed in the 1950s. A devastating fire in 1989 damaged much of the interior, but following restoration the dispensary was occupied by the London Russian Ballet School. Recently John Rigby and Co., the internationally renowned gunmakers have purchased the premises to use as their showroom, a production workshop and a training academy for its apprentices.

15. Battersea Park, Battersea, SW11

Battersea Park was opened to the public in 1858 by Queen Victoria on former market gardens land and reclaimed marshland from the Thames. At this time the area beside the river was covered with wharves, industrial works, and railway tracks and so the introduction of a 200-acre (83-hectare) expanse of parkland was a welcome addition. The park's layout was due to the architect Sir James Pennethorne and to the Parks Superintendent John Gibson. Pennethorne's plans included gardens, a lake, a cascade, an aviary, perimeter housing and carriage drives. As the lake and cascade required water, a pump house was built to the north of the lake in 1861. Designed by James and William Simpson in the fashionable Italianate style, it is a handsome, tall, one-storey brown-brick building with stucco dressings in which the pump and steam engine used to supply water to the lake and cascade were housed. It ultimately became neglected but was saved in the early 1990s when English Heritage and Wandsworth Council undertook its restoration. Nowadays the pump house has become a thriving visual arts exhibition space, a venue for civil weddings and is available for private hire.

Perhaps one of the best-loved structures in the park is its bandstand, located in the middle of Central Avenue. The present bandstand dates to the 1980s, a replacement for the original pavilion, and is both a popular meeting place and

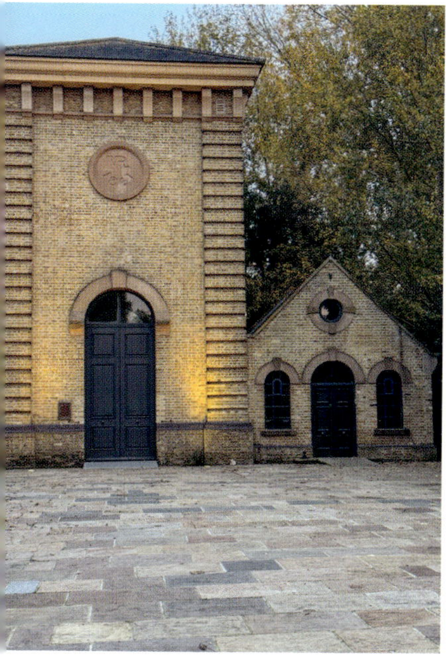

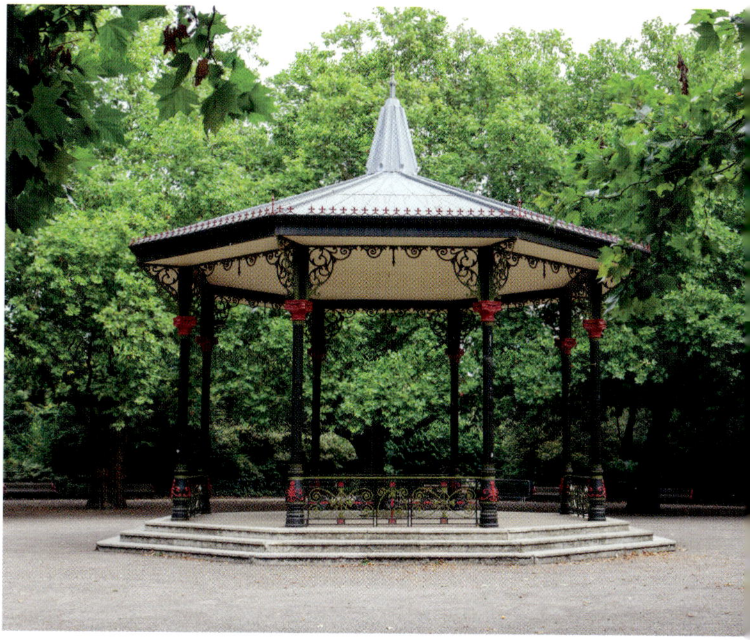

Above left: Former pumphouse.

Above right: Bandstand.

Below: Peace Pagoda.

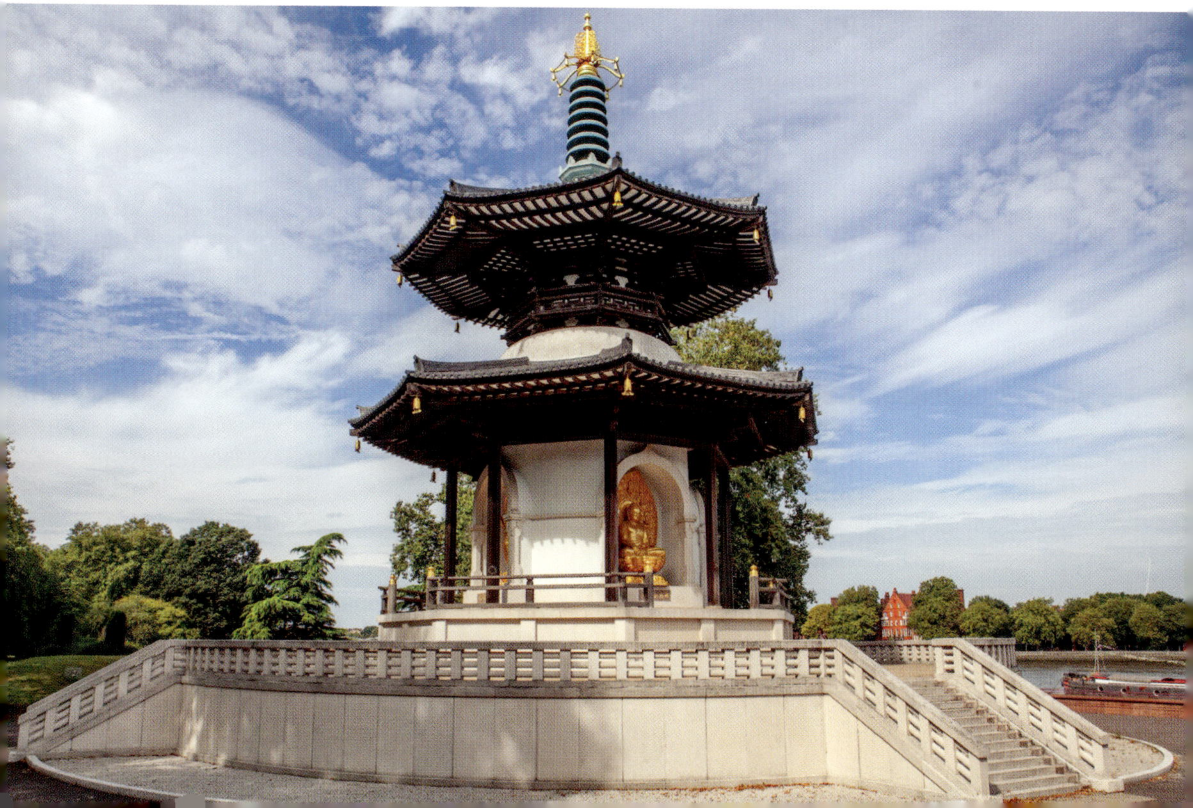

an events space. Another major feature of the park is its Peace Pagoda, which sits beside the Thames on the riverside walk. Erected in 1985, it was gifted to London by the Nipponzan Myohoji order of Japanese Buddhist monks and is cared for daily by one of the sect's Japanese monks. The pagoda is both a beautiful monument and shrine to peace and contains several gilt-bronze statues that detail the main stages of Buddha's life.

Battersea Park is also celebrated for its many interesting sculptures: the 24th Division War Memorial by Eric Kennington, an avant-garde sculpture comprising three infantry soldiers in military kit with helmets and rifles; and two twentieth-century sculptures, one by Barbara Hepworth and the other by Henry Moore.

16. Battersea Bridge, SW11

The current bridge was built before the motor car era and so the crossing's narrow 40-foot roadway is not entirely suitable for the traffic of the twenty-first century. Yet it continues in use after 135 years, and vehicles of every type as well as pedestrians cross the bridge daily. Joseph Bazalgette, the Chief Engineer of London's Metropolitan Board of Works (renowned for building central London's sewerage system), designed this plain five-arched bridge which was built in 1890. It replaced an earlier wooden bridge erected in 1777 which was the first of three bridges spanning the river between Chelsea and Battersea; the others, Chelsea and Albert, were built in the mid- to late 1800s.

The original timber bridge was simple but picturesque and characterised by its nineteen short spans. Interestingly, it was the first bridge to be lit by oil lamps across the Thames. It became the subject of paintings by the artists J. M. W. Turner and Walter Greaves as well as the American artist James McNeill Whistler. Whistler's *Nocturne: Blue and Gold – Old Battersea Bridge* when painted in the early 1870s caused great controversy for portraying the bridge apparently veiled in a ghostly mist and lacking clear details. Today, however, it is much acclaimed and hangs in Tate Britain on Millbank.

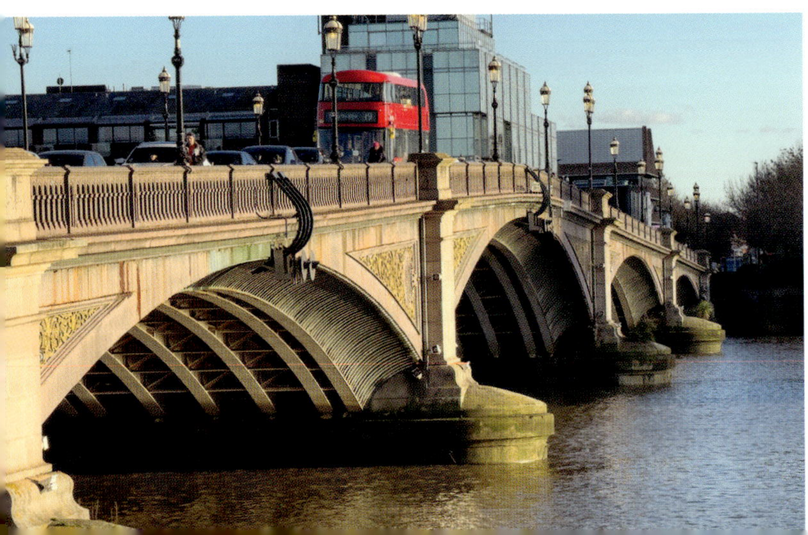

Battersea Bridge.

17. The Hibbert Almshouses, Nos 715–729 Wandsworth Road, SW8

This striking row of warm, red-brick almshouses was built in 1859 specifically to provide accommodation for eight elderly poor women who lived in the ancient parish of Clapham. The building was founded by two sisters, Sarah and Mary Ann Hibbert, in commemoration of their father, William Hibbert, who had been a Clapham resident. A foundation plaque recording this can be seen on the first floor at the centre of the terrace. Two storeys high, the cottages were built in a mixture of architectural styles; the upper windows being pointed and Gothic in style compared to those below which display Tudor characteristics.

The Hibbert Almshouses were designed by the noted architect Edward I'Anson and built as a symmetrical range. Residents did not have bathrooms until the 1960s when the buildings were updated but otherwise very few alterations have been made internally or externally since the dwellings were first built. Nowadays the criteria for residence have changed and applicants may be married couples or single men who are of state pensionable age. However, preference is still given to women should there be two applicants vying for a place here at the same time.

Almshouses have been a feature of towns and cities throughout Britain since medieval times and were a common provider of homes for the aged and poor before the state pension was introduced in the early 1900s. In the earliest times it was religious houses that owned and managed such accommodation but following the Dissolution of the Monasteries in the 1530s many buildings belonging to the religious orders were

Hibbert Almshouses.

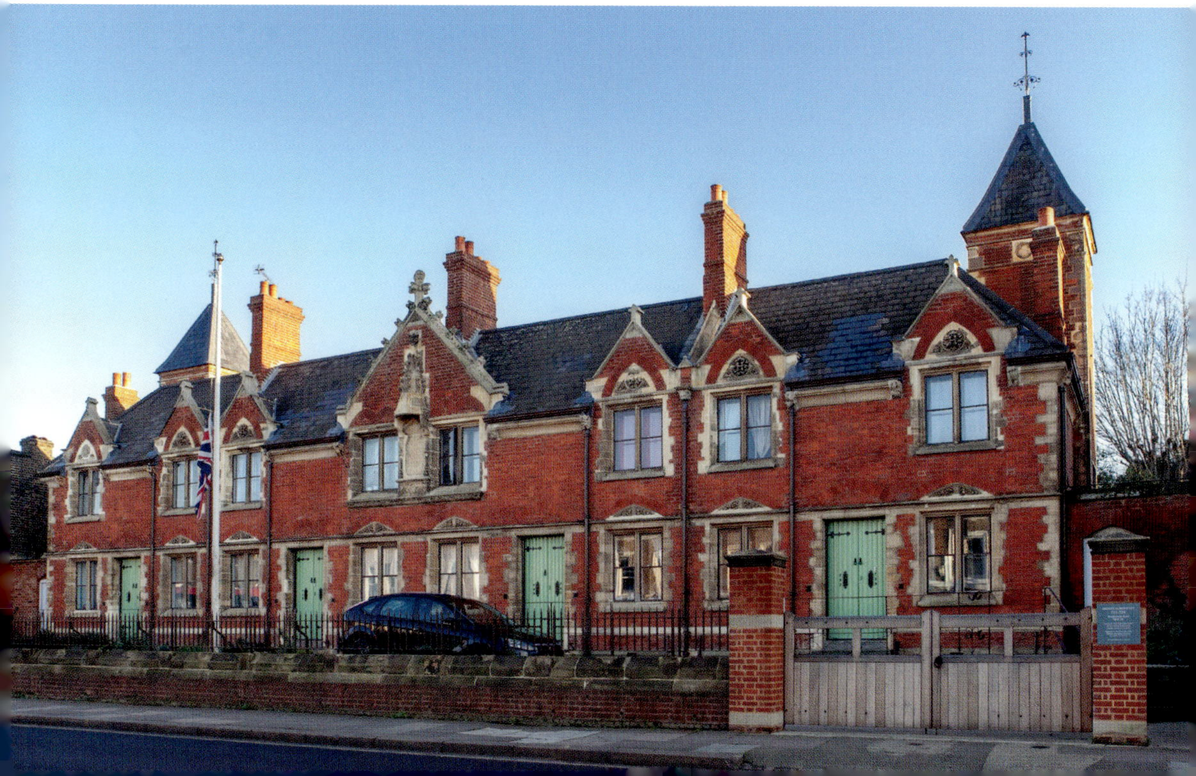

sold off to private landowners or fell into neglect. Fortunately, many livery companies and craft guilds of the City of London took over the role and set up 'hospitals' catering for the needs of the elderly and impoverished, many of which still exist today.

Nowadays, the Hibbert Almshouses are run by a trust of voluntary local trustees and a caretaker looks after the building's day-to-day needs and monitors the well-being of its residents. An annual garden party is held in the gardens each summer.

www.hibbertalms.org.uk

18. Nos 43-47 and 48–52 Cedars Terrace, Clapham Common North Side, SW4

In the latter part of the nineteenth century local architect James Knowles Jr (1831–1908) began developing an area, Park Town, which stretched from Clapham Common North Side towards the Thames. Knowles Jr's original intention had been to create an upmarket estate with wide boulevards and grand

Below and opposite: Cedars Terrace.

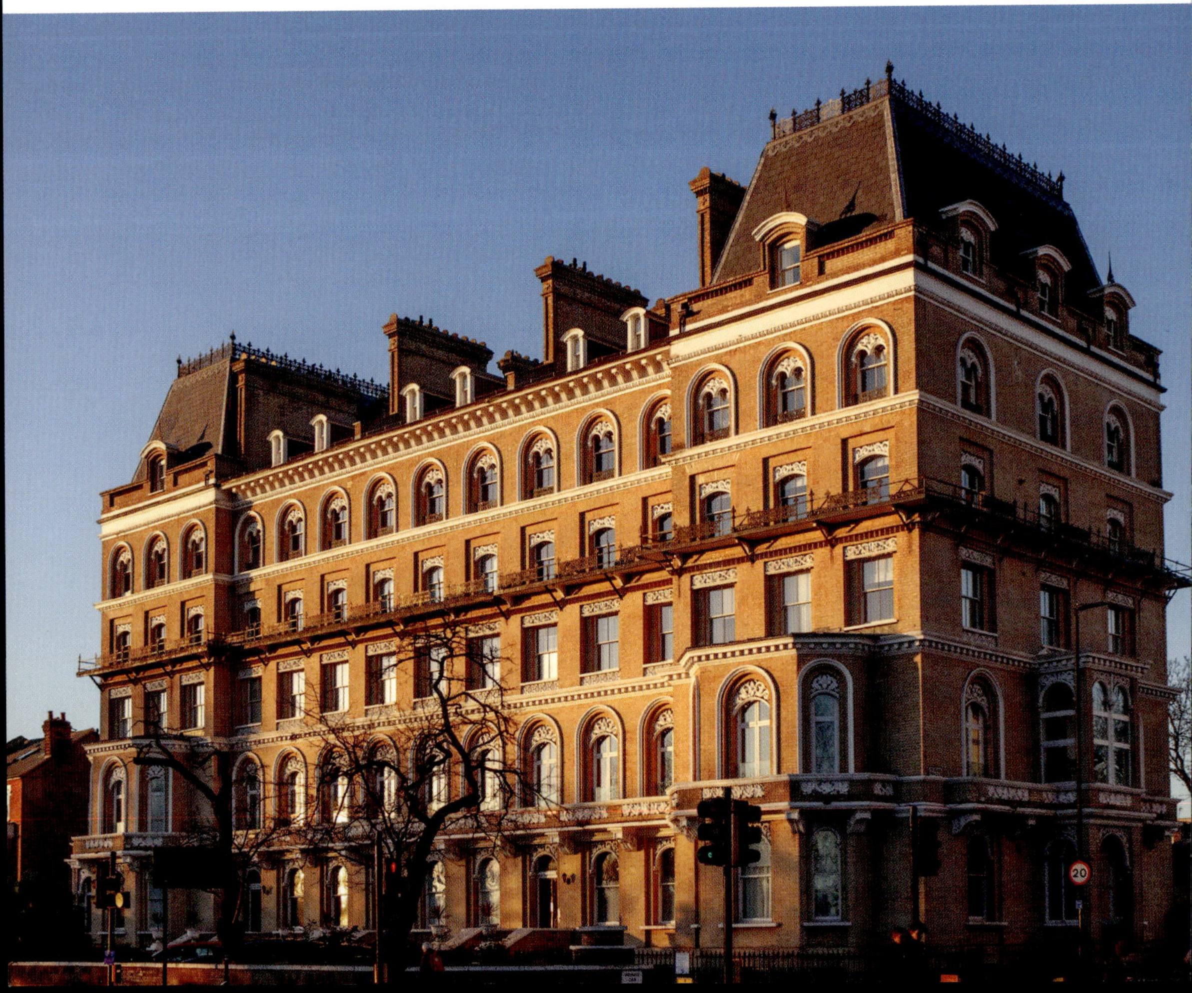

houses that would rival similar estates north of the river in Chelsea. Unfortunately, his plans were thwarted by the railway builders who were able to compulsorily buy up land, and proceeded to do so in the north of his estate which prevented him from developing it further as an upscale neighbourhood. However, he did manage to lay out Cedars Road and build some fine houses there, and in 1860 he erected two highly attractive apartment blocks at Cedars Road's junction with Clapham Common North Side. These blocks, positioned rather like a gateway on either side of Cedars Road, are impressive both for their height (five–six storeys) and for their lofty French pavilion roofs located at the end of the terraces. Knowles Jr

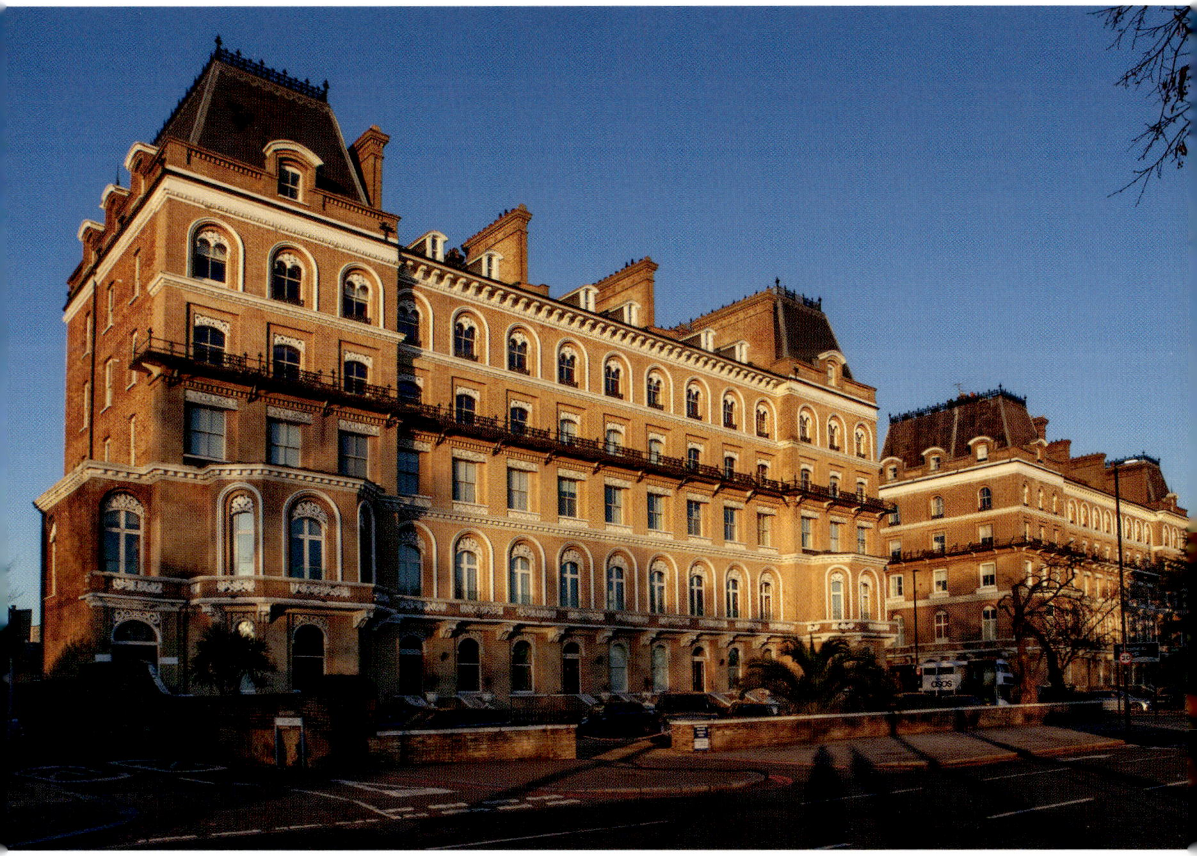

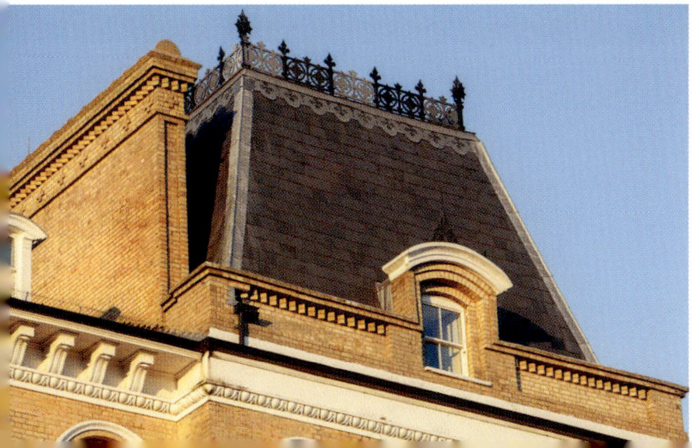

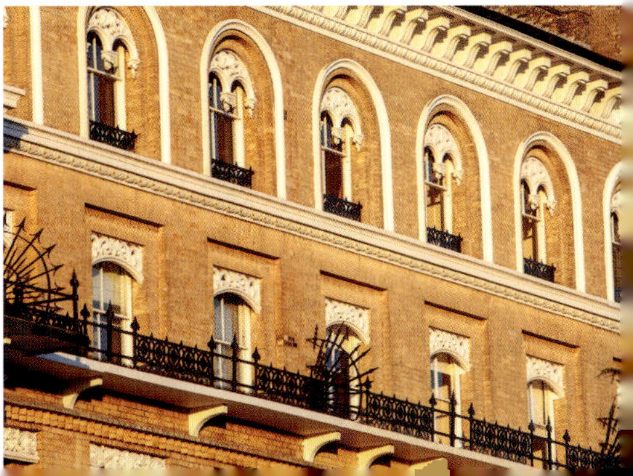

together with his father James Thomas Knowles became pioneers in this so-called French Renaissance Revival style and used it in their Parisian chateau design for the Grosvenor Hotel at Victoria railway station in London.

The Cedar Terraces are really a pair of magnificent buildings and simply dominate their locale. They can be seen from all parts of Clapham Common and when the sun goes down in the evening their façades change colour, and they are extraordinarily beautiful. Built in pale Suffolk brick, the terraces are embellished with cast-iron balustrades, steep-pitched roofs, elegant windows, a deep moulded cornice and ivy leaf decorations. The first-floor balcony is particularly attractive with its open work leafy panels. Today, as when they were first built, the apartments are greatly sought after.

Sadly, few of Knowles's forty-two grand houses in Cedars Road have survived; in fact, only Nos 113–19 remain. A 1960s local authority housing estate now occupies much of Knowles's former land. Built as low-rise blocks the development has been very successful and is set amid courtyards and mature trees, saved from the gardens of Knowles's large houses.

19. The Alexandra Hotel, Nos 12–16 Clapham Common South Side, SW4

The Alexandra, as it is known today, is a masterpiece of Victorian architecture with outstanding features on its façade. Four storeys tall with an attic, it sits

The Alexandra Hotel.

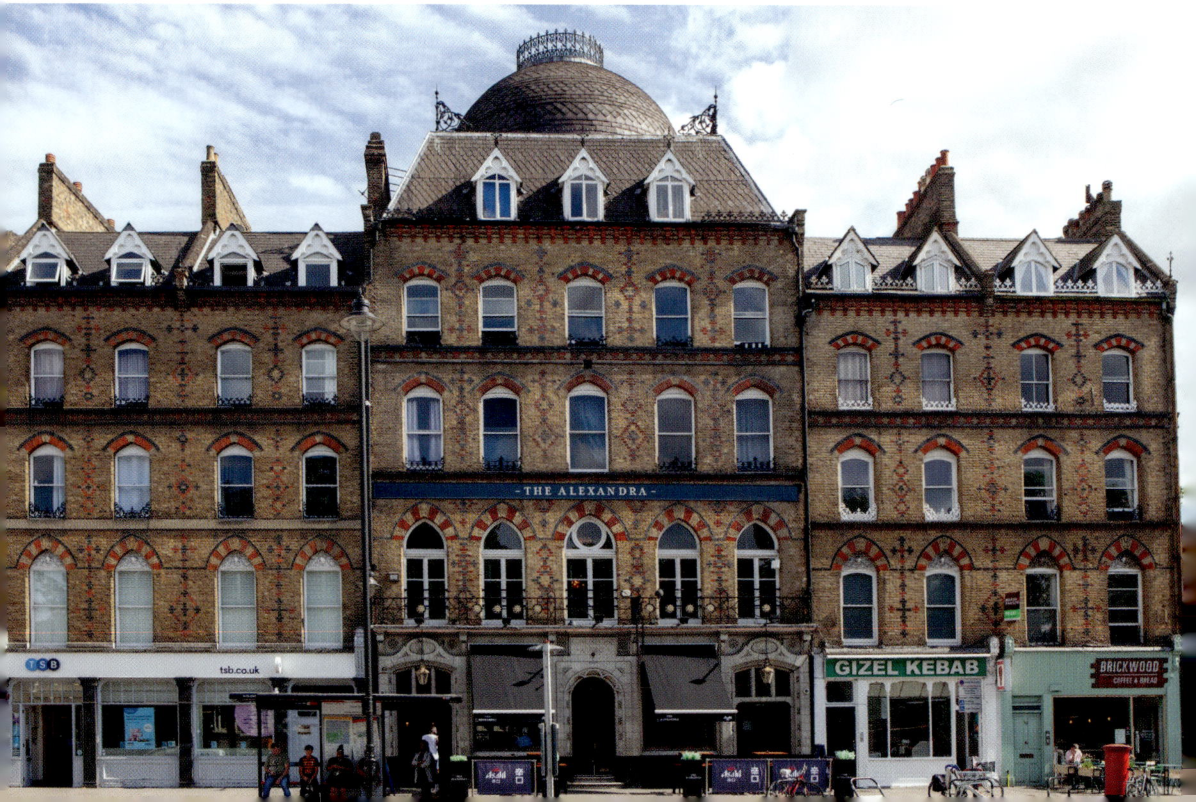

between two lower wings and the effect is one of perfect symmetry. Designed by Edward l'Anson, an architect who held office as president of both the Royal Institute of British Architects and the Surveyors' Institution, the building opened as an hotel in 1863. It was named after the then Princess Alexandra, wife of the Prince of Wales, later Edward VII. After thirteen years the hotel was converted into a pub, and at this point its flanking buildings were sold off.

Today, the Alexandra is a venue known for its good ales, and as a place to watch sports whether it be football (including Australian and Gaelic), rugby, or hurling, Interestingly, its popular first-floor function room, now the Darts Club bar, was once the site of the hotel's famous restaurant. Regrettably, nothing remains of its Victorian interior, but the building's striking exterior accentuated by its large dome decorated with fishtail slates, its cast-iron railings, and its elaborate polychrome patterned brickwork, suggests that the décor inside would have been equally as ornate.

www.alexandraclapham.com

20. Old Fire Station, No. 33 The Pavement, SW4

Renamed the Lodge, Clapham's old fire station is now a private residence and enjoys a prominent position just on the edge of Clapham Common towards Old Town. Built in the Gothic style, the building is immediately recognised by its two large ground-floor arches which originally supported the gates for the fire engines. When it was converted in the early twentieth century these arches were replaced, one into a doorway (painted red) and the other a window. The Lodge remains

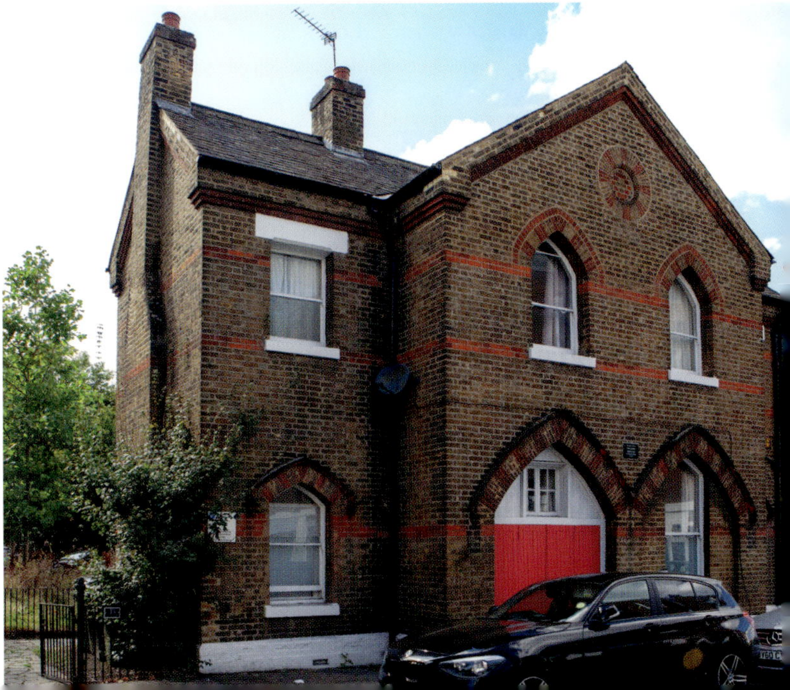

Old fire station.

much as it was built in 1868, extends over two floors and is constructed of stock brick and attractive polychrome brick. Its charming symmetrical frontage features a moulded brick cornice and plinth.

Prior to the construction of the old fire station there had been other buildings on the site owned by the parish of Clapham. The first of these was a seventeenth-century lock-up where drunks, vagrants and thieves would be detained overnight by the village watchman. In the early 1800s a one-storey fire-engine house replaced the lock-up, but following the establishment of the London Fire Brigade in 1866 the decision was taken to build a more substantial fire station. This was designed by the brigade's architect, Edward Cresy, and today is one of only three of his stations to have survived and is a unique example of a suburban station. This station was in operation for thirty-four years by which time both the appliances and population had grown markedly resulting in the need for larger premises. As the old fire station was built on a restricted site on Clapham Common, the new fire station was built at the corner of Old Town and Grafton Square in 1902 (which was itself rebuilt in the 1960s).

The need for coordinated fire services in London was only recognised following the Great Fire of London in 1666. This resulted in the arrival of private insurance companies who for a fee sent their own fire brigade to extinguish a fire at their policy-owners' premises. This privately run system continued until the early 1860s when a public fire service was called for following the horrific Tooley Street fire.

21. Former Sir Walter St John's Grammar School, Nos 28–40 Battersea High Street, SW11

This outstanding Gothic building is the work of the acclaimed Victorian architect William Butterfield and built for the Sir Walter St John's Grammar School in 1859. Butterfield, who is today remembered mainly for his design of All Saints' Church, Margaret Street, London, spent much of his working life designing ecclesiastical and educational buildings and his architectural style was greatly influenced by Augustus Pugin, the leader of the Gothic Revival movement.

The lavishly decorated asymmetrical school that fronts Battersea High Street is a real feast for lovers of the Gothic style: mouldings, stone dressings, pale gault brick diaper work, lancet windows and a magnificent entry arch, all set against a backdrop of warm red brick. It was built to replace the earlier school and nowadays many new modern buildings, a courtyard, a playground and playing fields have been added to the school behind its façade.

The school was opened in 1700 by Sir Walter St John, 3rd Baronet of Battersea and of Lydiard Tregoze, to educate twenty poor boys from the parish. It survived for 286 years, during which time girls joined the school. It was known as the Battersea School, but from 1860 it reverted to being Sir Walter St John's School,

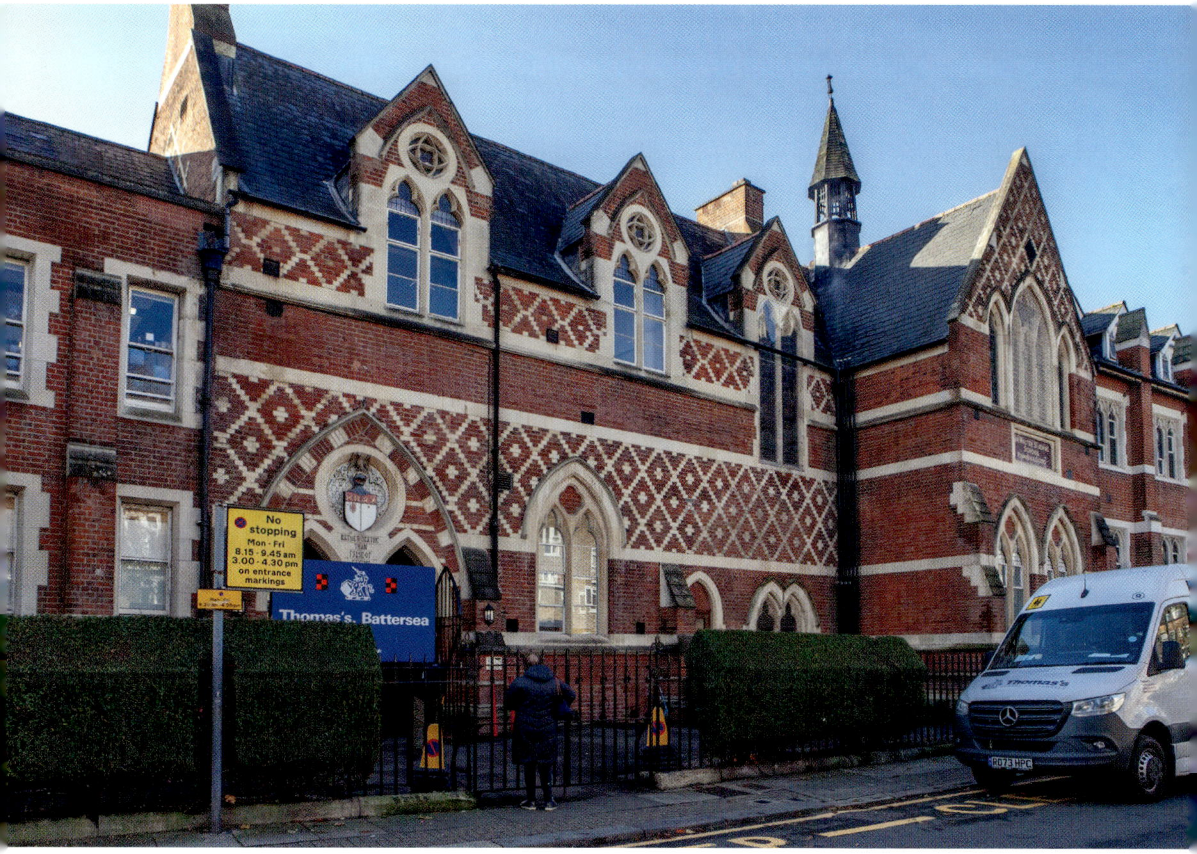

Former Sir Walter St John's School.

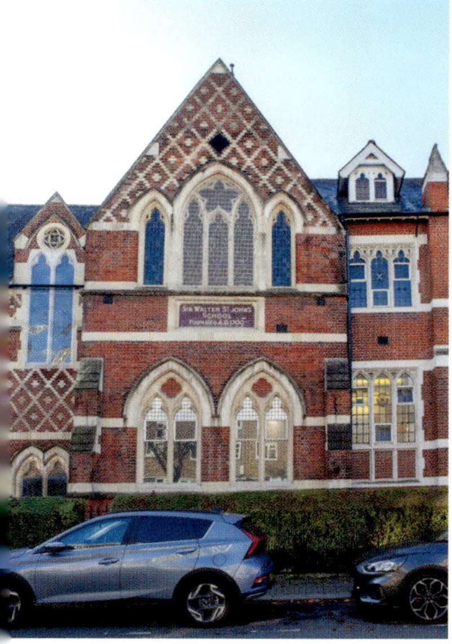

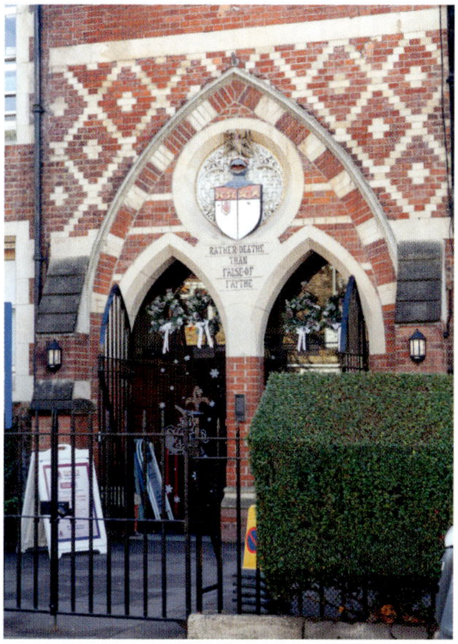

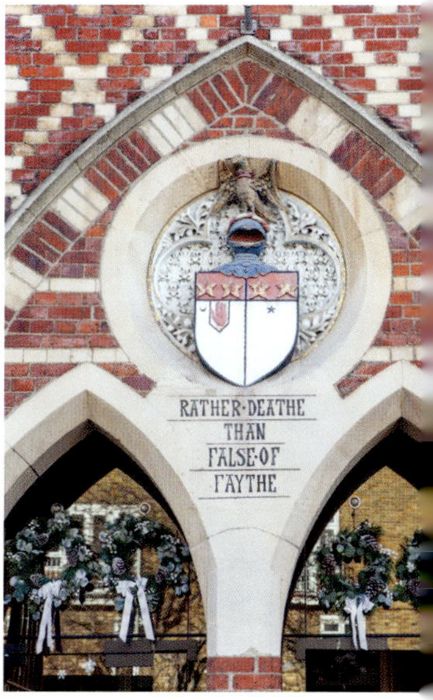

keeping this name until its closure in 1986. The school underwent numerous changes in its lifetime, becoming a secondary school in 1902, then a grammar school after the Second World War. In the 1970s it became a comprehensive school. In 1990 the premises were bought by Thomas's London Day School, and Thomas's continues to run the school today. Now a mixed prep school with 600 pupils aged between four and thirteen, it has an excellent reputation and produces, as its predecessors did, great artists, scientist, academics and athletes.

The novelist Martin Amis, actors Buster Merryfield and Melvyn Hayes, physicist Stanley Whitehead and Deep Purple musician Roger Glover were all alumni of the early school. More recently, before the family's move to Windsor, Thomas's was the school selected by the Prince and Princess of Wales to educate their eldest children, Prince George and Princess Charlotte.

22. Battersea Dogs and Cats Home, No. 4 Battersea Park Road, SW8

The Battersea Dogs and Cats Home (BDCH), now rebranded as 'Battersea', sits on the most awkward of sites beside the River Thames and is hemmed in by two railway lines.

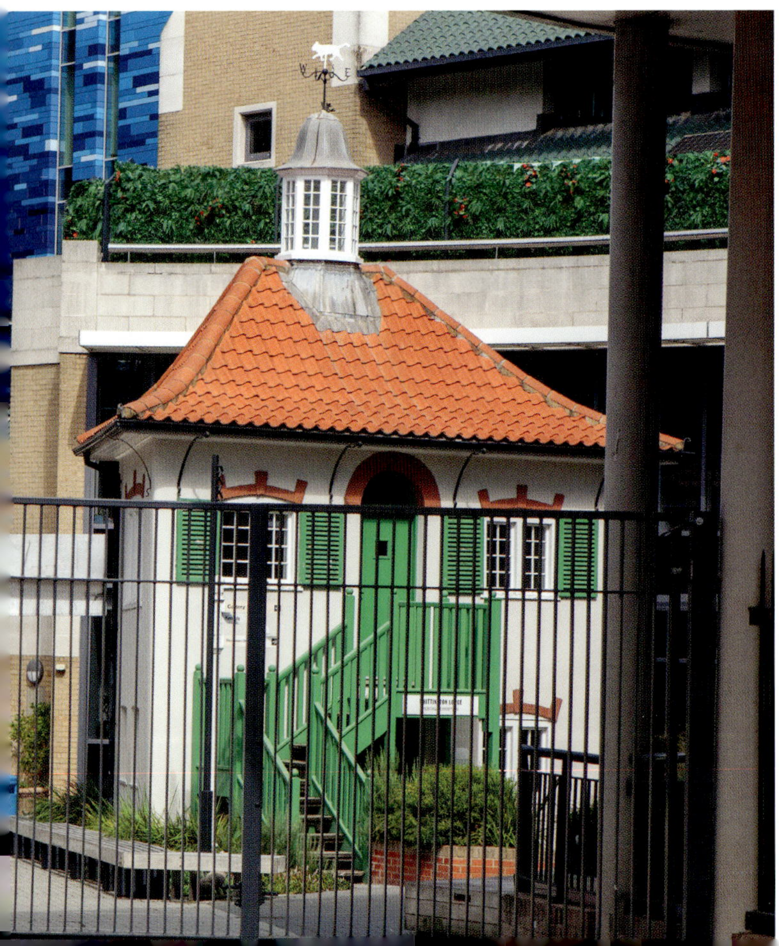

Whittington Lodge, Battersea Dogs and Cats Home.

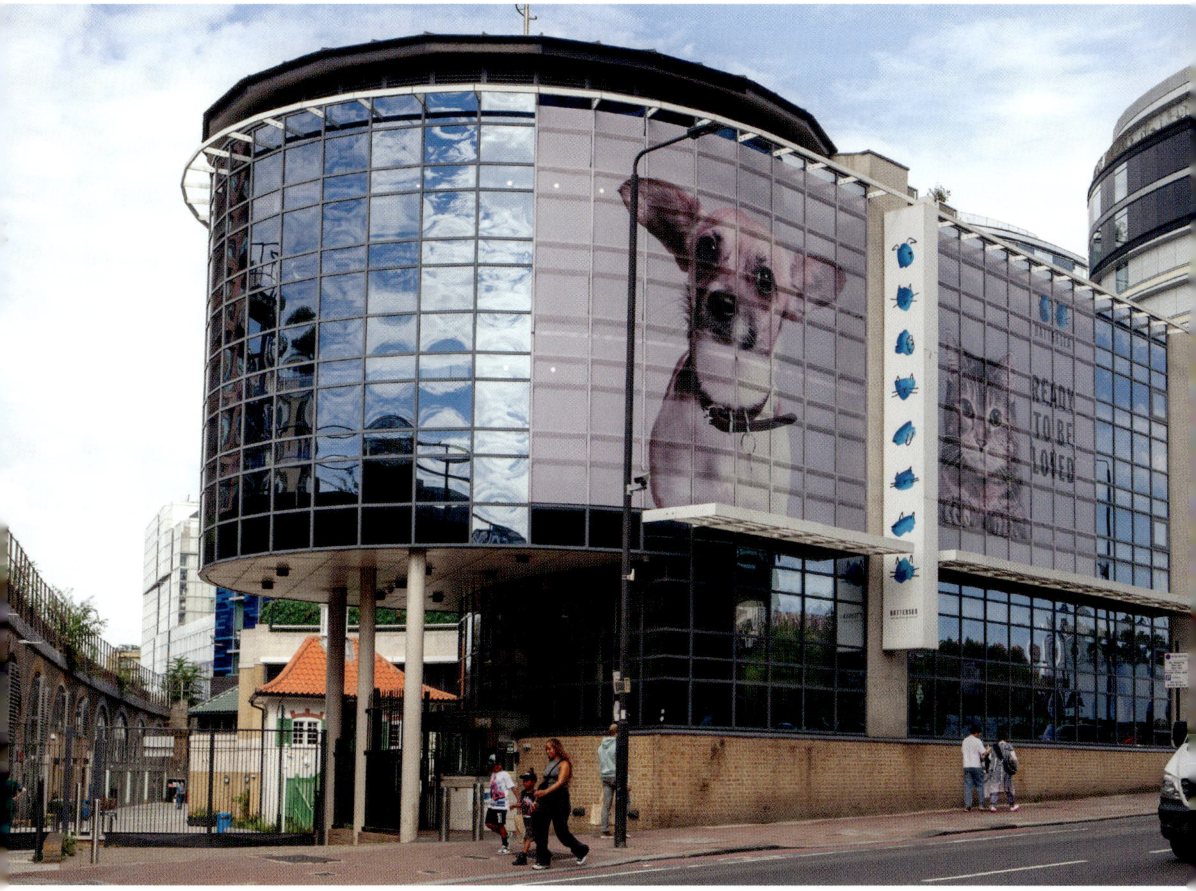

Above and below: Battersea Dogs and Cats Home.

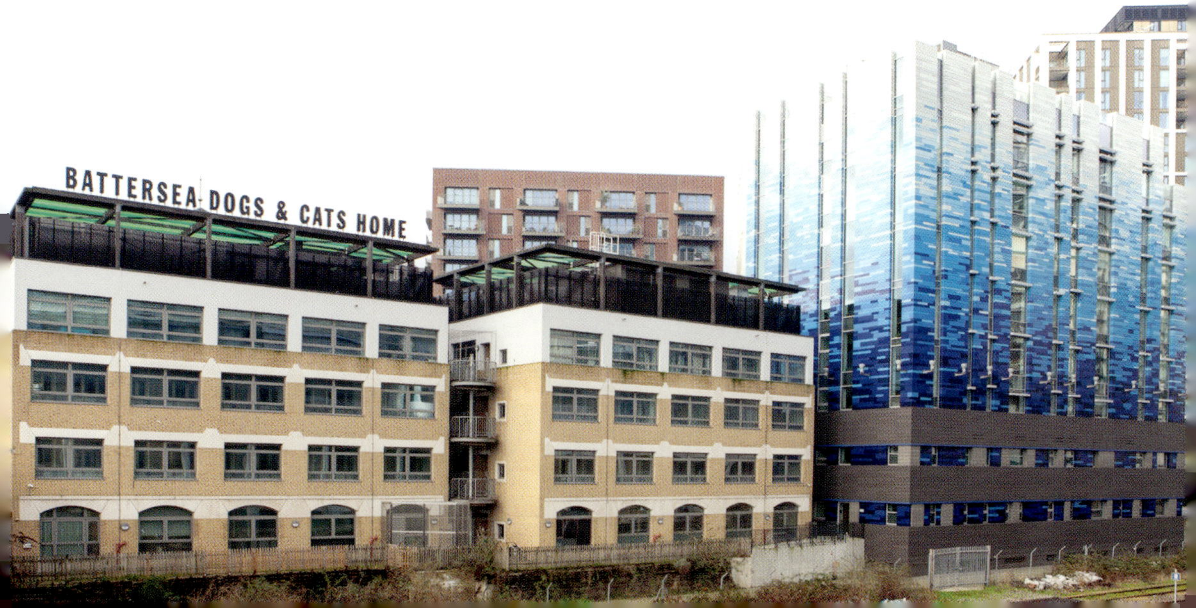

The charity was founded by Mary Tealby in 1860 as the Temporary Home for Lost and Starving Dogs and quickly obtained the support of the author Charles Dickens, which gave it greater credence – until this time, many in Victorian society had scoffed at the idea of rescuing dogs. From the early 1880s the BDCH was taking in cats, and Queen Victoria became the home's patron in 1885 (a role undertaken by Queen Camilla today). By the turn of the century the charity needed to expand its buildings, and the architect Clough Williams-Ellis, known for his Italianate village of Portmeirion in Wales, was commissioned to build a cattery, which was then named Whittington Lodge.This charming building still stands within the Battersea grounds and is now listed Grade II for its rarity – it may be the first of its kind to have been purpose-built in the UK – for its architectural and historic interest and because it is almost entirely complete except for the disappearance of the internal cat cages. Whittington Lodge is typical of the architect's idiosyncratic work and has some delightful Italianate and Arts and Crafts features, seen in its trapezoidal shape, flared steep pantile roof, octagonal cupola and weathervane.

In recent times Battersea commissioned Jonathan Clark Architects to build an intake and assessment wing, a kennel centre and a much larger block to accommodate a veterinary hospital, training centre and the charity's administration services. The latter, eight storeys high with a basement, was a real feat of engineering, erected just 3.6 metres from the rail tracks. It has the most beautiful façade made from glazed terracotta tiles, described by the architects as 'a pixelated patchwork of blues … intending to make the building act as a distinctive beacon'.

Today, this is one of several sites run by Battersea; the other two are based in Old Windsor and Brands Hatch. All three depend on public donations to support their work caring for the animals.

www.battersea.org.uk

23. The Shaftesbury Park Estate, Battersea, SW11

Battersea's population increased rapidly in the 1800s due to the capital's massive industrial expansion and the area, like much of London, suffered from poor, unsanitary and overcrowded housing. The working classes were living in dire conditions and were unable to find alternative decent accommodation at rents they could afford. Their plight was well documented in Charles Dickens' books, but there was no co-ordinated government help to improve the situation. Fortunately, philanthropists such as Anthony Ashley-Cooper, 7th Earl of Shaftesbury, MP, addressed the problem in Parliament while George Peabody, Sir Edward Guinness and other patrons began building affordable, healthy and sturdy housing for the respectable working poor.

In the 1870s an area of flat land close to the Thames, renowned previously for producing high-grade asparagus, was purchased by the Artizans', Labourers'

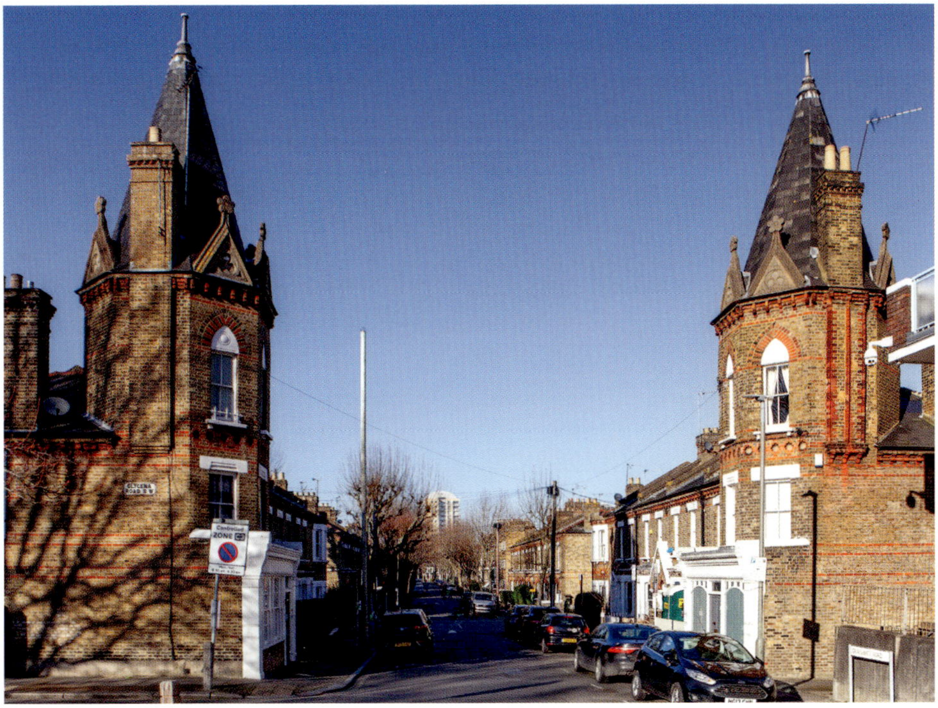

Gateway to Shaftesbury Park Estate.

and General Dwelling Company (ALGDC), a housing co-operative. Its founder, labourer William Austin, planned to provide solid, quality housing for the working poor which would provide community facilities such as a washhouse, baths, a school and a large recreational space. In keeping with prevalent temperance attitudes of the time, no pubs were to be built on the estate. Lord Shaftesbury laid the foundation stone in 1872, and the development promptly adopted his name.

Responsibility for the attractive design of the Shaftesbury Park estate lies with Robert Austin (no relation to William), the ALGDC's architect. Its southern entrance on Grayshott Road is stunning, framed by two turreted houses, and remarkably little has changed since the development was constructed. Austin built tree-lined streets and laid out the estate as a grid with long parallel streets crossed by shorter streets. These he filled with low-rise terraces of brick cottages which came in slightly different designs. With interesting and distinctive features such as canopied paired front doors and pointed Gothic arches of red and black brick, the estates' cottages have an overall uniformity which makes them so visually charming. The 1,200 homes constructed were of four sizes which affected their cost (between £170 and £310) although many were rented from the outset. Today very popular and far from cheap, the homes are in both private and Peabody Trust ownership.

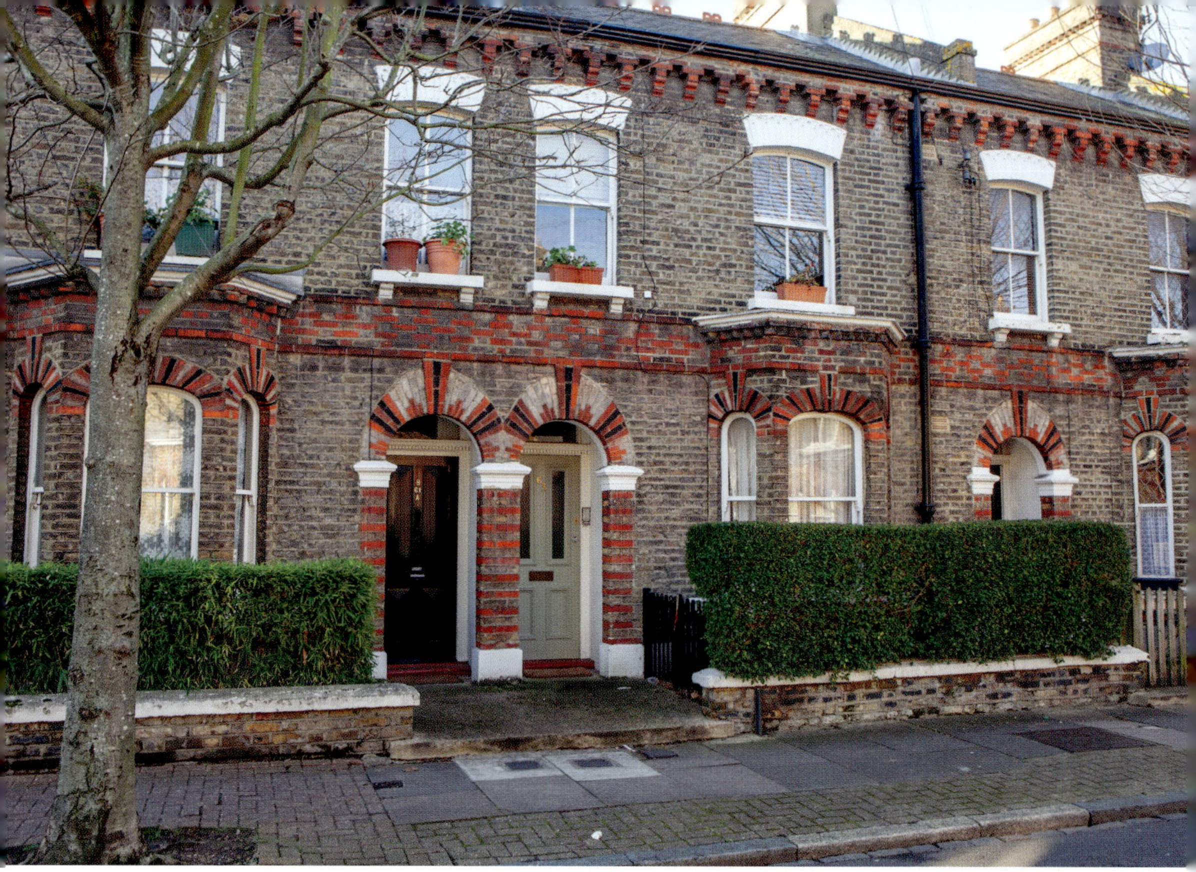

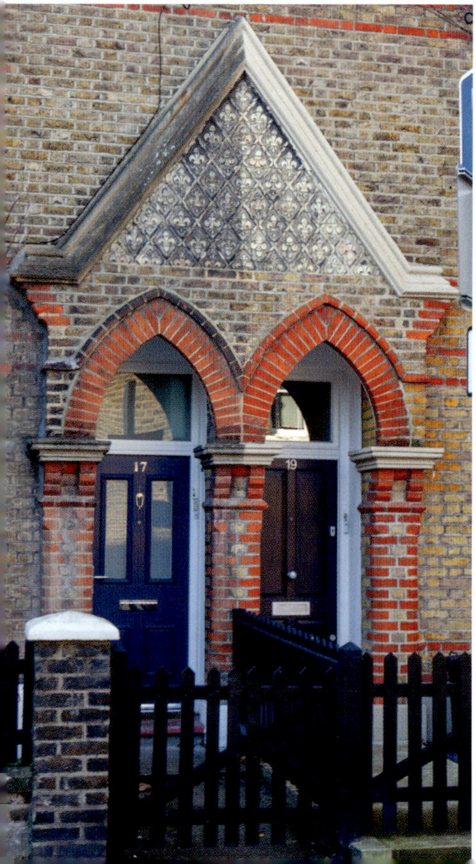

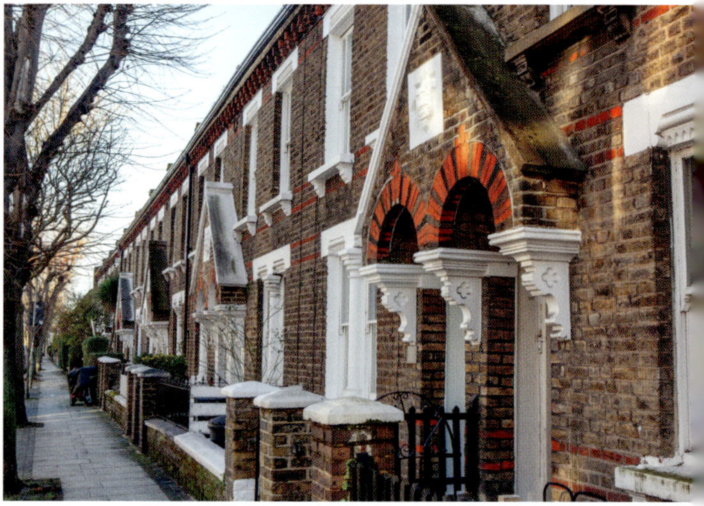

Top, left and above: Shaftesbury Park Estate.

24. The Falcon, No. 2 St John's Hill, Battersea, SW11

It is impossible to miss this splendid Victorian pub sitting beside Clapham Junction railway station. Its position on the corner of such a busy road junction, opposite the former Arding and Hobbs department store and amid shops and offices, makes it highly accessible. Today it is known as much for its fine ales as its sports entertainment; it frequently attracts a large crowd, especially on match days and

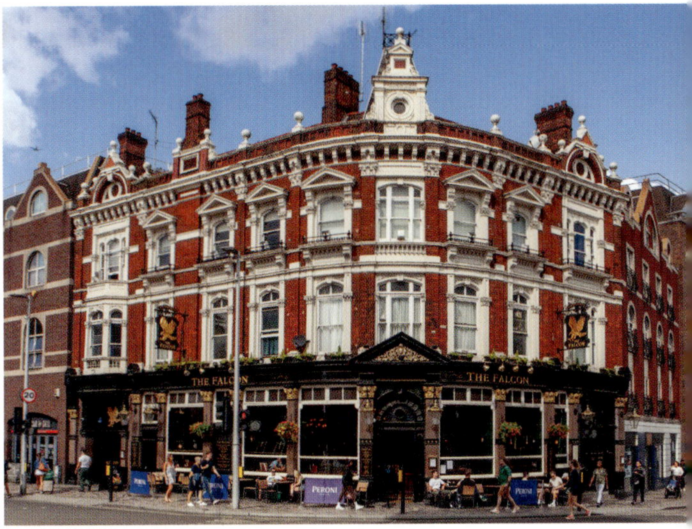

Right and below: The Falcon public house.

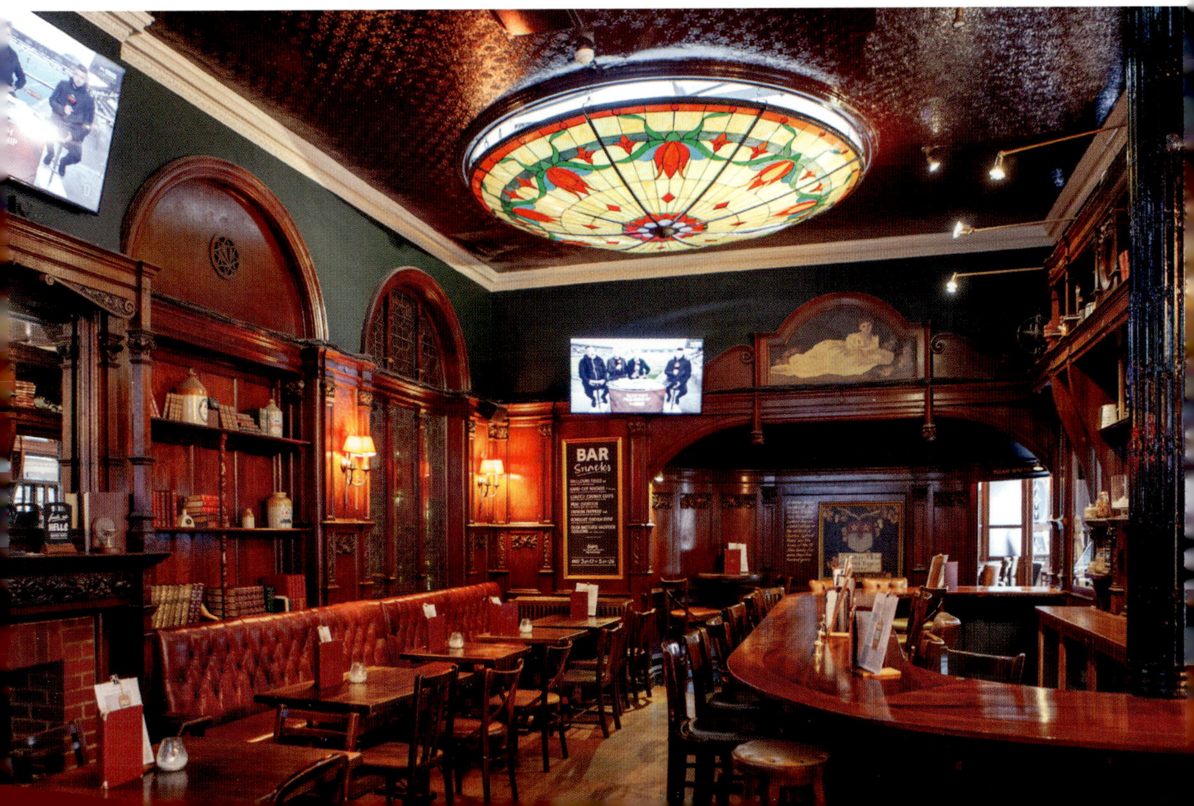

on weekends when there is live music. The Falcon comes under the umbrella of Nicholson's Pubs and like many pubs in their portfolio it has its own delightful ambiance and distinctive style.

The Falcon was opened as a hotel in the late 1880s. The building, with its gorgeous curved front, straddles Falcon Road and St John's Hill, both of which have their own entrances. A further entrance that is embellished with an elaborate pyramidal roof and flagstaff on the rooftop, faces directly towards the road junction. The pub's red brick and white stone façade is striking, and its architecture undoubtedly reflects that of the Victorian age – with grand stone and granite pilasters, pediments, fanlight windows, beautiful hanging lamps and prominent chimneys.

Its interior is equally as notable; the public bar is an enormous space with dark wood panelled walls and at one time held the record in the Guinness Book of Records for containing the country's longest pub counter. A main feature is its glass, some cut-glass as is found behind the bar display, in partitions between the bars, and some original glass in the snug on the left-hand side of the pub that depicts a falcon, the bird of prey after which the pub is named (it appears on the crest of the St John family, the lords of Battersea manor from 1644 to 1763).

The interior of the Falcon is embellished by fluted cast-iron columns with capitals and certainly lives up to CAMRA's Heritage Pubs group's description of being 'mightily impressive'. It appears in CAMRA's National Inventory of Pub Interiors of Outstanding Historic Interest and moreover, is designated a Grade II listed building.

https://www.nicholsonspubs.co.uk

25. No. 7 Alexandra Avenue and Prince of Wales Road, Battersea, SW11

Built in 1879–80 as a vicarage for the Church of St Saviour Battersea, the house is unusual in having two main frontages: one onto Alexandra Avenue, the other facing Battersea Park on Prince of Wales Drive. It is a house that immediately catches the eye due to its brickwork which is elaborately patterned with diamonds and geometric designs on the first and second floors, and the cast- and wrought-iron gate and gate screen in front of the Alexandra Avenue entrance. Built as three storeys in grey and red brick, the house features tall chimneys, a stepped gable roof on its northern side, sash windows and dormers in the attic space. Some features, such as the moulded stone string courses beneath the roof line and the brick band between the basement and ground floor, continue across the building. The entire house has an impact on the streetscape and its design and quality of build are much acclaimed.

No. 7 Alexandra Avenue was designed by John Oldrid Scott, the second eldest son of Sir George Gilbert Scott, best known for his design of the Midland Hotel, St Pancras station. Oldrid Scott's career was mainly spent on ecclesiastic design, and he was renowned for his work at St Sophia's Greek Orthodox Cathedral in Bayswater. Following his death in 1913 *The Times* newspaper obituary

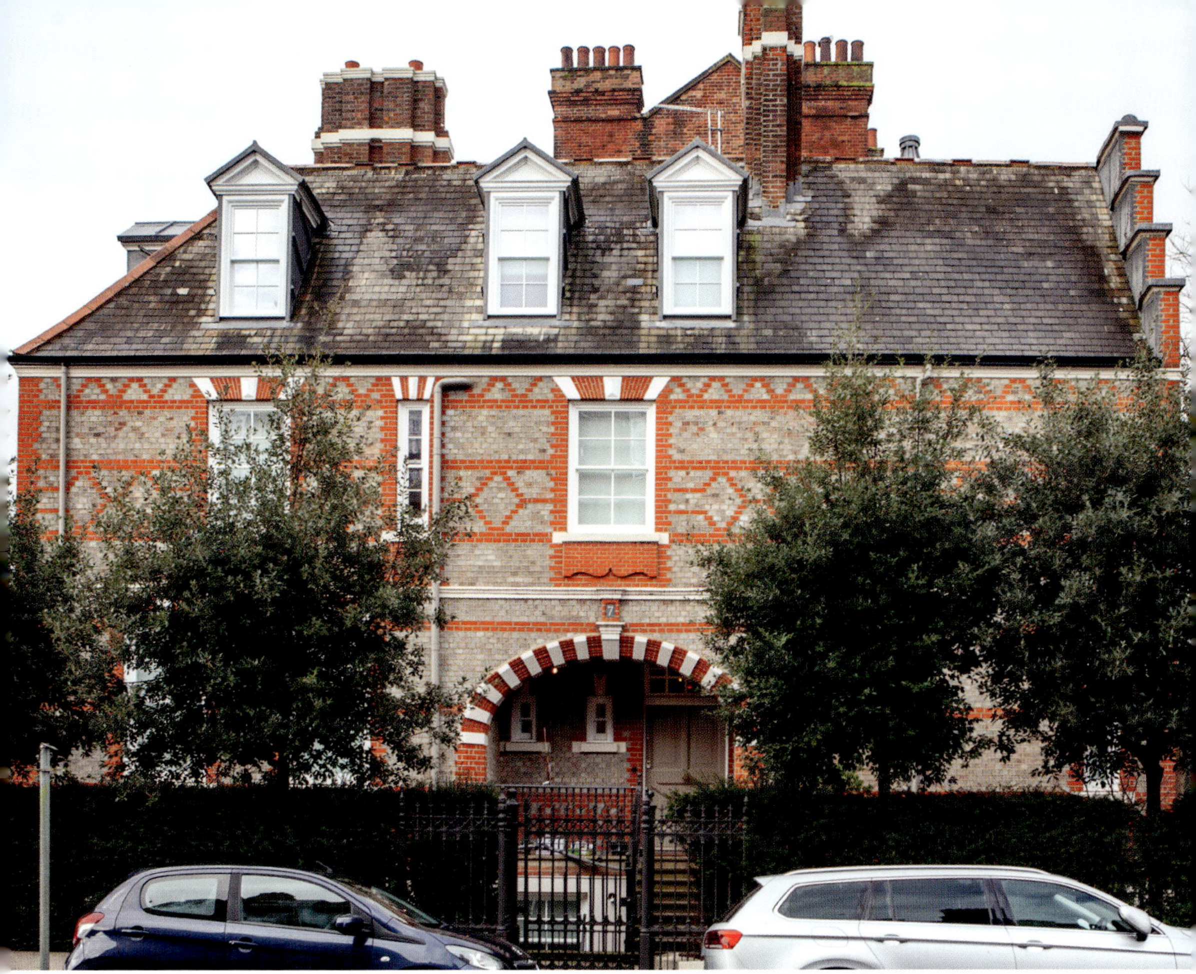

Above: No. 7 Alexandra Avenue.

Below: No. 7 Alexandra Avenue on Prince of Wales Drive.

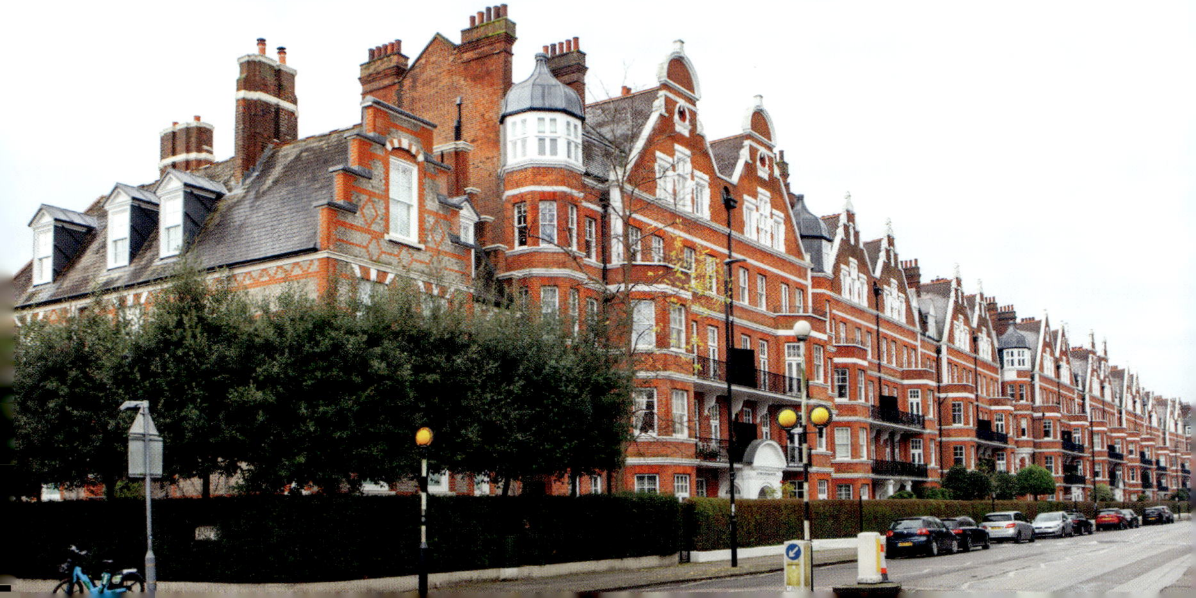

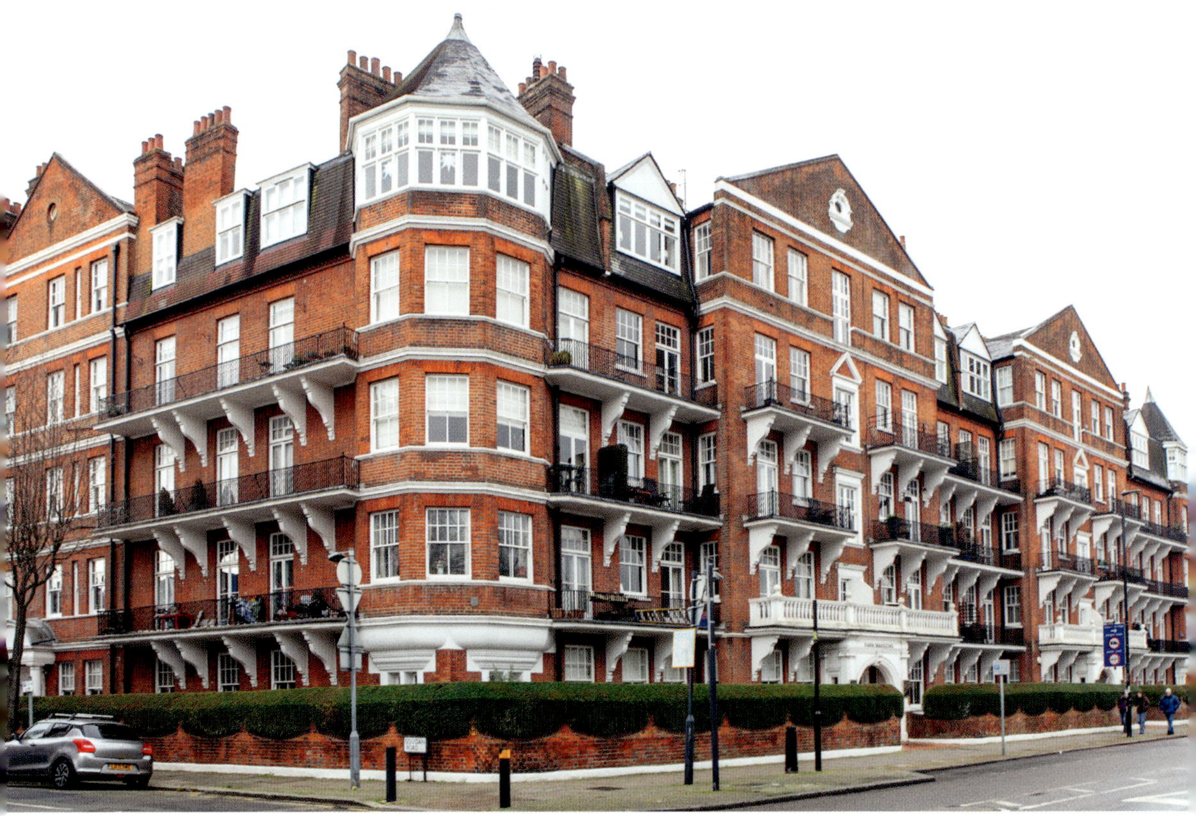

Park Mansions on Prince of Wales Drive.

said: 'He was not an architectural genius ... but he was a sound workman in his own chosen province of architecture.' Certainly, No. 7 Alexandra Avenue demonstrates Oldrid Scott's great attention to detail – and in the words of Historic England it as 'an interesting example of his domestic style'.

The former vicarage stands out even more on Prince of Wales Drive as most housing here is in mansion blocks that overlook Battersea Park. There are seven groups all individually named, and each of five storeys in height. Although at first glance they appear uniform this is not so. Look closely and you will see distinct differences in decoration, on the roofline, in the windows, balconies and entranceways. All were built between 1892 and 1902 and are nowadays part of the Battersea Park Conservation Area.

26. Bolingbroke Academy (Former Hospital), Wakehurst Road, Battersea, SW11

Since its foundation in 2012, Bolingbroke Academy has occupied the site of the former Bolingbroke Hospital which was a vital part of Battersea's community for more than 132 years. The school is part of the education charity Ark, one of the UK's leading academy providers, and is a four-form secondary school and sixth form establishment. Most recently awarded 'outstanding' status by Ofsted, the academy was praised for its excellent curriculum, high-quality teaching and its

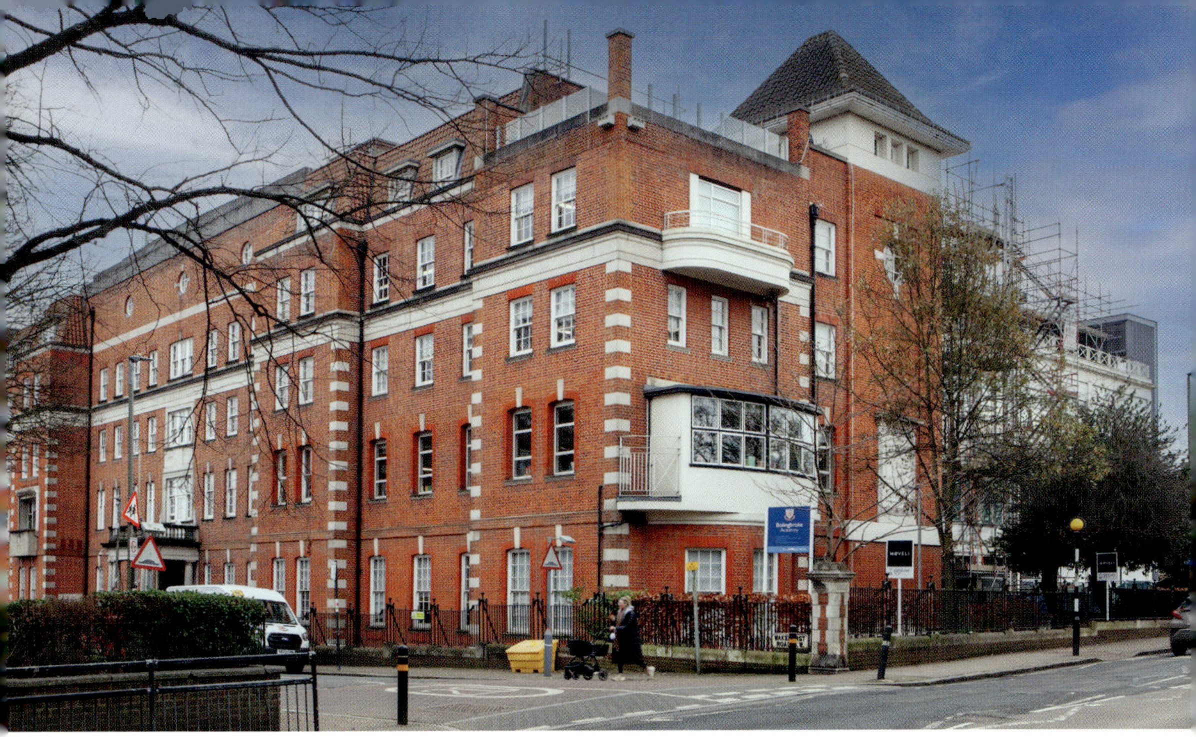

Above and right:
Bolingbroke Academy.

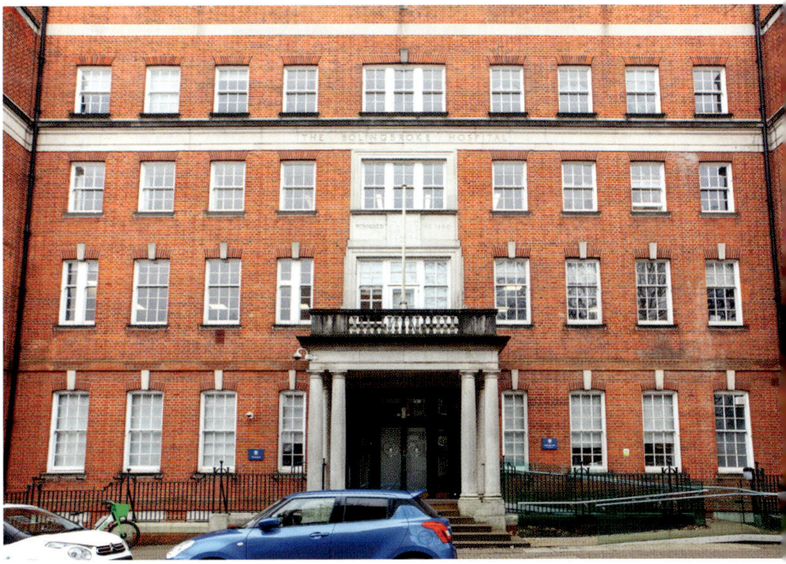

broad personal development of pupils. Pupils are fortunate in being schooled at a modern school that combines contemporary buildings and facilities with heritage, evident in its older twentieth-century Grade II listed buildings.

Bolingbroke Hospital's first patient was admitted in 1880 after Bolingbroke House was purchased from Viscount Bolingbroke. Named the Bolingbroke Self-Supporting Hospital and House in Sickness, it became a small general hospital and was one of the very first to serve the artisan and middle classes. Until this time the wealthy received private treatment in their own home and the poor were treated in workhouse infirmaries, but nothing had been available for those who fell in-between the two. From the early 1900s new wings were added housing an Out-Patients Department (1901) and a three-floor building with basement accommodating an operating theatre, mortuary and wards (1906). The Bolingbroke Wing, a ward block then opened in 1914 and was used to treat military patients during the First World War.

One final building was added in 1927 by which point the hospital contained beds for 120 patients and included a children's ward. Ten years later the original house was demolished to make way for an administration building and to build a main entrance for Bolingbroke Hospital. The design of all the twentieth-century extensions was by the architectural practice Young and Hall and is of particular interest as it shows how they introduced new styles of architecture for each phase, ranging from Edwardian Free style to neo-Georgian and then to 1930s Moderne.

Today's school library was once the children's ward and still displays an exceptional set of tiles that depict nursery rhymes and animals.

www.arkbolingbrokeacademy.org

27. Victorian Churches: St Mark's and St Luke's

These two Anglican churches were built in entirely different architectural styles despite opening within years of one another. The first to be built between 1872 and 1874 was St Mark's on Battersea Rise, near Clapham Junction. The church, designed by the architect William White in the Early English Gothic style of the thirteenth century and sitting at the top of a hill, is a large and imposing building built in yellow stock bricks with red dressings and diapering. At its south-west corner the church tower with its wooden belfry and spire can be seen for miles around and dominates the local area. The church interior is equally as impressive; the nave with its choir stalls, pulpit and raised font (on a stone and tiled stepped plinth) were all built to White's designs while the concrete piers and carved capitals were the work of Harry Hems. Perhaps its most unusual feature is the ambulatory at the east end which descends to the crypt.

In the 1980s St Mark's fabric was crumbling and the church suffered from a waning congregation. Fortunately, with assistance from Holy Trinity Brompton it was able to recover, and the church began a programme of restoration which has resulted in the establishment of a welcome hall and an enlarged meeting hall. Both are now venues for a multitude of community activities and have contributed greatly to the revival of St Mark's.

St Luke's, like St Mark's, is a Grade II* listed building but is built in the Italian Romanesque, basilica style. Work began on it in 1883 and the church was completed in 1892 to the designs of F. W. Hunt. It is a most handsome building constructed of red brick, decorated with moulded and shaped brick string courses

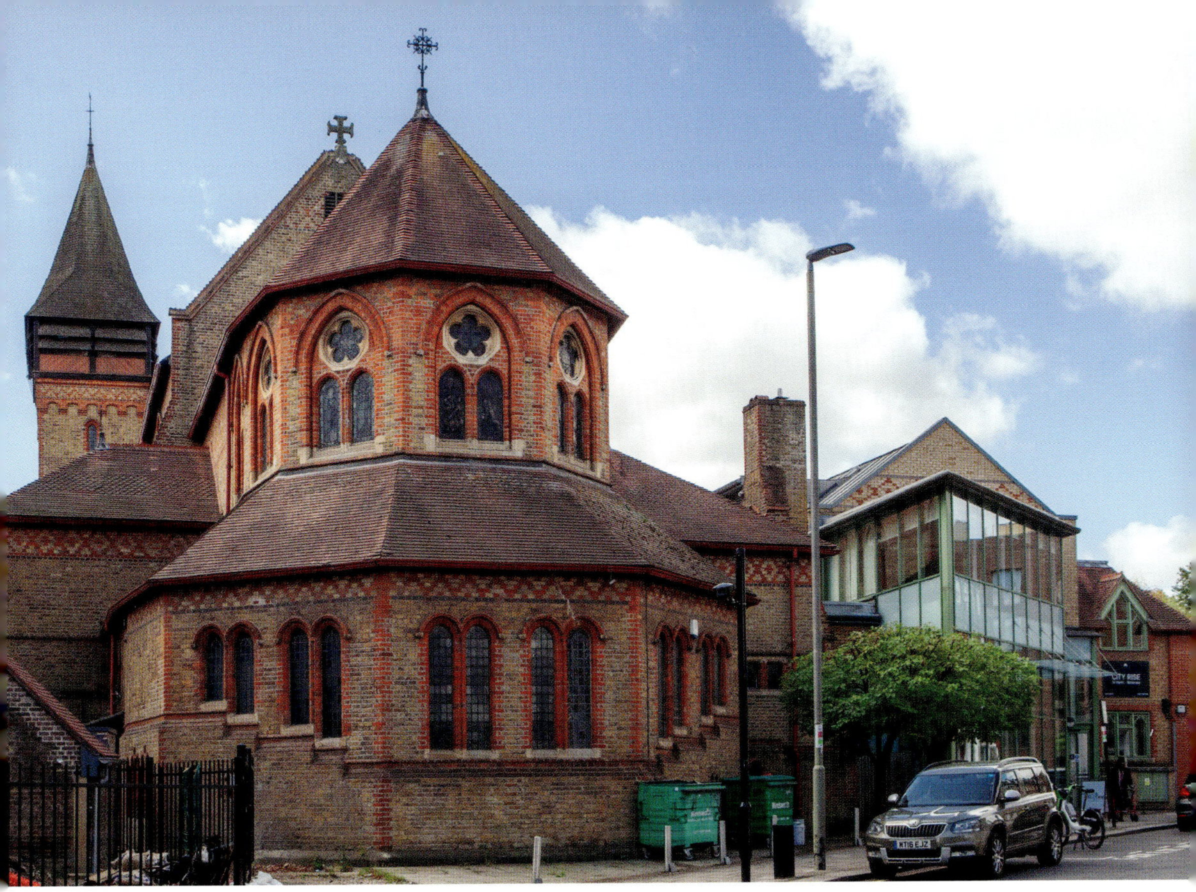

Above and below: St Mark's Church.

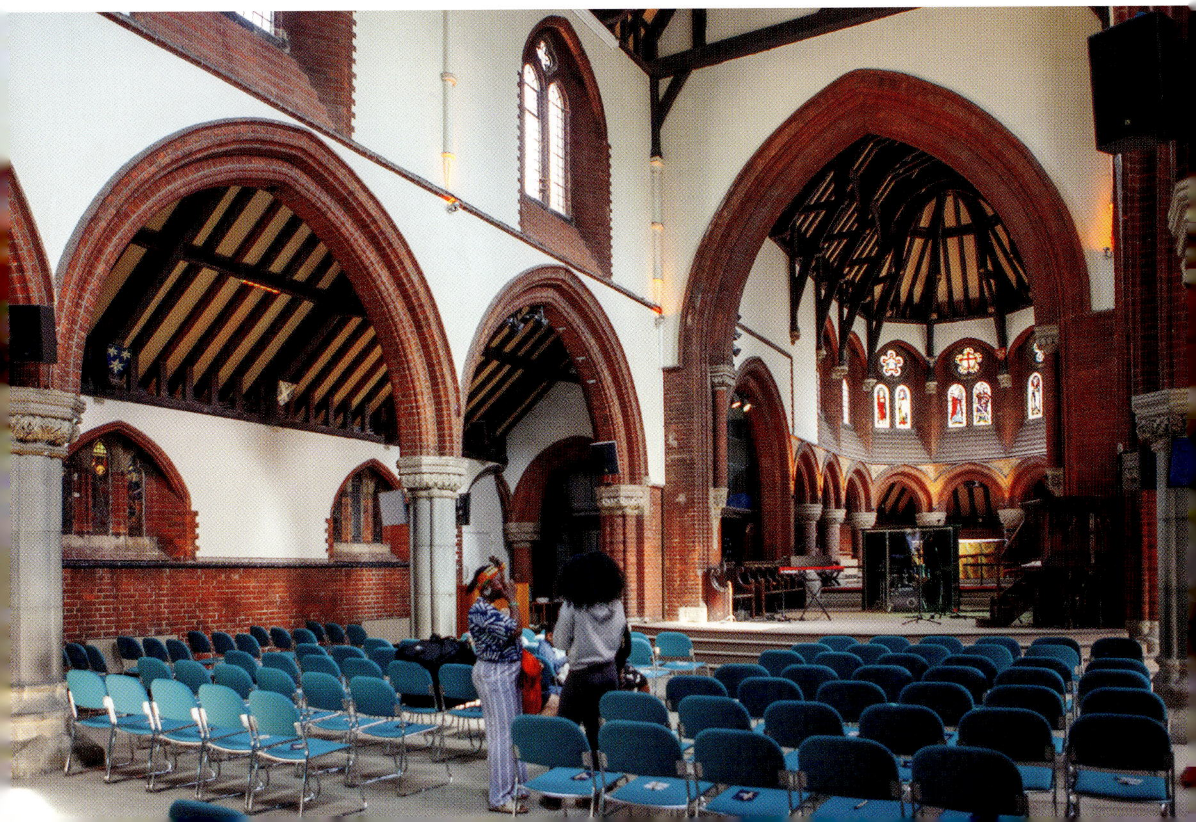

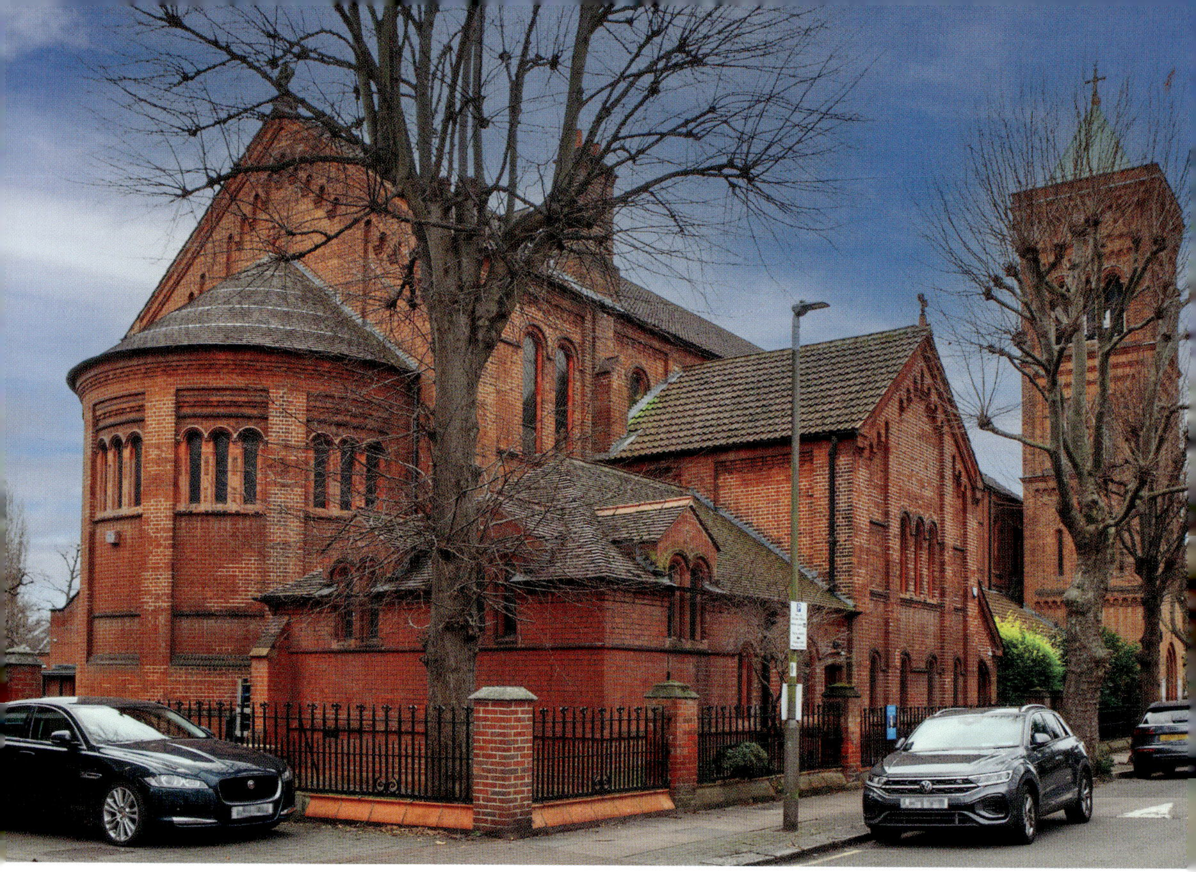

Above and below: St Luke's Church.

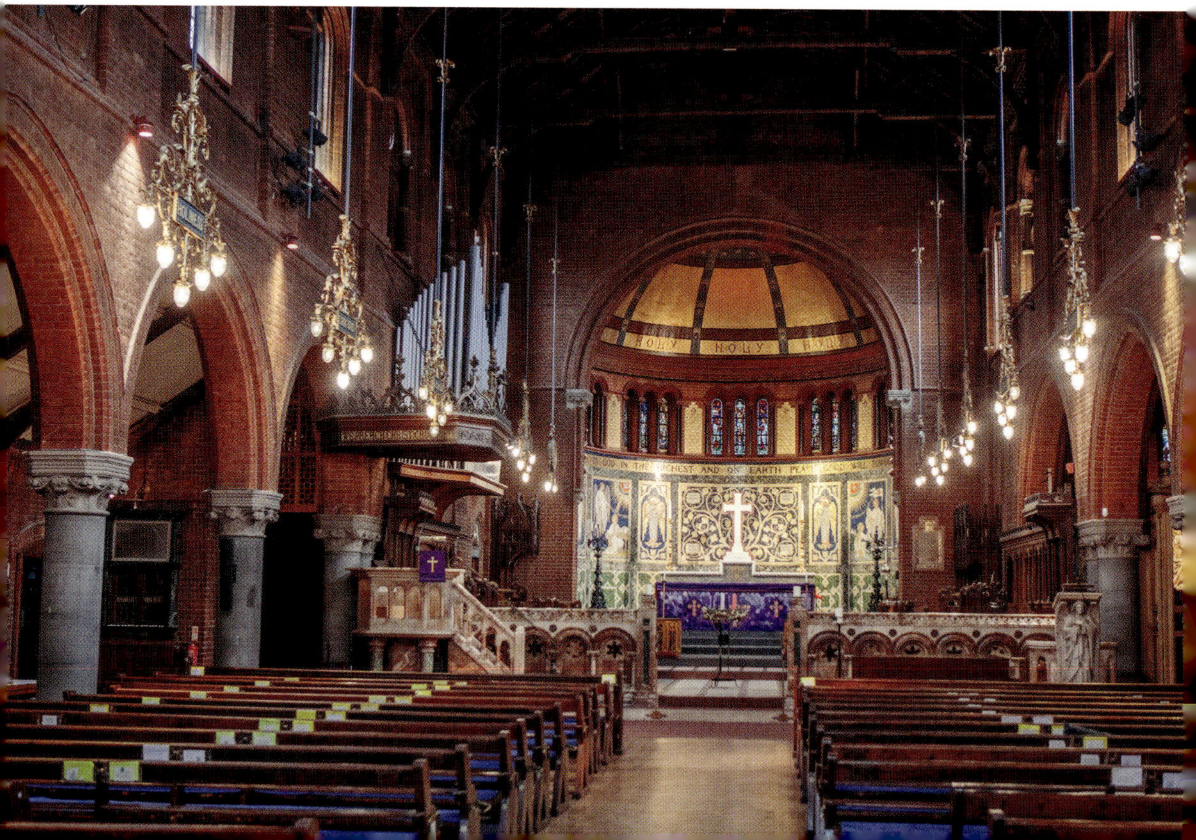

and has a tall campanile over its north-west entrance. Its magnificent interior includes William White's handiwork – seen in the lantern, alabaster and marble pulpit and chancel wall – and that too of Harry Hems, who was responsible for the bishop's throne, sedilia and choir stalls. St Luke's is celebrated moreover for its wonderful pointed arched arcades, its apse mosaic and original metal electroliers installed in the early 1900s.

smbr.church
www.stlukeschurch.org.uk/welcome.htm

28. Clapham Junction Station, Battersea, SW11

Probably the most unusual fact about Clapham Junction is to be found in its name, for in reality it lies in Battersea, not Clapham, which is about a mile away. Naturally this has caused much confusion to travellers over the years, so much so that the famous Bradshaw railway timetable felt compelled to add a footnote advising travellers of the misnomer. It is still a mystery as to why it was so named, but the most convincing argument is that the railway companies felt that the former was a wealthier area and would thus attract more customers at a time when Battersea, although full of market gardens was also quite industrial. In other words, Clapham Junction sounded more respectable than Battersea!

Clapham Junction station.

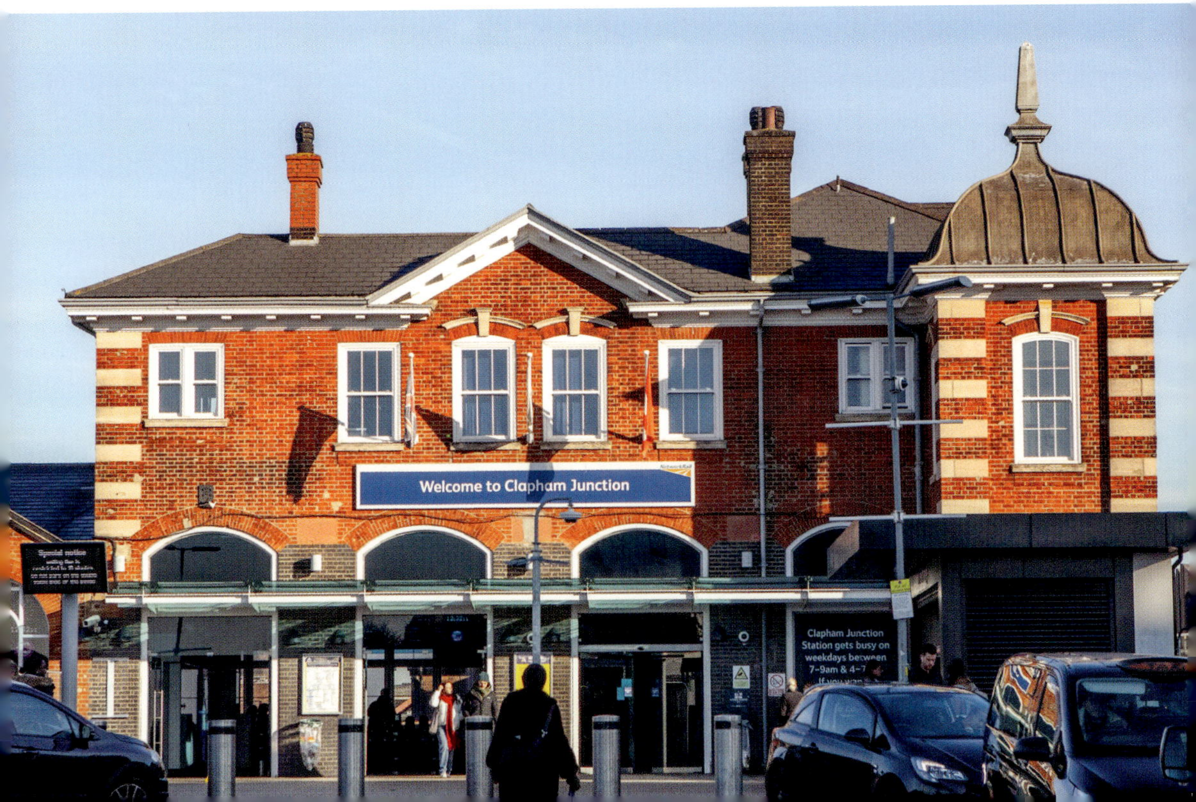

By 1860 the intersection had become so busy that the railway companies pooled resources and built Clapham Junction station much as it is now. With all trains from Waterloo and Victoria passing through the station, it has always been exceptionally busy and today it is alleged to be the busiest interchange in the UK. The station's original Victorian built entrance on St John's Hill with its attractive red-brick façade is in daily use and passengers reach the platforms (eighteen in total) via a covered footbridge.

29. Former Arding and Hobbs Department Store, Lavender Hill and St John's Road, SW11

Arding and Hobbs (A&H), dubbed the 'Harrods of the South', began its life in Clapham Junction as a department store in 1885 specialising in drapery and furnishings. It was the third shop owned by Henry Arding and James Hobbs to open in the area in a decade. The new enterprise combined all three shops into one store and A&H became an exceptionally successful retail centre as the population around Clapham Junction grew in the late 1800s. Calamity hit in 1909 when A&H was burnt to the ground in a dramatic fire; eight lives were lost and many injured. Yet within a year the store was up and running and the reconstruction resulted in a much larger and grander building. Designed in the Edwardian Baroque style by the architect James Gibson, it was stunning: set on four floors in red brick with warm Bath stone. It was built to rival the recently launched Selfridges store on Oxford Street, so great attention was paid to its internal design and to the range of its departments and services to entice

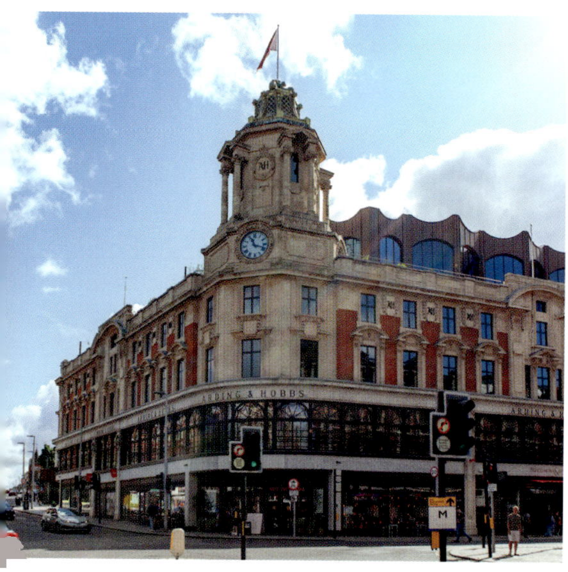

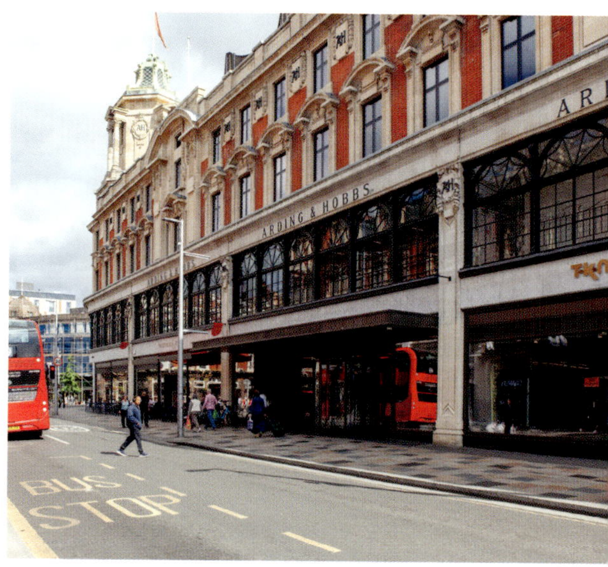

Above left and above right: Former Arding and Hobbs department store.

customers through the doors. Externally, too, the store was most attractive, adorned with carvings, façades, centrepieces and display windows with beautiful round-headed fanlights. Above the main entrance at the apex of the store a majestic Baroque roof cupola and green copper belfry was added that to this day is a local landmark.

After James Hobb's retirement in 1905 the store remained in the hands of Henry Arding and his family until the late 1930s. From then on, the store changed hands several times until 2005 when Debenhams PLC took it over. Sadly, the Debenhams chain collapsed in 2020, putting the A&H's future in jeopardy, but following major renovation carried out by its new owner, W.RE, this wonderful Battersea institution has reopened and now offers a mix of shops, a restaurant and bar, a health club and offices. The latter are housed in a new roof extension and in the building's upper floors. A&H's restoration has been exceptional, and the building now looks as glorious as it did when it opened in 1910.

30. The Omnibus Theatre (Former Clapham Library), Clapham Common North Side, SW4

Public libraries first appeared in Britain after the passing of the 1850 Public Libraries Act, which permitted free libraries to be established by local authorities. The Act stipulated that a local poll had to be conducted and required two-thirds of those voting to be in favour of establishing a library. Prior to this time there were philanthropic libraries (free to their users) and others that were paid for by subscription. Clapham's library on Clapham Common North Side was erected in 1889 following a concerted effort by three men, namely the vicar of St Paul's Church, a churchwarden of Holy Trinity Church and a wealthy gentleman, William Guesdon who lived in the neighbourhood.

Edward Blakeway l'Anson (1843–1912), a renowned London architect who lived in Clapham, won the commission for the library's design. The library he built is easy to recognise for its handsome red-brick gabled façade in the neo-Flemish style. The original interior consisted of a ground-floor borrowing area and a section where newspapers, periodicals, and railway guides could be read. Upstairs was a room large enough to accommodate public meetings and the librarian's own living quarters. Throughout its lifetime (1889–2012) the library remained popular with the locals but as readers' habits changed Lambeth Council decided to replace it with a purpose-built library in Clapham High Street. Local opposition to the closure was enormous and for a time the building's future was uncertain. However, the council was finally persuaded to lease the premises again agreeing to its use as an arts centre.

Since 2013, the building has been home to the independent Omnibus Theatre and has been supported by patrons such as Sir Michael Gambon, Sir Richard Eyre, Dame Judi Dench and Matthew Warchus. It is a registered charity and with Marie

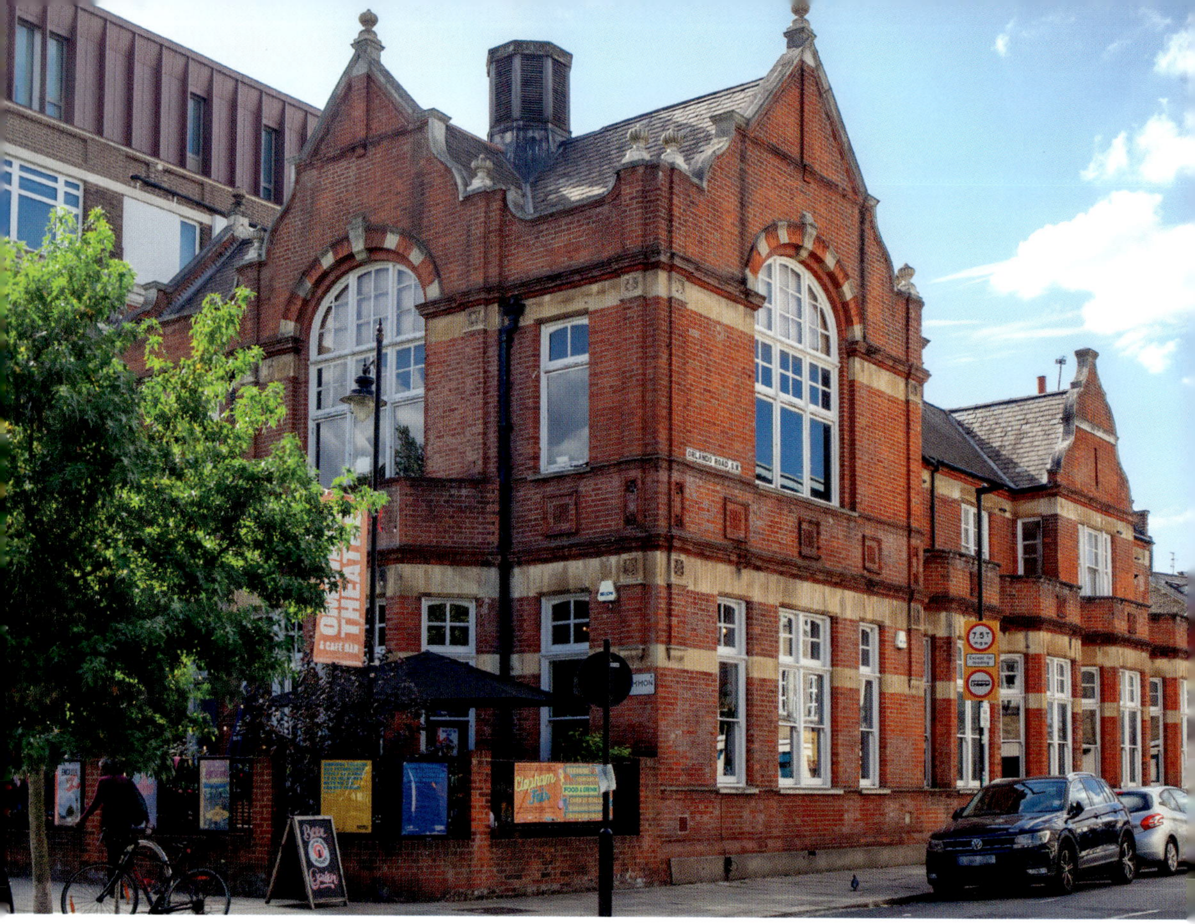

The Omnibus Theatre.

McCarthy as its Artistic Director it has gone from strength to strength. Offering two main performance spaces, the Theatre and the Studio Upstairs, two rehearsal areas and a café-cum-bar the Omnibus is extremely successful. It puts on theatre of every genre and has won many awards for its productions which are not only affordable but all-inclusive. Today it is a thriving off-West End venue.

www.omnibus-clapham.org

31. Clapham Common Bandstand, SW4

This glorious structure stands in the very heart of Clapham Common and is one of its most loved landmarks. It was built in 1890 to the designs of the London County Council's (LCC) architect Thomas Blashill and is a brightly painted circular construction with coupled iron columns. Designated a Grade II listed building by Historic England, the listing describes the bandstand's roof as 'a Greek cross on plan with quadrants filling the angles. Above is a shallow drum of pierced ironwork supporting a … lead dome'.

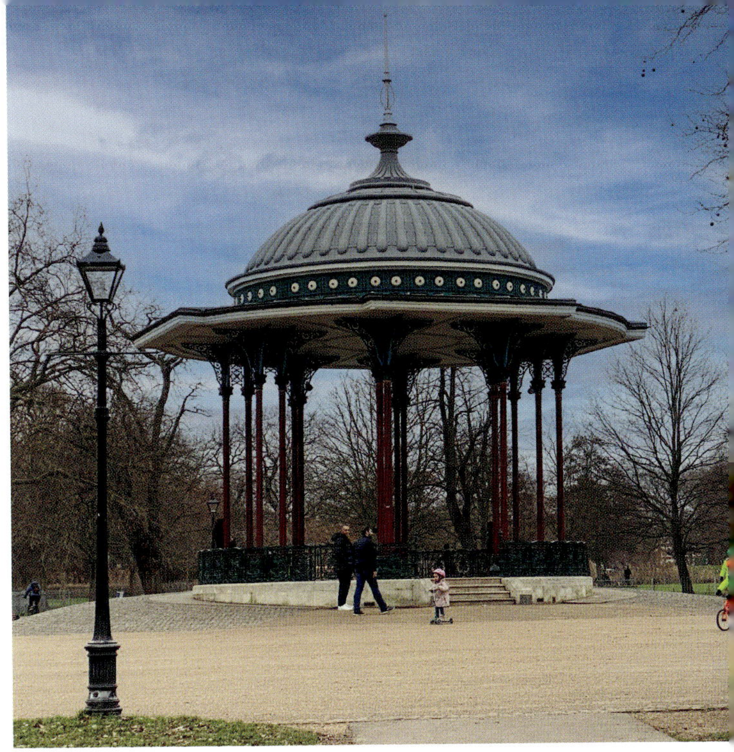

The bandstand, Clapham Common.

Clapham's bandstand was built in response to a local petition and was in constant use until after the Second World War. Concerts took place here every Wednesday, when there was half day closing for local shops, and again on Sundays. Over the course of time its popularity waned and by the early 2000s the iconic bandstand was in a sorry state, daubed with graffiti, with rusted columns and its crumbling cupola was home to nesting birds! Fortunately funding for its refurbishment was received from the Heritage Lottery Fund, through local fundraising and from Lambeth Council. The bandstand, now returned to its former magnificence is in constant use throughout the summer months.

32. Battersea Library and Reference Library, No. 265 Lavender Hill and Altenburg Gardens, SW11

Battersea Central Library, with its striking corner turret, was built by the Battersea Vestry in the late 1880s at a similar time to the library in nearby Clapham. Constructed in warm red brick its façades are embellished with Portland stone and there are a series of attractive terracotta relief panels beneath the second-floor windows. The building is an excellent example of the Baroque Revival architectural style and has a great presence on Lavender Hill. The library was built to the design of E. W. Mountford, the architect of the Old Bailey, who won an architectural competition for the project. His entry, the only one to fulfil the Vestry's budget criteria was selected from a group of ten proposals and his

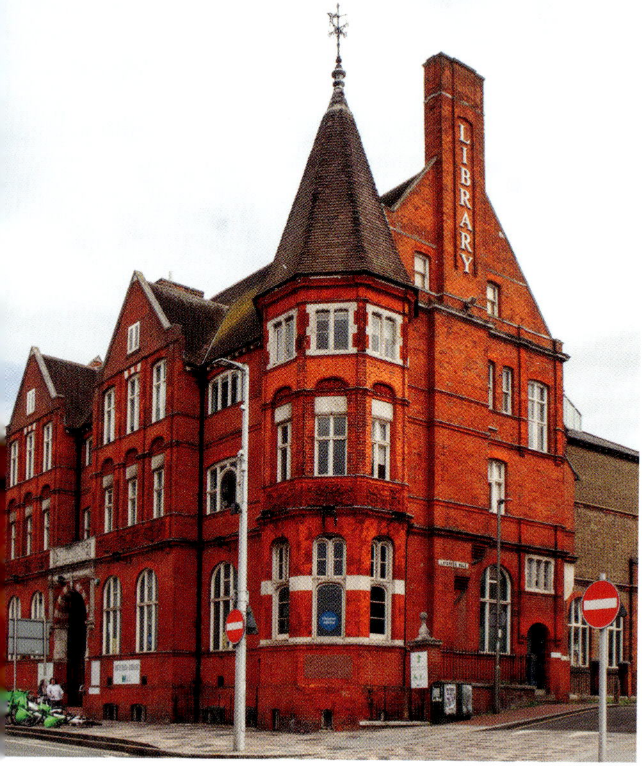

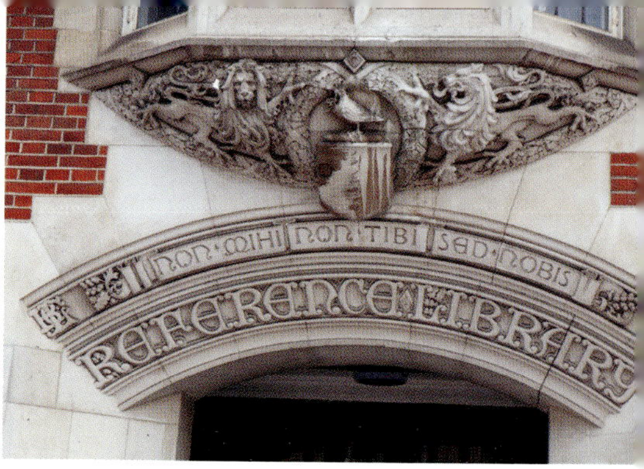

Above: Battersea Central Library.

Left and below: Battersea Reference Library.

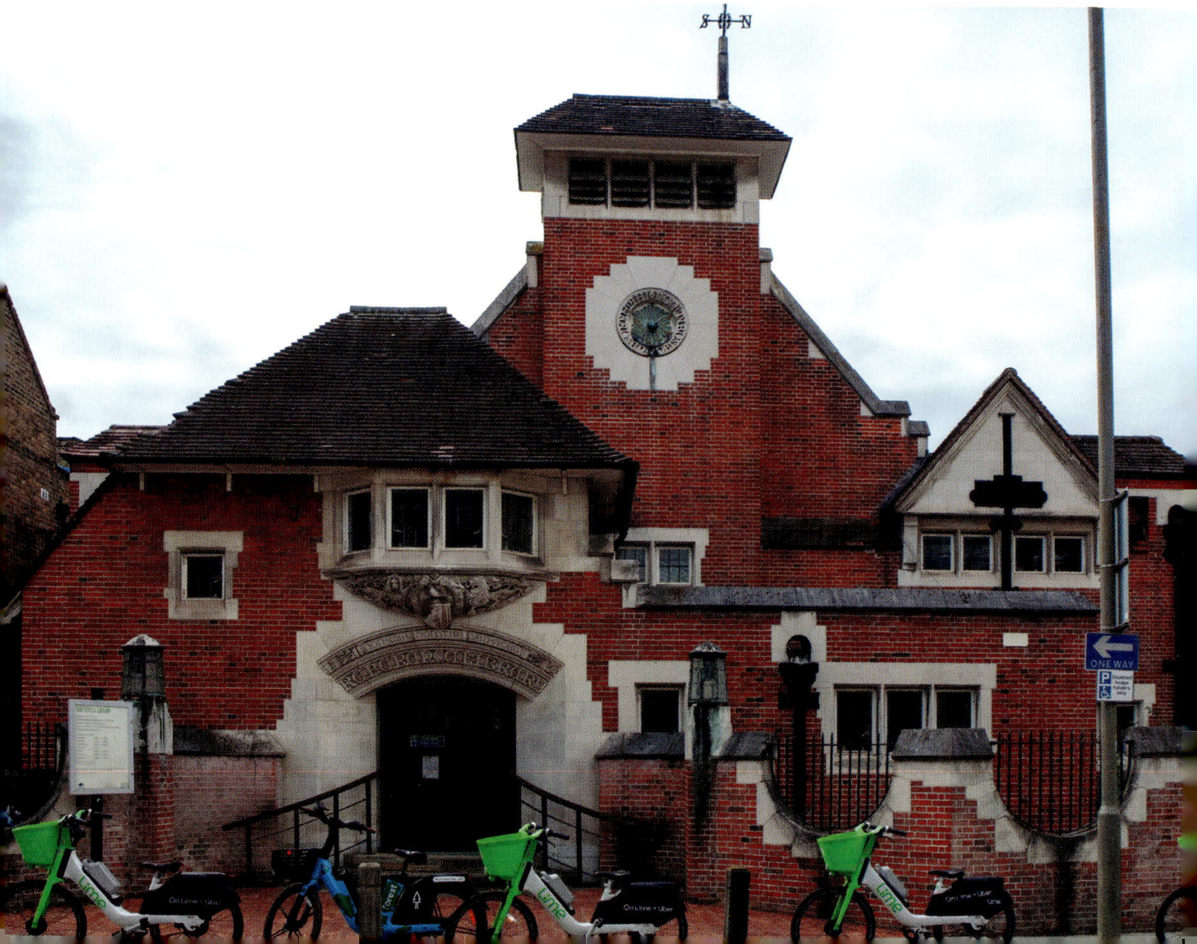

design was so successful that the local authority subsequently engaged him as the architect for several other buildings in the borough.

From the outset the library was hugely popular, especially the reference section, which was very well used but lacked the space it required. The Public Libraries Act passed in 1919 paved the way for the local authority to construct a separate reference library in 1924 in Altenburg Gardens nearby. Unlike the earlier building, the new reference library was designed by Henry Hyams an advocate of the Arts and Crafts style that had been so prevalent in the country in the late nineteenth and early twentieth centuries but was uncommon in Battersea in the 1920s. Hyams's belief in quality craftsmanship and the use of traditional practices rather than mass produced materials is displayed throughout the building, both externally and internally. The library's main entrance, full of interesting features, catches the eye instantly. Its ornate oriel window hangs above oak porch doors and the motto of Battersea Council 'Non mihi, non tibi, sed nobis' (meaning, 'Not for me, not for you, but for all of us') is inscribed on its archway. A central turret sits beside the main entrance and is topped by a weathervane with what appears to be a bearded man reading a book. Perhaps the building's greatest feature however is its vaulted glass roof that lights up the room for readers.

www.better.org.uk

33. Trinity Hospice, Nos 29–32 Clapham Common North Side, SW4

The hospice is an imposing building, set back from the road, where it occupies attractive Georgian buildings overlooking Clapham Common. It was established in 1891 by Colonel William Hoare of the famous banking family who in addition to donating £1,000 of his own money to set up the enterprise, made an appeal for a further £1,000 through *The Times* newspaper to provide a home 'for the man who is neither curable nor incurable but simply dying'. At this time end of life care was not understood to be a healthcare priority so physicians working in the voluntary hospitals concentrated their efforts on curing patients, whilst the workhouses, where many of the chronically sick and terminally ill spent their last days were without the facilities to give them the care they required.

When it opened in 1892 the hospice was called the Free House for the Dying and was managed first by one, and then by another order of nuns. It moved from its original site on The Chase to No. 29 Clapham Common North Side in 1900 and a few years later purchased the adjacent house, No. 30, whose previous famous occupants had been the banker Robert Barclay and Sir Charles Barry, architect of the Houses of Parliament. Further houses at Nos 31 and 32 were acquired by the hospice during the twentieth century.

In 1917 the hospice changed its name to the Hostel of God and was known by this name until 1980. By this time its association with the nuns had ceased and it

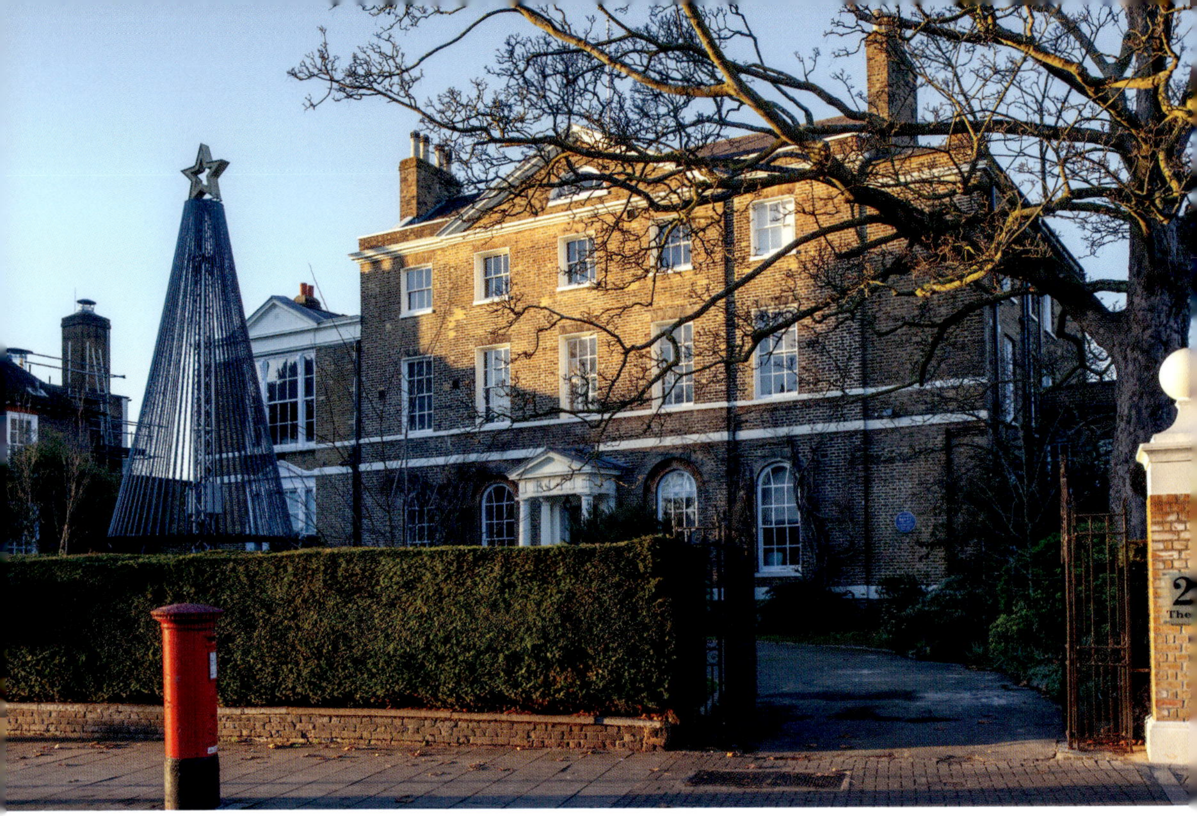

Above and below: Trinity Hospice.

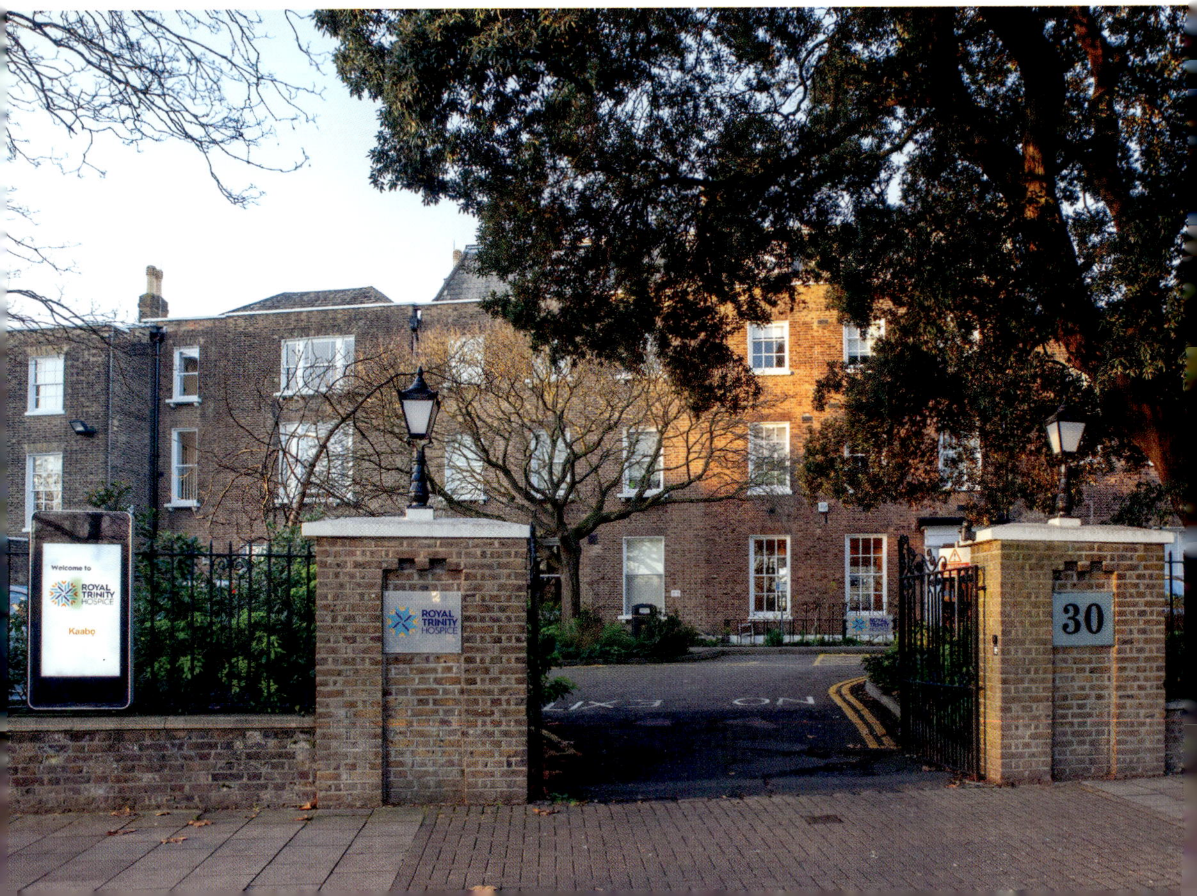

became a charitable trust, known as Trinity Hospice. In recent years, the hospice has been renamed Royal Trinity Hospice due to its long association with the royal family. Relying upon public donations it now serves the communities of south-west and central London providing free palliative and end of life care to all, and its role today is as much about helping the living as it is the dying.

Patients and their families both appreciate this modern approach and take comfort in visiting or simply looking at the hospice's delightful and award-winning gardens.

www.royaltrinityhospice.london

34. Former Battersea Polytechnic Institute, Battersea Park Road, SW11

One cannot fail to notice this building when walking along Battersea Park Road as it extends over a long block, displays some fabulous ornate features and is, moreover, symmetrical. Its red-brick frontage decorated with bull's-eye windows, Dutch gables, statuary and its splendid main entrance dominate the street, even though the building is separated from the road by railings. Built as a higher education establishment, the Battersea Polytechnic Institute was founded in 1891 and was designed by the architect E. W. Mountford (see Building 32) in the Northern Renaissance style. The polytechnic was built in the grounds of what had previously been the Albert Palace, an enormous iron and glass structure, similar to the Crystal Palace of 1851. The palace, originally located in Ireland, was rebuilt at Battersea in 1885 as an entertainment and exhibition centre with a programme of concerts, animal and flower shows, snake charmers and craft stands. Although initially popular, the attraction was forced to close due to low visitor numbers (there was an admission charge here, while nearby Battersea Park was free) and the land was then developed for housing and as the site for the new polytechnic.

The Polytechnic Movement began life in the late 1830s and concentrated on the teaching of technical and science subjects as opposed to the traditional classical university education. Battersea Polytechnic Institute was set up with the distinct object to provide London's poorer inhabitants with access to further and higher education and became a specialist technology centre early in its existence. In 1956 it was among the first such institutions to be designated a 'college of advanced technology', and the following year its name changed to Battersea College of Technology.

Over the years the range of subjects offered grew and courses validated by the University of London were taught at the college. This led to the need for larger premises which coincided with a government report recommending that colleges of advanced technology become technological universities. In 1966 the college was closed in Battersea and moved to Guildford as the University of Surrey. Its magnificent building has since been converted into apartments and renamed Kingsway Square.

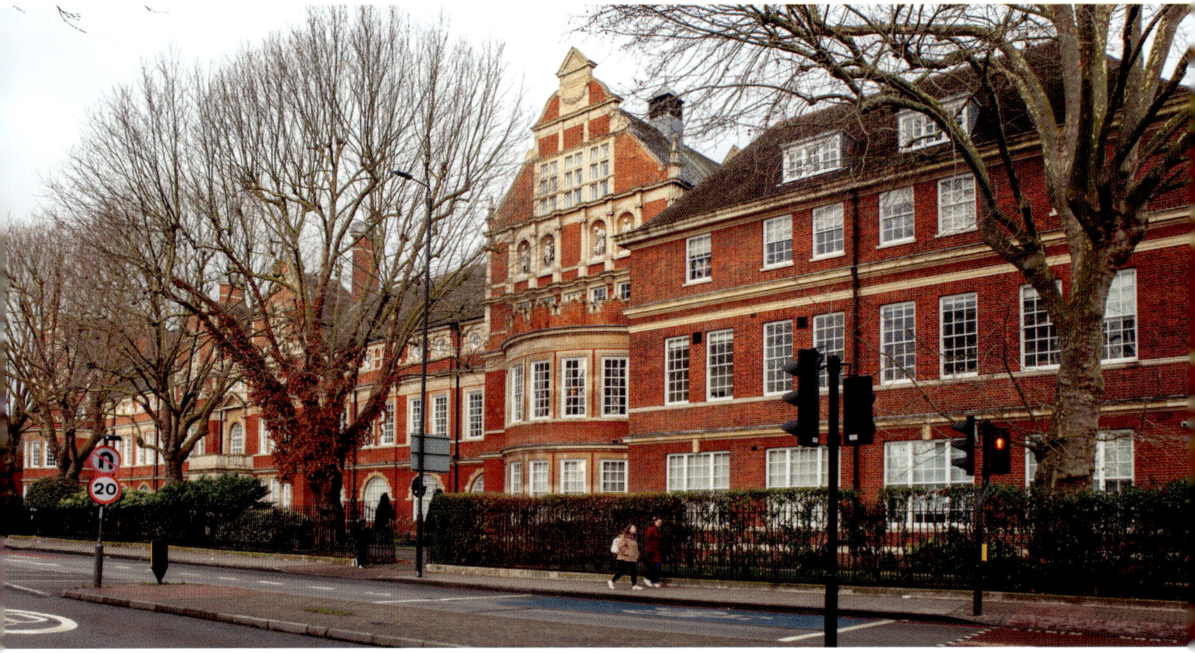

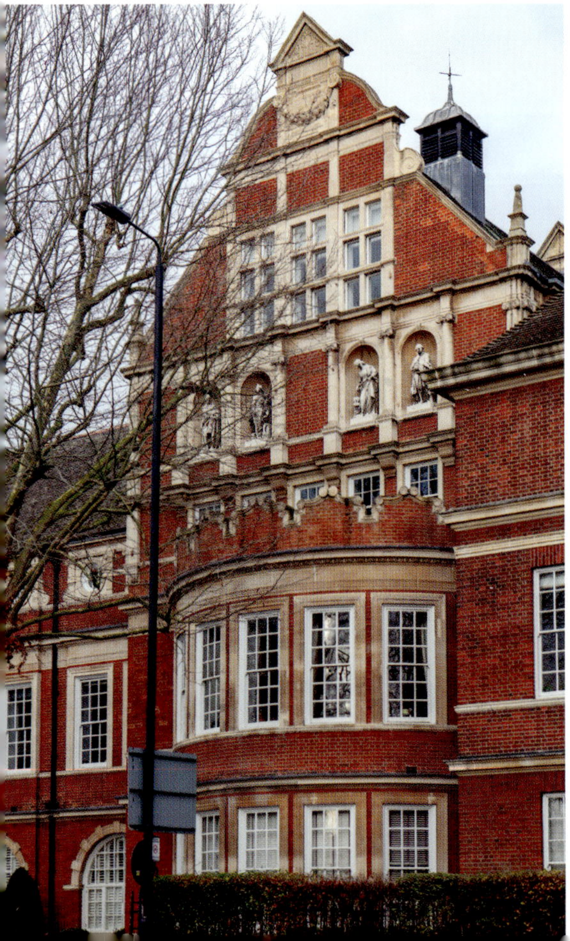

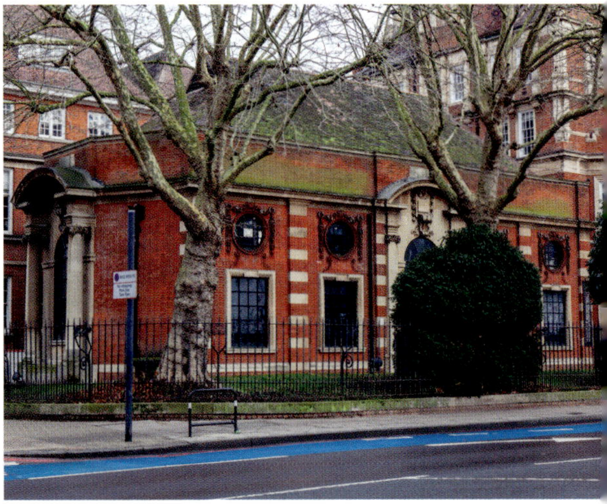

Top, left and above: Former Battersea Polytechnic.

35. Battersea Arts Centre (Former Battersea Town Hall), Lavender Hill, SW11

The former Battersea Town Hall is the third of architect E. W. Mountford's commissions in Battersea and, like the Central Library and Polytechnic Institute (Buildings 32 and 34), it is a building of great distinction. Grade II* listed it contains some exquisite internal rooms including a council chamber, public hall, lobby, and a monumental stair hall, a wealth of exterior decoration and relief sculpture and the largest surviving Hope-Jones organ in the world. It was built by the Battersea Vestry in 1893 to serve Battersea's ever-growing population and

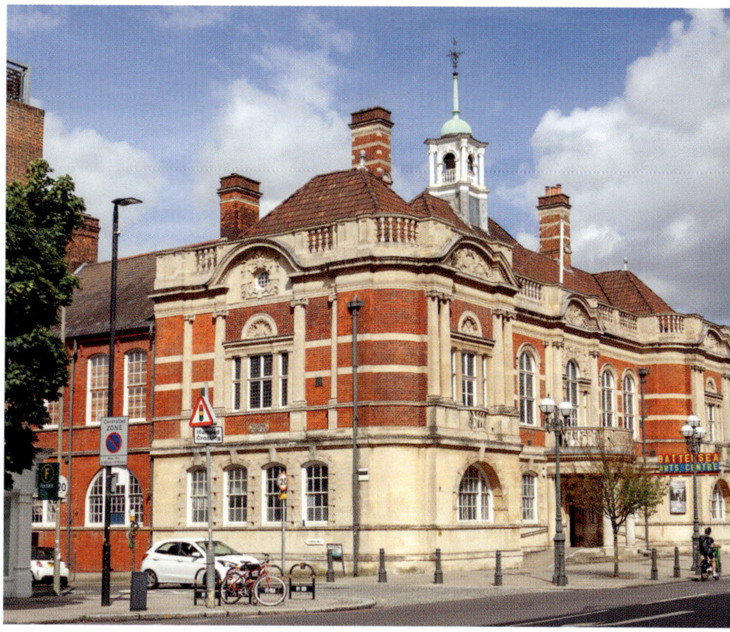

Right and below: Battersea Arts Centre.

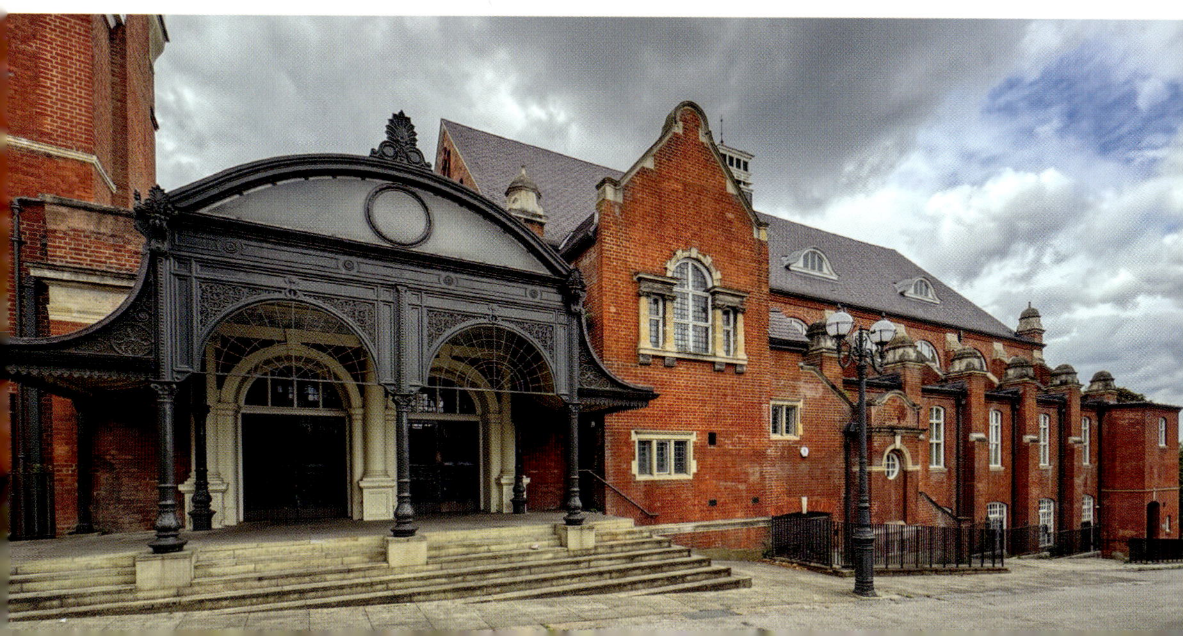

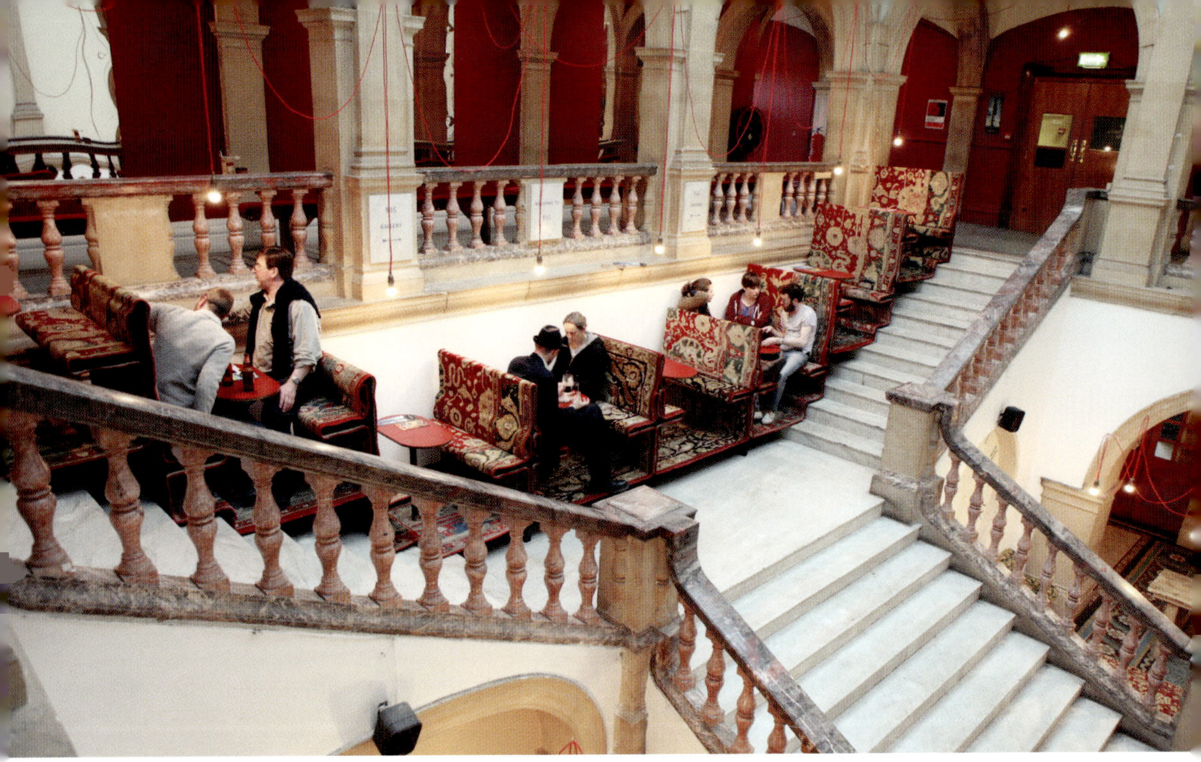

Battersea Arts Centre. (Courtesy of Nicholas Hartwright)

occupies a commanding position at the top of Lavender Hill located on a sloping site. Prior to its construction Elm House, a villa and home to Jeanie Nassau Sr (one of the area's most eminent social campaigners of the mid-1800s) stood here. She was the country's first female civil servant and is particularly known for her work in helping to establish the modern system of foster care. Her circle of friends included Octavia Hill, Florence Nightingale and Alfred Lord Tennyson. Today her name lives on in one of the rooms within the Town Hall.

In the twentieth century many assemblies of a radical nature occurred within Battersea Town Hall's walls. The suffragettes Christabel and Emmeline Pankhurst held meetings here and the Town Hall was frequently the venue for political rallies. In 1913 it was in the building that Britain's first Black mayor, John Archer, was elected. The Town Hall was also renowned for its programme of activities in its main hall which included boxing tournaments, ballroom dancing, concerts and exhibitions.

In 1965 when the borough of Battersea merged with Wandsworth to form the London Borough of Wandsworth the building's future was put in jeopardy. However, a successful public campaign averted its demolition, and the Town Hall was given a second lease of life when Battersea Arts Centre (BAC) was created. BAC has been, and is, phenomenally successful and has a commitment to being 'A Home for Extraordinary Artists'. It offers an exciting and varied schedule presenting drama and shows and encourages young people to engage in the arts by running Beatbox and Dance Academies and organising a Young Producers programme.

bac.org.uk

36. The Clapham Grand, Nos 21–25 St John's Hill, Battersea, SW11

Over the 125 years it has been in existence, the Clapham Grand has seen both good and bad times, especially in the 1980s when it was closed for more than a decade. However, today it is booming again and now styles itself as 'The Grand, Clapham Junction – A Palace of Modern Variety'. People flock here throughout the day and well into the early hours of the morning to see live acts

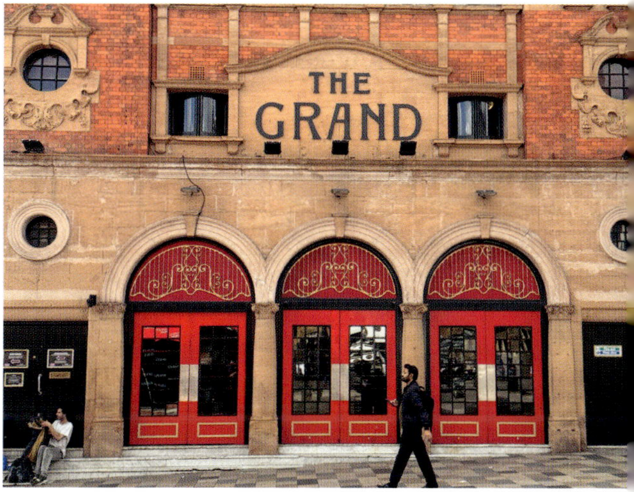

Right, below and overleaf: The Clapham Grand.

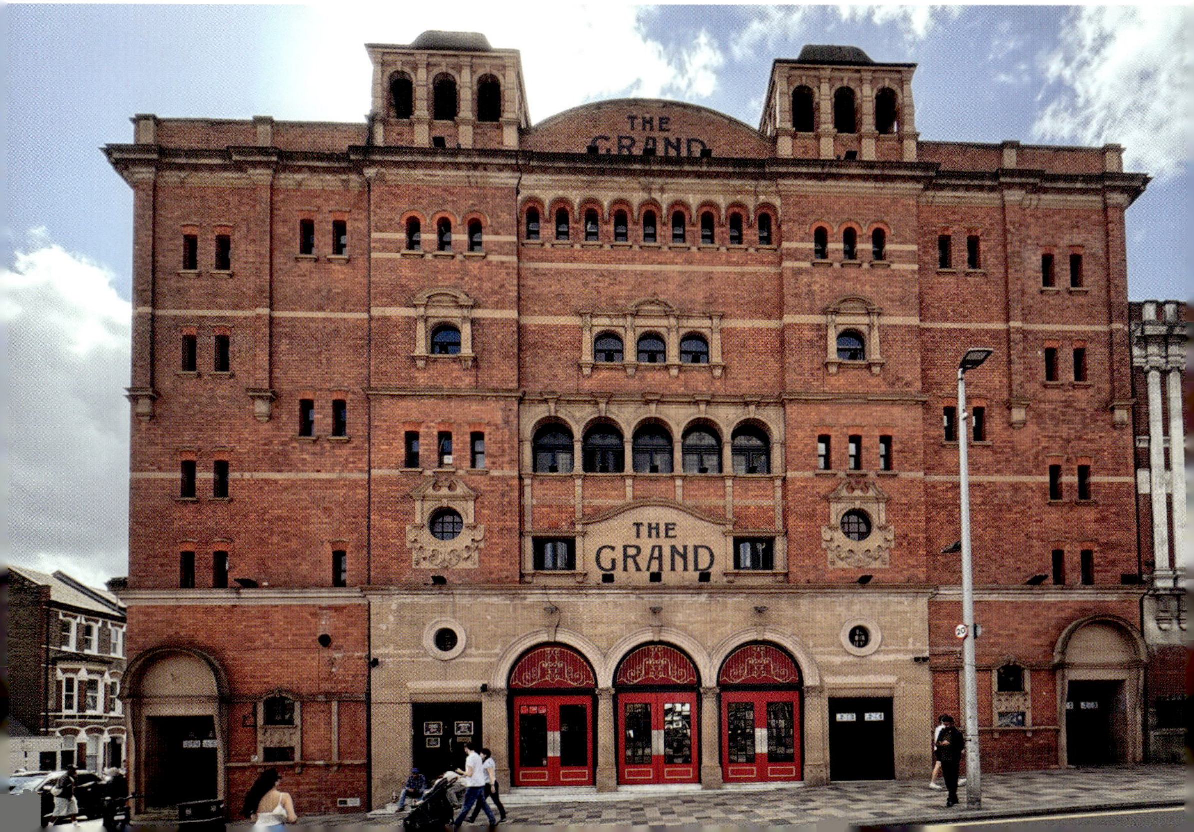

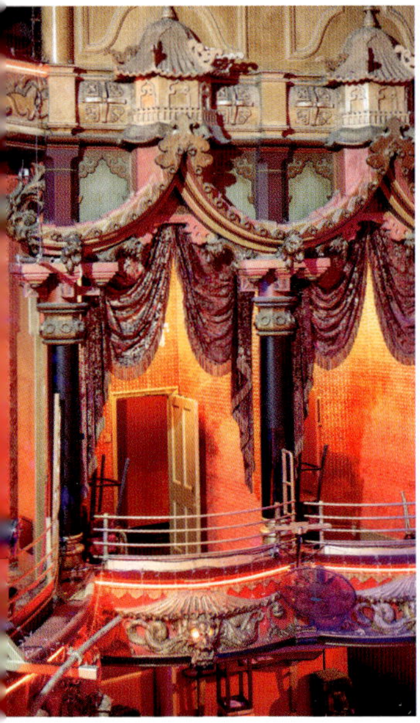

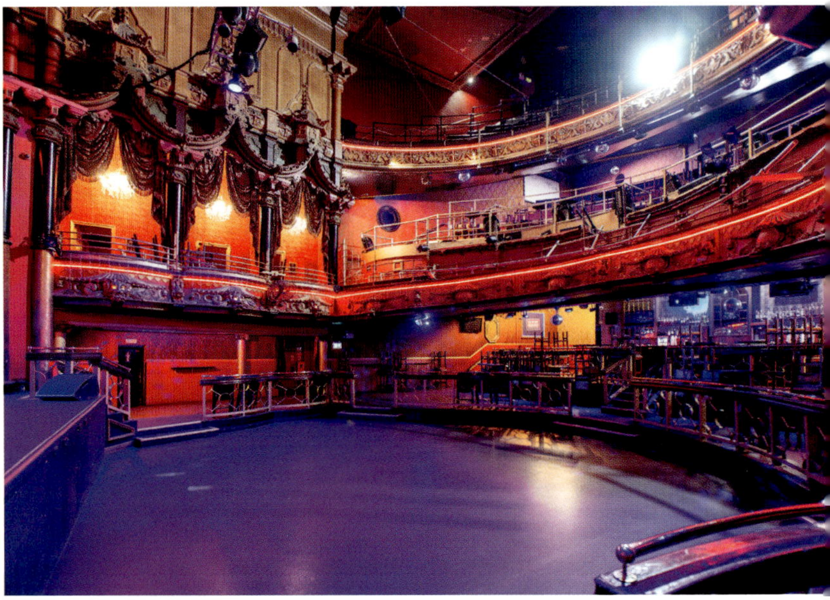

like George Ezra and Rag & Bone Man for the venue's Club Nights, Brunch Parties, theatre, comedy, movies, drag shows, the incredible Bongo's Bingo and even White-Collar Boxing matches. It is a place that never sleeps and makes itself accessible to all. People come here to be entertained, just as they would have been when the building first opened in 1900. Then, it was called the New Grand Palace of Varieties and was set up by Dan Leno, one of the best-known music hall artistes of the day (it was he who created the role of the pantomime dame). Here, crowds saw their favourite stars, like Marie Lloyd, Charlie Chaplin and the comedian and acrobat Little Tich. However, in the 1930s the building was adapted for the cinema market; a projector room was added on the fifth floor and the venue became known as the Grand Theatre and Essoldo Cinema. Thirty years later, the owners turned it into a bingo hall, which lasted until 1978. New owners restored and renamed the building the Clapham Grand in 1991, transforming it into a live music venue with acts like the Kinks and the Verve. It then turned into a clubbing destination before returning to its music hall and variety roots in 2016.

The interior of the Clapham Grand is remarkable with extravagant Chinese decoration such as dragon's heads with glistening eyes and pagoda canopies above the boxes. It is a vast and opulent auditorium with a mix of spaces that lends itself to all types of entertainment. The exterior too is outstanding, designed in the Colonial Indian style in red-brick and pink stone with two domed, arcaded towers it is impossible to miss.

claphamgrand.com

37. Clapham Common Station and Clock Tower, The Pavement, SW4

The world's first underground railway, the Metropolitan Railway, was opened in 1863 and ran between Paddington and Farringdon using steam-powered locomotives. The line was such a success that it provided the impetus for other lines to be built, all owned by separate companies. Towards the end of the century The City and South London Railway (C&SLR) introduced the world's first electric underground railway that ran from the City to Stockwell, but it was not until ten years had passed that the line was extended to Clapham which then became the line's new southern terminus and remained so for the next twenty-six years.

Today, the station has two entrances: one on the west dating from 1924 that is the handiwork of the renowned London Transport designer Charles Holden, and a more modern curved-steel and glass pavilion to the east. The former is immediately recognised for its glazed dome and wings and is located on an island between the Pavement and Clapham Common South Side. The station sits on the south-east corner of the common and was initially called Clapham Road, but in 1926 when it became part of the Northern Line it changed its name to Clapham Common to differentiate it from Clapham North nearby. These two stations are the London Underground's only remaining deep-level stations, with an island

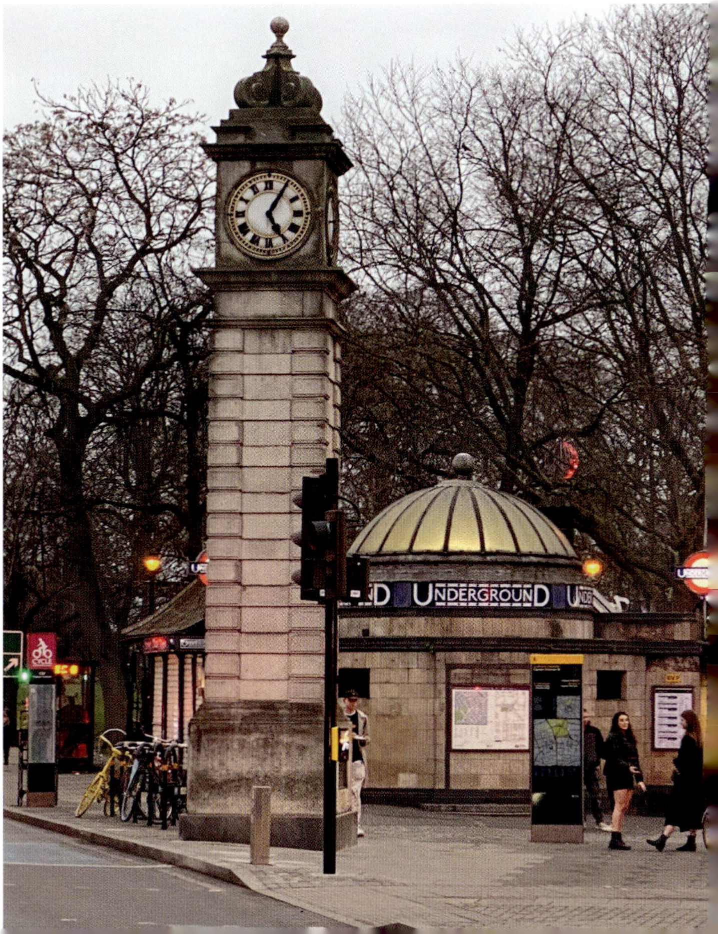

Clapham Common station and clock tower.

platform serving both northbound and southbound trains. Their platforms, at just 3.7 metres (12.14 feet) wide, have been the subject of much controversy over the years due to concerns about passenger safety. However, to date no plans have been put in place to widen them, although the Mayor of London has pledged to keep the platforms and their safety under review.

The iconic clock tower that stands outside the station on Clapham High Street was a gift to the people of Clapham in 1906 by Alexander Glegg, the Mayor of Wandsworth (which included Clapham at the time). It is a 9.44-metre-high (31-foot) free-standing Portland stone tower with a granite base, above which is a four-faced clock. The tower, a handsome structure, is characterised by its banded rustication and the ball finial at its peak.

38. Former Temperance Billiard Halls, No. 47 Clapham High Street, SW4 and No. 66. Battersea Rise, SW11

The reason why south-west London saw a rise in the construction of temperance billiard halls in the early 1900s has been attributed to the huge growth in public houses in this part of the city in the late Victorian period. The

Former Temperance Billiard Hall, Battersea.

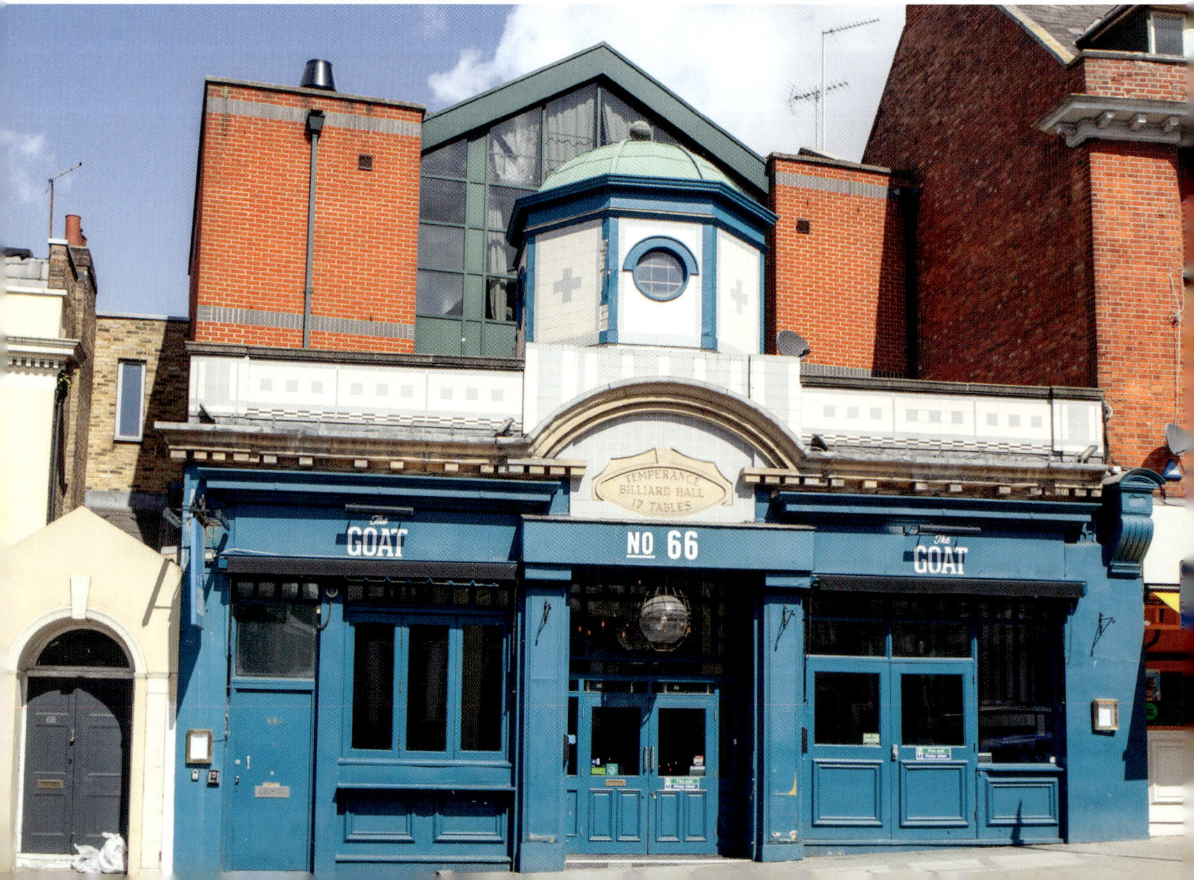

construction of these 'dry' halls was the Temperance Movement's answer to curtailing the rise of alcoholism, particularly amongst the working classes. The new pubs that appeared in the area were sociable places, often extravagantly decorated with exquisite etched glass, stained-glass windows, tiled façades, and marble, cast-iron and wooden furnishings. To attract customers to the temperance billiard halls many of the pub features were replicated in the hope that customers would feel at home in these halls, which, although devoid of

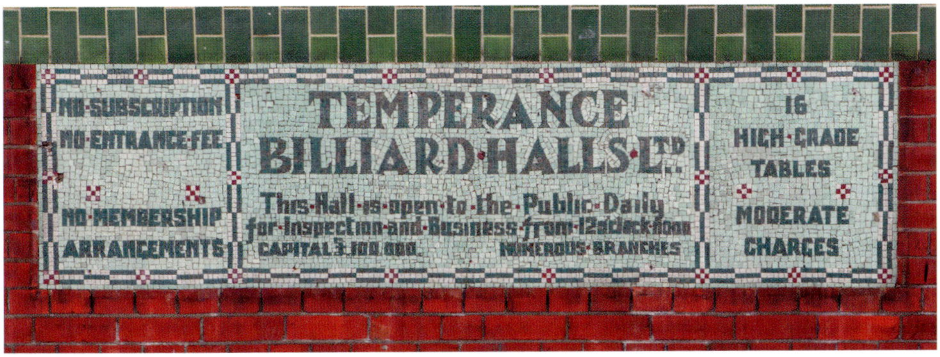

Above and below: Former Temperance Billiard Hall, Clapham.

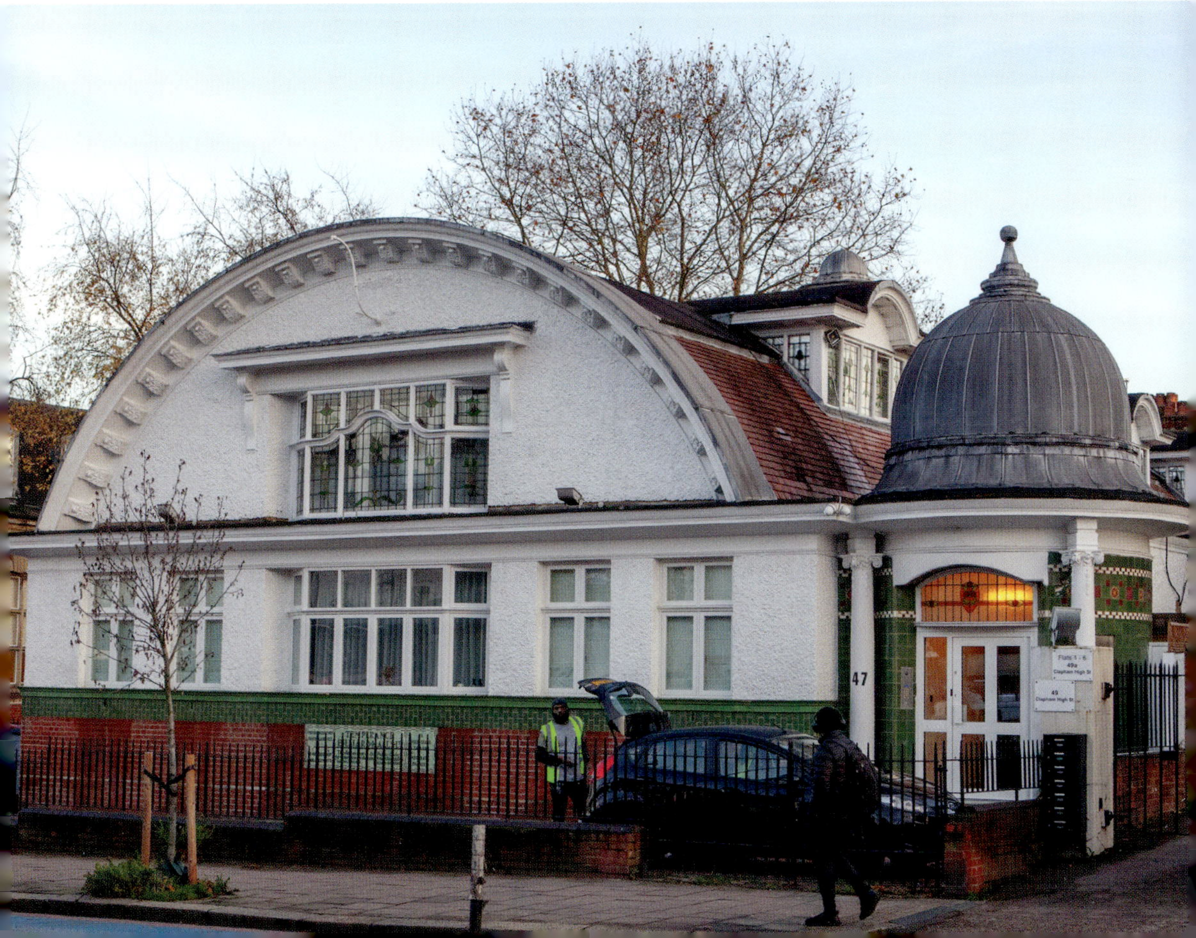

alcohol, provided a similar atmosphere to the drinking palaces they were used to frequenting.

The Temperance Movement originated in north-west England where it set up Temperance Billiard Halls Ltd to build its billiard halls in the north and London. The two halls in Battersea and Clapham were constructed in the early years of the twentieth century and the hall in Clapham was designed by the company's in-house architect Norman Evans. Evans also designed a hall across the river in Fulham, which, like several other temperance billiard halls around the country, is now a Grade II listed building – ironically, today it is a Greene King pub and named 'The Temperance'!

Clapham's temperance billiard hall on Clapham High Street is the most striking of buildings, with a curved roof, beautiful windows, green tiling and Art Nouveau detailing. It has a domed entrance vestibule to one side (a feature of many of the halls) and is set back from the road behind railings. The building has had several uses over the years but now contains residential apartments.

In contrast, Battersea's temperance billiard hall has, like its sister hall in Fulham, changed usage to become a restaurant and pub and is called The Goat. Its entrance, though not original, is still quite prominent on Battersea Rise and there is a plaque above it stating 'Temperance Billiard Hall, 17 tables'.

39. Former South London Hospital for Women and Children, Clapham Common South Side, SW4

Since 1995 this impressive Baroque-style building, once a general hospital, has been converted into use as a supermarket for Tesco and today functions as a residential complex too. Its original 1929 frontage designed by one of the twentieth century's key architects, Sir Edwin Cooper, remains in situ but only after a prolonged and acrimonious campaign was carried out to prevent the supermarket chain from demolishing the building to replace it with a tower block of housing and a new Tesco store. Unfortunately, without listing by Historic England the interior was completely lost in Tesco's refurbishment but at least this iconic building has not disappeared as it has a unique and most interesting history.

The idea for the hospital was conceived by two female surgeons in the early 1900s who had worked at the New Hospital for Women (later, the Elizabeth Garrett Anderson Hospital and now incorporated as a wing of University College Hospital in central London). The New Hospital for Women (NHW) had been the first hospital to treat women and children with only female practitioners and staff. It was vastly over-subscribed, so surgeons Eleanor Davies-Colley and Maud Chadburn were determined to open another hospital in South London run on similar lines. On receiving a very generous donation of £53,000 for the building along with a £40,000 endowment they were able to open the South London Hospital for Women (SLHW) in 1916 on Clapham Common South Side

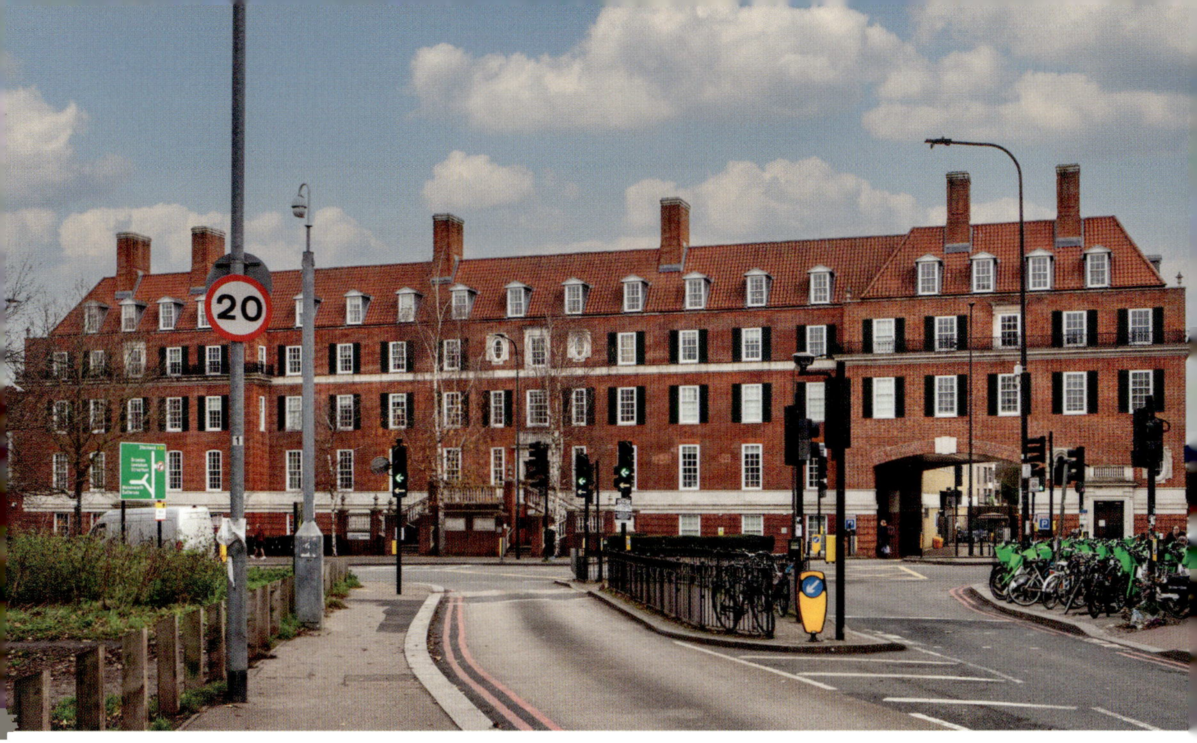

Former South London Hospital for Women and Children.

(in a building that has since been demolished). The hospital treated all female patients and boys under the age of seven and was led entirely by female staff, with the only exception being the gardener and porter, leading to the hospital receiving the nickname 'Adamless Eden'.

From its inception SLHW aimed to train women doctors to become specialists as the medical profession was extremely male dominated and many women practitioners were barred from hospital employment. The hospital was finally closed in 1984 despite a major fight to keep it open. Remaining true to the terms of its endowment SLHW was always run by its female staff for women and children, except in wartime when it treated male soldiers too.

40. Battersea Power Station, Circus Road West, SW11

Battersea Power Station is perhaps one of London's most loved and cherished industrial buildings of the twentieth century. Its chimneys have dominated the capital's skyline since the 1930s and smoke belching out from the stacks is said to have guided RAF planes back home during the Second World War. After its closure in 1983 the building, despite being Grade II listed, was left in a state of great neglect and the fabric of the power station – its chimneys, brickwork and roof simply began to crumble away. Many proposals for its repurposing were put forward including one as a visitor attraction, but every redevelopment plan failed until 2012 when the site was bought by a consortium of Malaysian investors. They had the money and the vision to bring about the power station's transformation and turn it, and the surrounding land, into a new 'city' in south London.

After an enormous regeneration and conservation programme Battersea Power Station was opened to the public in October 2022 as an area for entertainment, dining, shopping, living and working. The interiors of the original vast turbine halls have been transformed by the architects Wilkinson Eyre into a high-class shopping mall now with its own cinema, a visitor attraction – Lift 109 – cafés, restaurants, bars, and offices. Apartments have been built on the roof and sides of the building and in the surrounding area too there are exciting contemporary residential developments (see Building 49) and even a new high street, Electric Boulevard. The adjacent railway line arches have been occupied by a variety of eateries and bars and the area outside the power station is used for sport, festivals, ice-skating and screen events.

The power station is in fact divided into two parts. The first, A, was built in the 1930s, and the work was carried out by the engineer Leonard Pearce. The station's splendid brick exterior was designed by the architect Sir Giles Gilbert Scott and J. Theo Halliday was responsible for its art deco interior. Station B, built in the austere post-war years, mirrors A but is less lavish. If you are interested in learning more about the power station's history and architecture, take the excellent guided tour which gives you entry to the power station's awesome 1930s Control Room A.

batterseapowerstation.co.uk

Battersea Power Station. (Courtesy of Charlie Round-Turner)

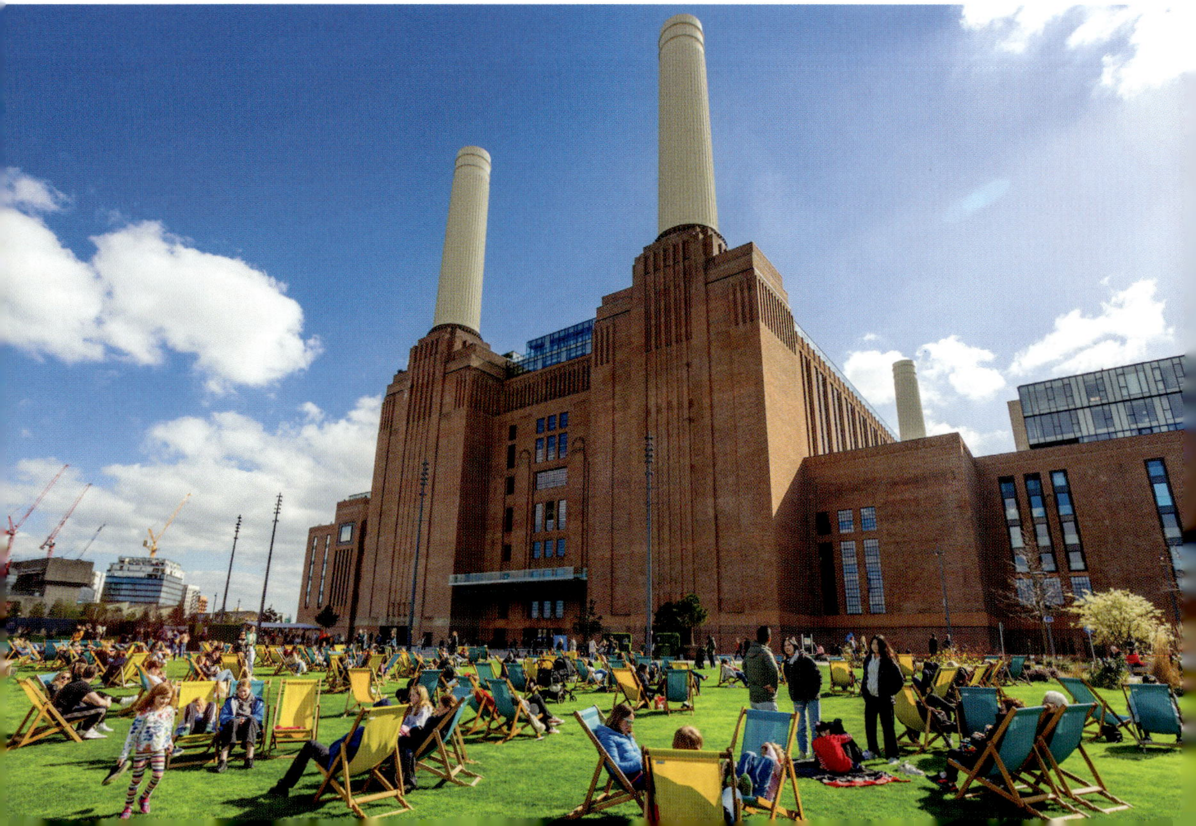

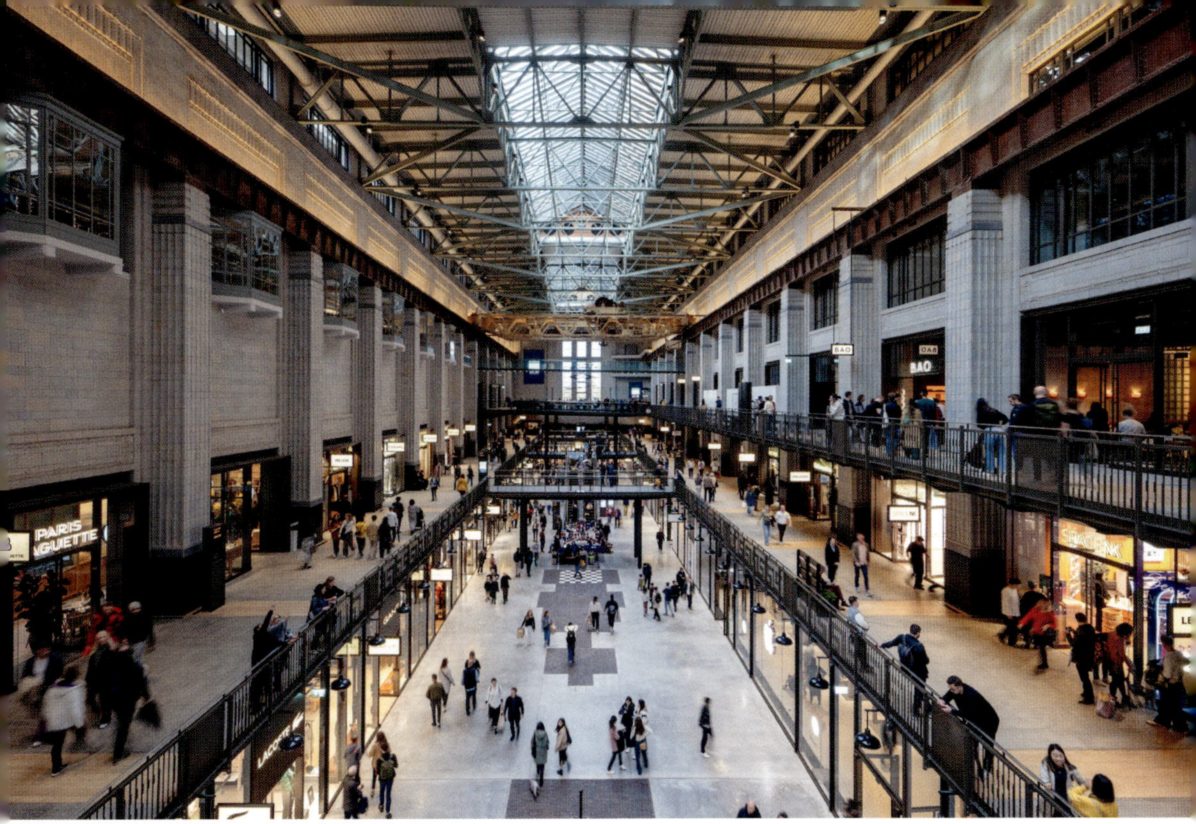

Above: Former turbine hall A, Battersea Power Station. (Courtesy of Charlie Round-Turner)

Below: Apple UK headquarters in Battersea Power Station. (Courtesy of Apple UK)

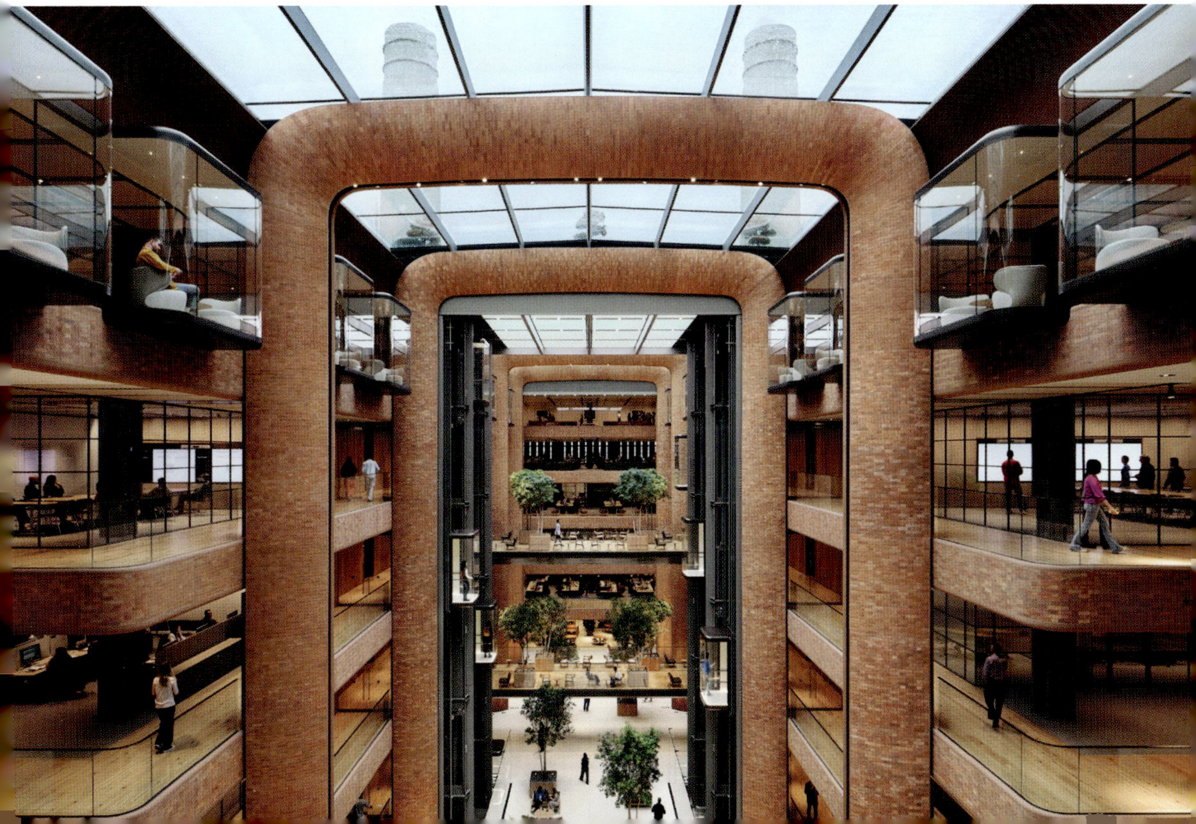

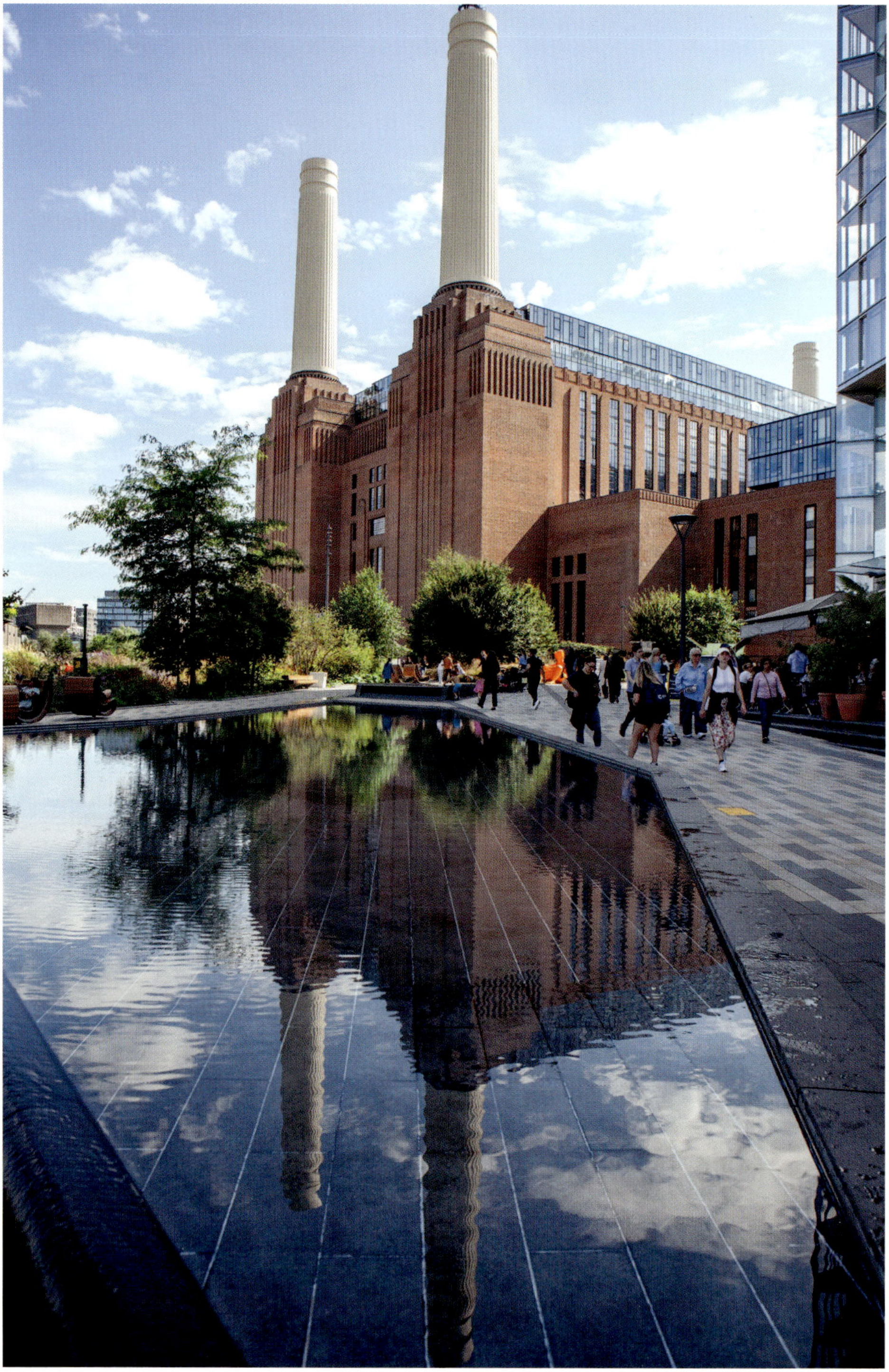

Battersea Power Station from Circus West Village.

41. Hightrees House, Nightingale Lane, Clapham Common South Side, SW4

This 'International'-style apartment block was constructed in 1938 and was built to replace an eighteenth-century mansion here of the same name. Using the most modern materials and fittings the apartments were designed by Richard William Herbert Jones, who, although barely known for his works in London, is much celebrated for his art deco Saltdean Lido, near to Brighton on the south coast. The block forms a double 'E' shape with its longer sides overlooking Clapham Common and the shorter sides facing Nightingale Lane. It was originally five storeys tall, although a penthouse floor was added in the 1970s which is set back from the floors beneath it.

Hightrees House is typical of the Modernist architecture of the period with little exterior decoration apart from its white curved balconies, metal windows and its central 'thermometer' glass stairwell above the main entrance. Inside there are 110 units in a range of sizes and when built the flat's lounges were fitted out with a radio, clock and electric heater, all very modern for the time. To attract residents to the fashionable development the basement was filled with communal facilities including a restaurant, bar and swimming pool, but today only the latter remains.

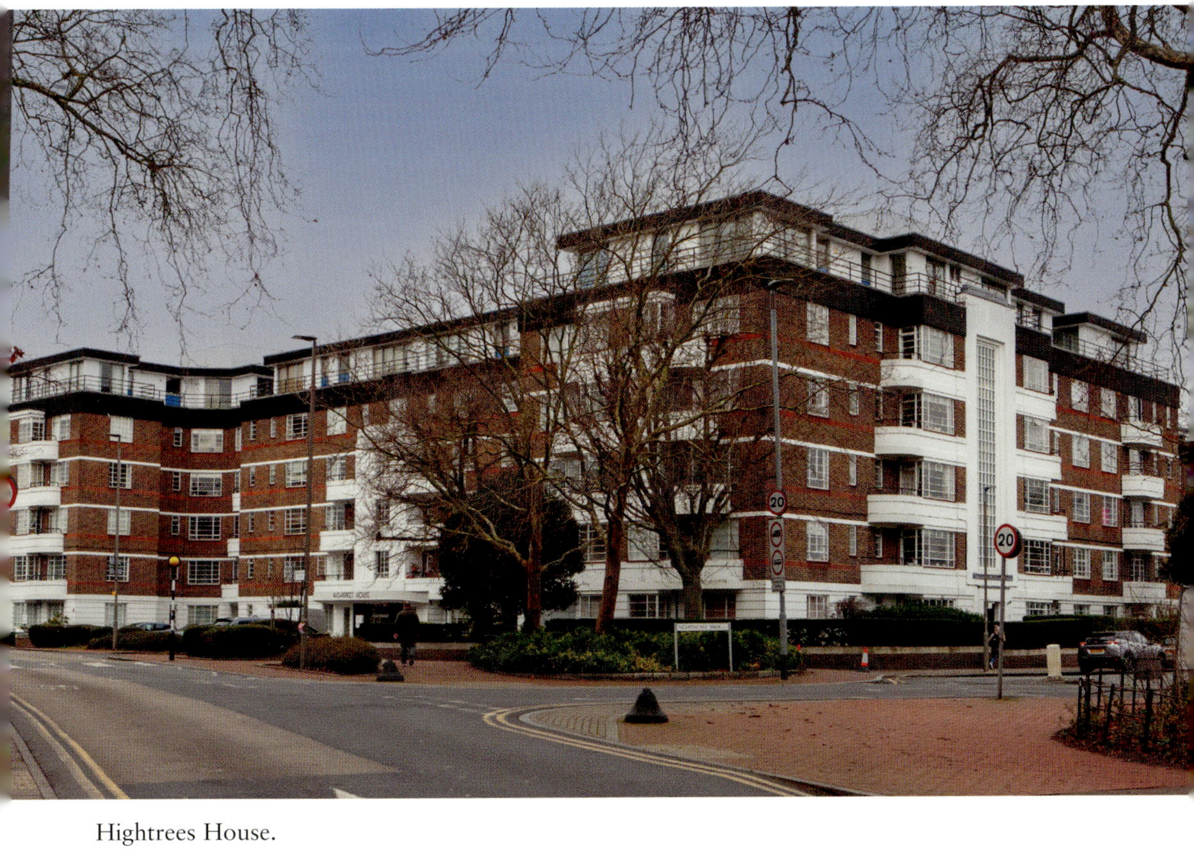

Hightrees House.

42. Former Granada Cinema, No. 58 St John's Hill, Battersea, SW11

Described for its grandeur, scale and style as being one of the 'super cinemas of the 1930s' the building became an immediate landmark in the area when it opened at the top of St John's Hill as the Granada Theatre in 1937. The building's owners, brothers Sidney (later, Lord) and Cecil Bernstein, had already established a chain of Granada theatres and were determined that their new enterprise should be the largest and luxurious of its kind in the area. To this end the Bernsteins commissioned three eminent architects – H. B. Horner, Cecil Masey and Leslie Norton – to design the cinema and brought in Theodore Komisarjevsky to be responsible for the interior decoration. Komisarjevsky, probably the finest interior theatrical designer of the day in Britain, certainly left his mark on the building, which he fitted out in the Italian Renaissance style. Using mirrors, pilasters, paintings, a grand stairwell, a deeply coffered ceiling and glass chandeliers, he created a magnificent foyer and a vast auditorium capable of seating 3,000. The latter was equally as spectacular as the former with extravagant classical decoration in fibrous plaster and a highly decorated roundel in the ceiling above the front stalls. Not only was Komisarjevsky's work carried out to the highest standard, but it remains a superb example of the elaborately decorated entertainment centres of the period.

The architecture of the exterior of the building which extended along both Plough Road and St John's Hill was in total contrast to the cinema's interior displaying many art deco features and an eye-catching curved entrance facing the junction. Sadly, the popularity of television saw visitor numbers fall, and the building was then divided up into several screens in the hope that this would stem

Former Granada Cinema.

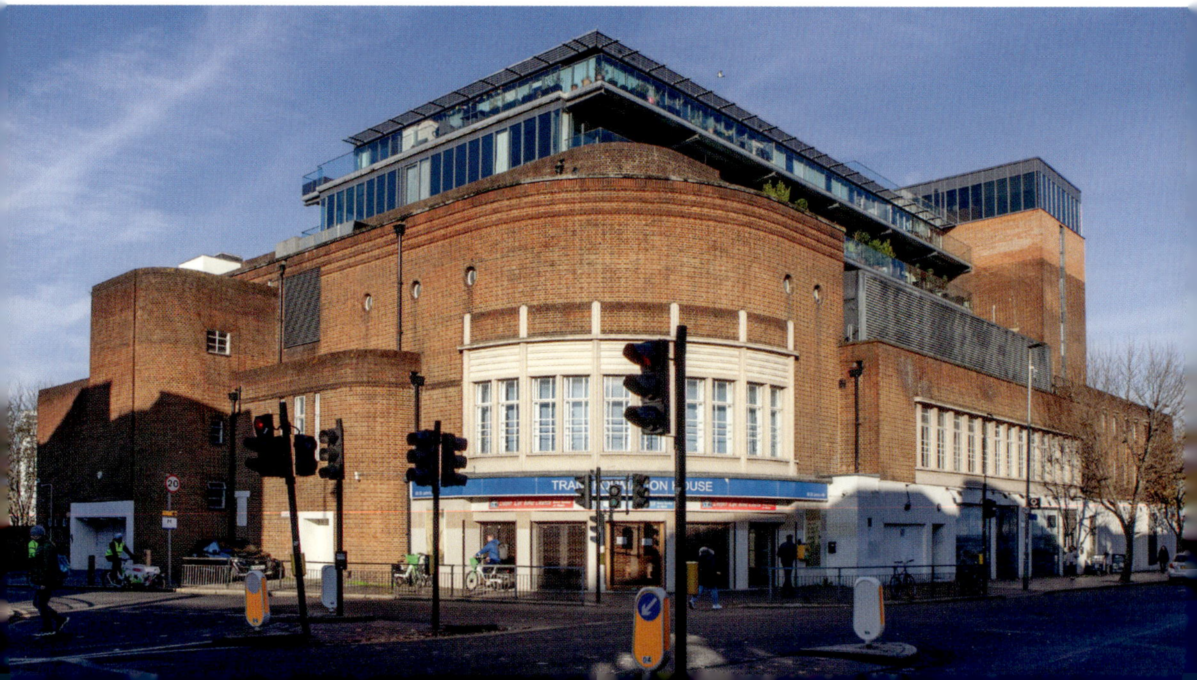

its decline. This wasn't successful and nor was the cinema's reincarnation as a Granada Bingo Club. The building closed in 1997 until finally planning permission allowed new apartments to be built above the former cinema and within the stage fly-tower (today known as Lumiere House) and for the thorough restoration of the former Grade II* listed auditorium and foyer to be used by a church group in what is now Transformation House.

43. Deep Shelters, Clapham Common, SW4

Around Clapham Common there are several conspicuous circular cement structures that have little in the way to commend them apart from being daubed in brightly coloured graffiti. However, despite their apparent ugliness the structures have an interesting story to tell. They were erected in 1942 during the Second World War by the government in response to the need to provide night shelter for local people, many of whom had lost their homes in bombing raids. These prominent portals are both the vents and entrances to pairs of underground tunnels that were built 91 metres (295 feet) below ground, and measure 5 metres (16.6 feet) in diameter and are 365 metres (400 yards) long. The tunnels were intended to accommodate up to 8,000 people and were fitted out with bunk beds and basic facilities. They ran beside Clapham's Tube stations at Clapham North, Clapham South and Clapham Common and when the decision was made to build them it was thought that the deep shelter tunnels might be converted for future use as an express underground railway, but this idea never came to fruition.

A deep shelter, Clapham Common.

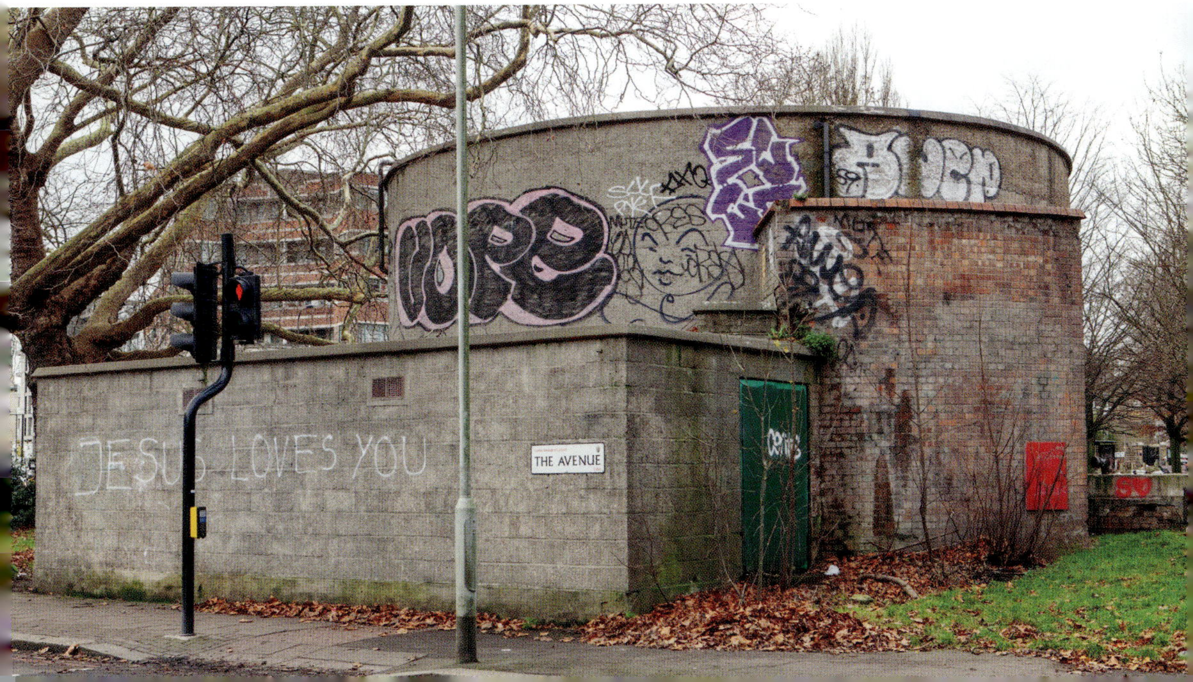

By the time the deep shelters were up and running the need for them had mainly passed, although they were used in 1944–45 during the V1 and V2 raids. The tunnels have subsequently been employed in a variety of ways, most commonly as storage for archive materials, but in 1947 the Clapham South shelter welcomed the very first group of Caribbean immigrants to the UK, who had arrived in the country on the SS *Empire Windrush*. The 240 guests spent their initial days living in the shelter until, having found work, moved to accommodation elsewhere. Many ultimately settled in south London and set the foundations of its multi-racial community.

Most recently Clapham Common's shelter was set up as the country's first hydroponic farm growing subterranean salad leaves. Run by two entrepreneurs their company, Growing Underground, occupied the tunnels for almost a decade, growing and harvesting crops in a pesticide-free environment using the latest LED technology. During this time the company's produce was sold to New Covent Garden Market, and other retail outlets such as M&S, Waitrose and Whole Foods Market.

44. Albion Riverside, No. 22 Hester Road, Battersea, SW11

Located between Albert Bridge and Battersea Bridge on the south side of the Thames, Albion Riverside has won since its construction in 2003 a host of awards for its quality of design. The deluxe mixed-use development was designed by Foster + Partners and sits beside Foster's own studio which he established beside the river in 1990. Norman Foster's design has contributed to the formation of a new urban

Below and opposite: Albion Riverside.

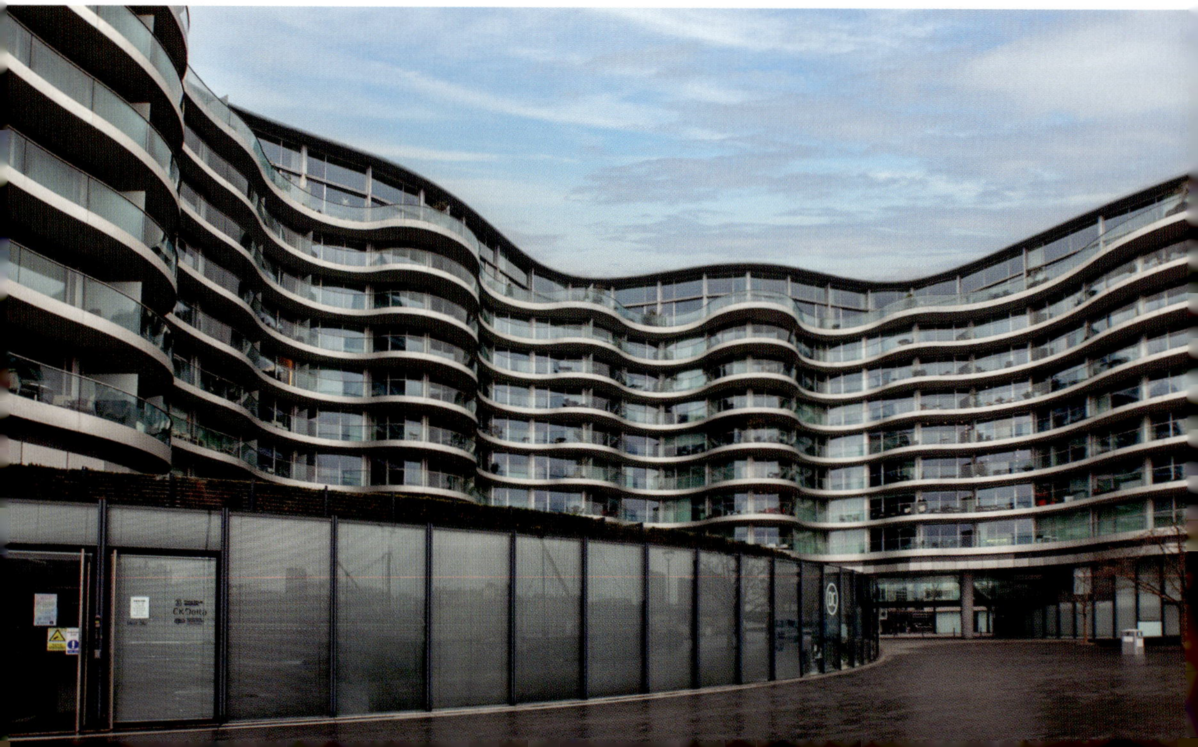

neighbourhood in Battersea right beside the river, and one where people not only live and work but can also access a range of shops, art galleries, health and leisure facilities, and cafes. The retail outlets are sited at ground level along the waterfront where there is a wide promenade and seating. Albion Riverside is designed in the high-tech modernist style with façades mainly of glass and made up of four separate buildings connected by public spaces. True to many of Foster's works the buildings are curvaceous; this can be seen on the river side in the asymmetrical crescent of the development's main building and on its southern side, in its spaceship-like

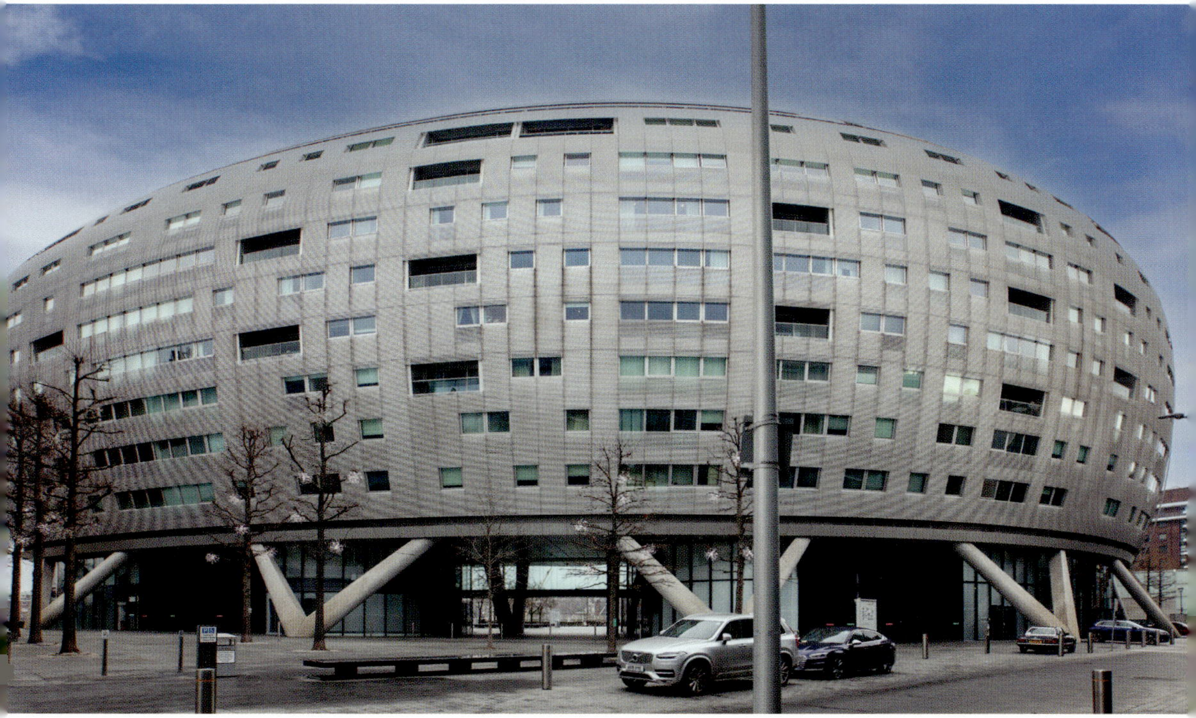

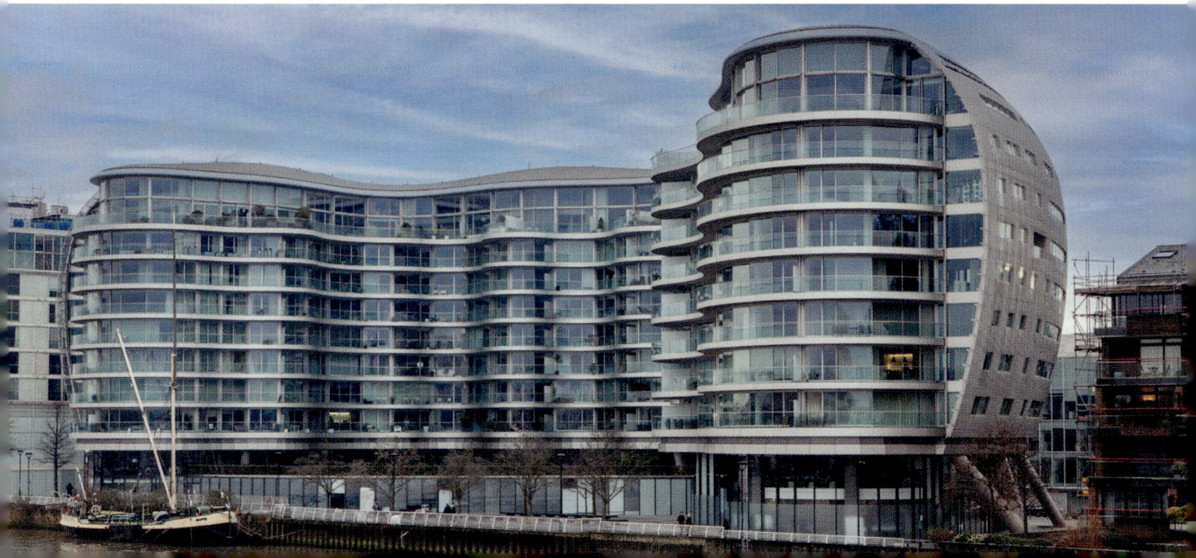

aluminium structure. Its spacious apartments and duplex penthouses are filled with natural light and those facing the Thames have the added benefit of balconies.

45. The Montevetro Building, No. 112 Battersea Church Road, SW11

The Montevetro Building west of Battersea Bridge was designed by another very famous architect, Baron Richard Rogers of Riverside. Like Norman Foster (see p. 84), his collection of high-tech architectural buildings since the late twentieth century has made an enormous contribution to the capital's architecture as well as to its skyline. In London his best-known works are probably the Lloyd's building and the Millennium Dome (now rebranded The O2) but he is acclaimed throughout the world for buildings such as the Pompidou Centre in Paris, The European Court of Human Rights Building in Strasbourg, Park 1 Tower in Seoul and a host of other buildings across the continents of North and South America, Asia and Europe. Sadly he passed away in 2021, but his architectural practice, Rogers Stirk Harbour + Partners endures and is now re-branded RSHP.

Montevetro, an Italian word meaning 'Glass Mountain' perfectly describes the residential development Rogers designed overlooking Battersea Reach. Sitting beside St Mary's Battersea (see Building 4) it is a most imposing structure built over five linked blocks and varies in height between four and nineteen storeys, the tallest of which lies on the north-east side. The building is almost entirely made of glass, and all the apartments are fitted out with floor to ceiling windows. Many of them are fortunate to have large balconies and thus have marvellous views of the river. Facilities are top class and Montevetro offers its residents a health and leisure club with its own outdoor tennis courts, gym and saunas, a twenty-four-hour concierge service, as well as private gardens.

The Montevetro Building.

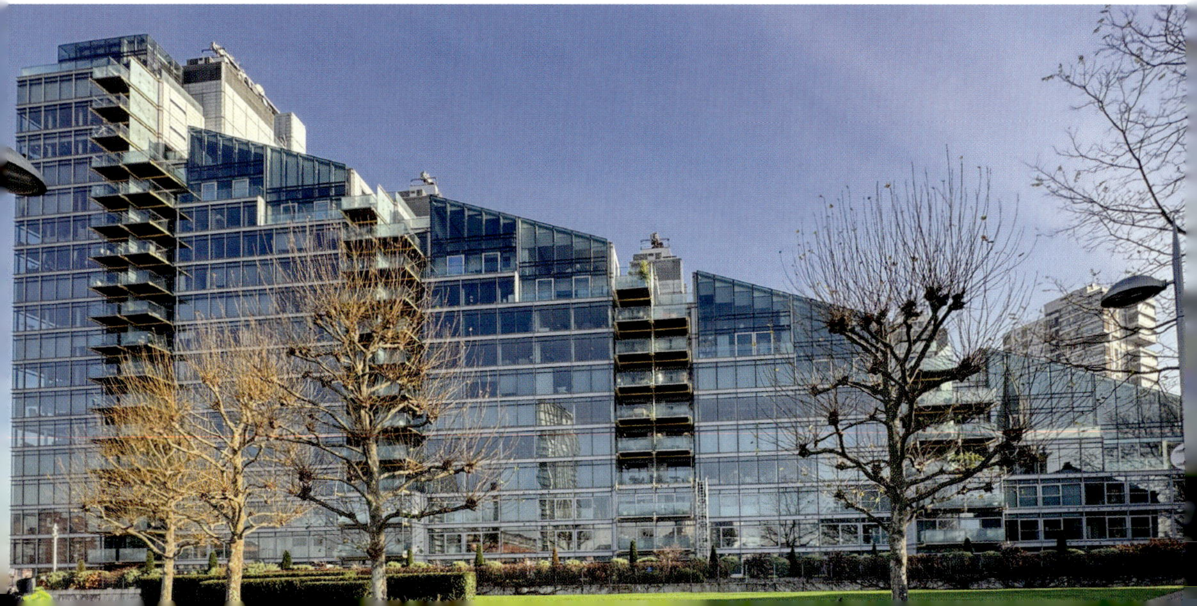

It is difficult to believe that this area beside the Thames was once heavily industrialised. In the late nineteenth century it was home to factories, chemical works, a foundry, a corn mill, a malt house, Price's Candles factory and many wharfs for shipping. From the late 1780s until 1997 there was a mill where Montevetro stands today, initially grinding linseed to produce linseed oil but latterly it produced flour, part of the Rank Hovis McDougall group. It finally closed in 1992 and was demolished five years later paving the way for the future regeneration of the area.

46. St John's Therapy Centre, No. 162 St John's Hill, Battersea, SW11

With its name prominently displayed on the building's façade and clad in warm reddish-brown wooden panels, St John's Therapy Centre really stands out in the street. It was designed by the architects Buschow Henley, renowned for their work in the health care sector and commissioned under a government initiative which involves the Primary Care Trusts (PCTs) and private companies working together to improve GP surgeries and community health buildings. It is both an attractive and functional building that is defined by its rectilinear frontage, its large expanse of wall and the asymmetry of its windows. The inside too has a definite character – the architects have designed a building that is constructed around two cloistered courtyards, making it easier for patients and staff to navigate around the centre, and ensures that natural daylight floods into the interior rooms.

St John's Therapy Centre is home nowadays to two GP practices, specialises in looking after accident and stroke victims and runs a mental health unit for alcohol and drug addiction. The present building dates to the early 2000s but there has

St John's Therapy Centre.

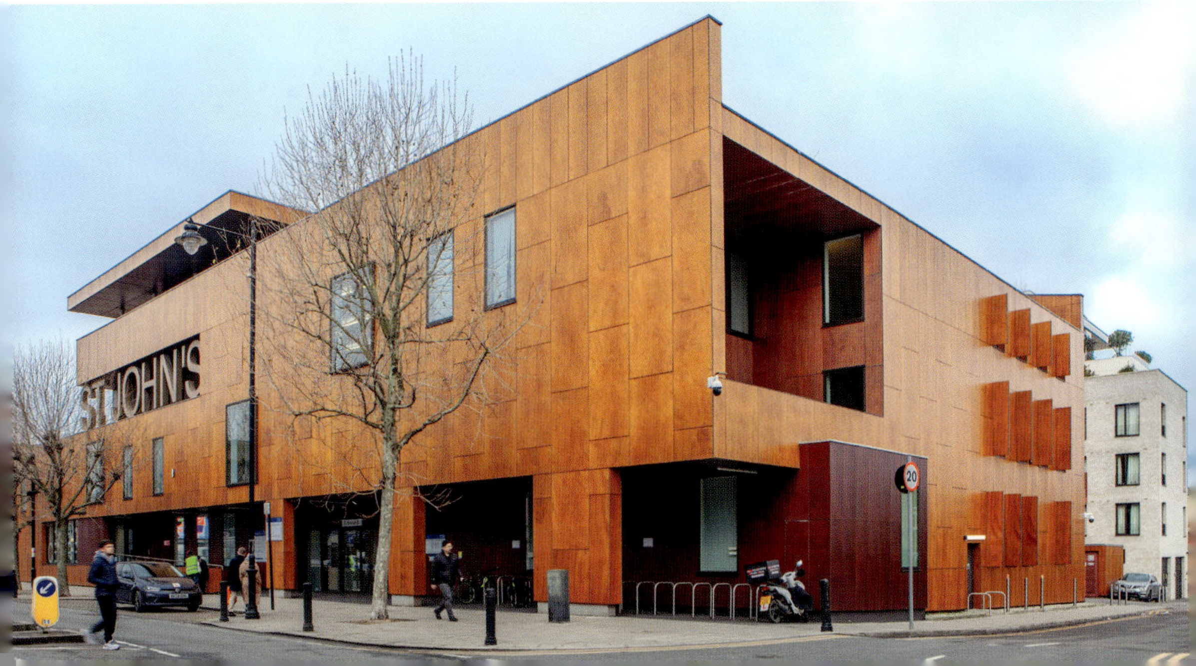

been welfare provision on this site since the early nineteenth century, originally as a workhouse, and subsequently as St John's Hospital.

47. Clapham Manor School, Belmont Road, Clapham, SW4

Clapham Manor School was built in the late nineteenth century when society was undergoing major transformation due to industrial and social changes of the time and the need to educate children became increasingly pressing. This led to the passing of the Education Act 1870, the first piece of legislation to deal specifically with the provision of education in England and Wales. Following its enactment 'board schools', the earliest state-run schools, were established. These schools, managed by elected school boards and funded through the rates, gave their name to schools up and down the length of the country. The Clapham Manor School on Belmont Road was typical of the period; a handsome building, three storeys high and brick built, set up to educate children living in and around the surrounding streets.

Today, the school is a primary school and designated 'outstanding' by Ofsted. As a result of its prestigious ranking in the early 2000s, the school grew from being a one-to two-form entry school, which naturally put pressure on its facilities and classroom space. So much so, that it commissioned the architectural practice dRMM to build it a wing that would not only extend the learning spaces within the site but also complement the old building. Consultations held with the local community and local authority revealed that the success of the school was largely

Clapham Manor School.

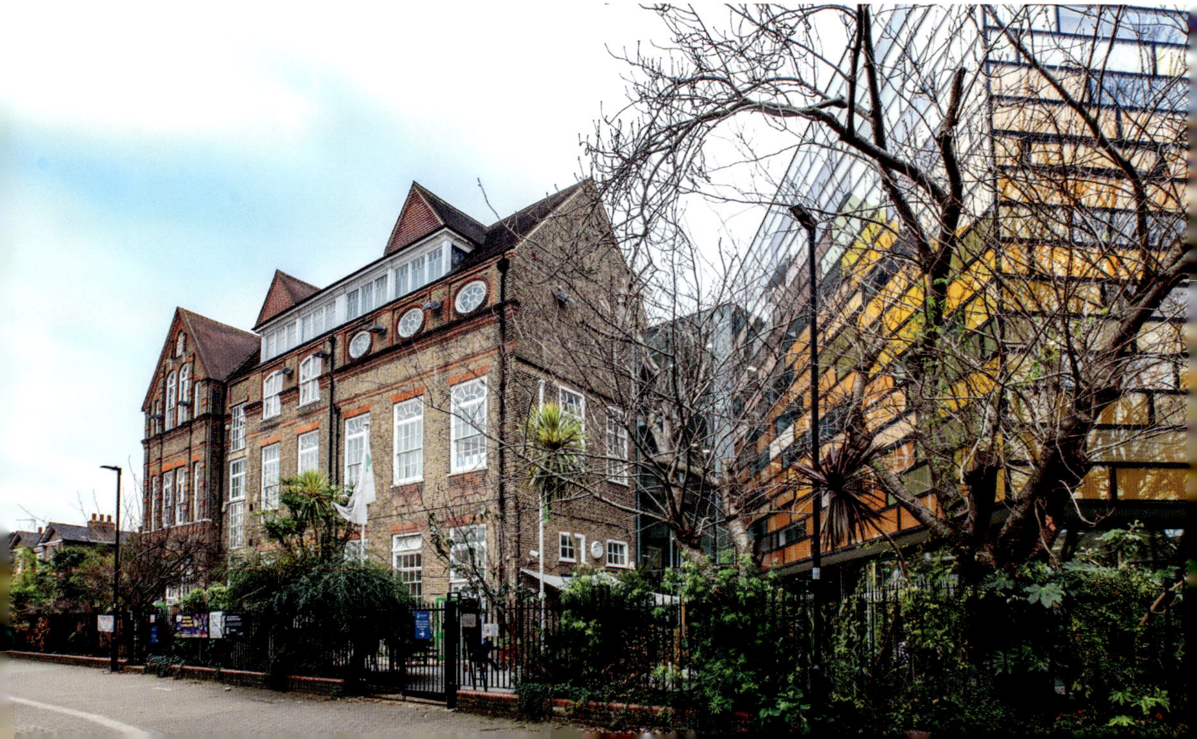

thought to be because everything was under one roof. So, the architects proposed a freestanding building that would connect directly into the existing school and provide a new and more secure school entrance. The extension built consists of a dynamic triple-height atrium that divides the new building from the old and includes a glazed lift with a fully exposed mechanism. The four new contemporary floors simply merge with the original three-storey school via walkways and stairs.

Undoubtedly the most stunning feature of the new wing is its polychromatic façade made from fritted glass in a wonderful melange of oranges, yellows, greens and blues. Remarkably, this highly modern glazed building sits well beside the Victorian school and has won many architectural awards for its design.

48. Mary Seacole House and The Library Building, Clapham High Street, SW4

For more than a decade this unique structure, now a real Clapham landmark, has dominated both the street and skyline around Clapham High Street with its exceptional curves and building blocks. Designed by architects Studio Egret West, the building is quirky in that it has no corners, is comprised of three sculpted masses and is 'stepped' in shape. There are some interesting semi-circular roof terraces as well as a communal roof garden on the seventh and

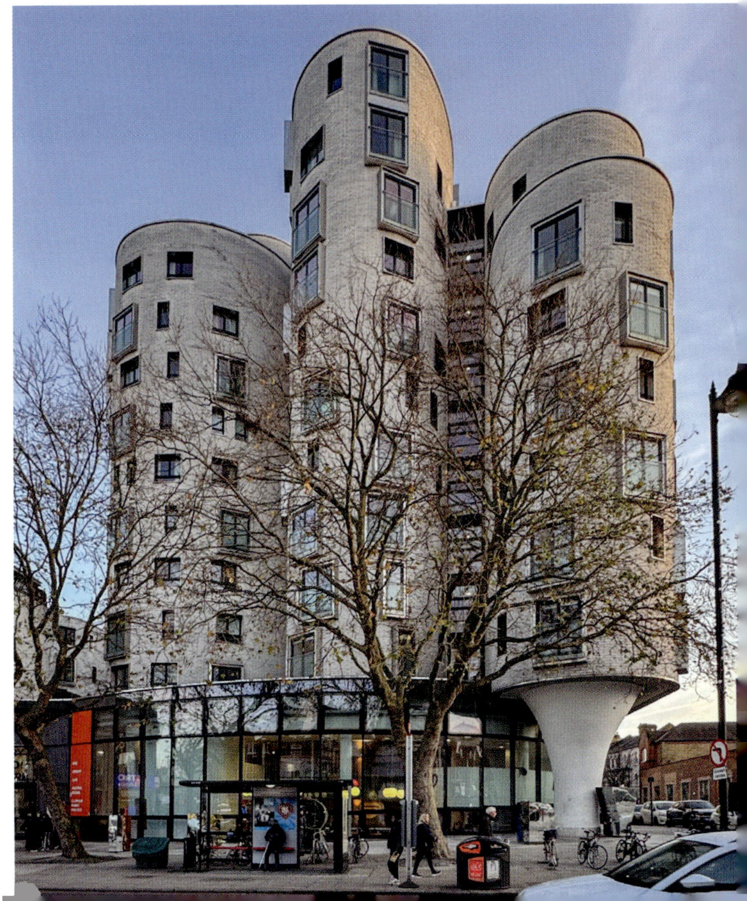

Mary Seacole House and the library building.

eighth floors. Known as Mary Seacole House (it replaced a former office block of the same name) its name commemorates the celebrated Jamaican-born nurse who looked after sick and wounded British soldiers during the Crimean War in the mid-1850s.

The building was a joint venture between Lambeth Council and the Cathedral Group to improve facilities in the neighbourhood and today provides a range of community amenities including a state-of-the-art library, a nursery, a café and a Primary Care Trust (PCT). These facilities are all based in the building's lower floors whilst the PCT is located at the back and occupies a single-storey building. The library entrance with its high atrium is a vast area, sometimes used as a performance space. Its bold spiral drum-shaped design is probably the library's most distinctive feature, with a ramp swirling down to the children's library and upwards to the reading room above. The eleven residential floors above this are known as the Library Building and filled with one- and two-bedroom apartments. All have great character with at least one room containing a curved wall, and some even offer dual-aspect rooms from which there are excellent views of the area. The apartments are stylish, built to a high standard and residents have access to bicycle storage, basement car parking and concierge services.

Since opening in 2012 Mary Seacole House and the Library Building development has proved to be a great success for the local community, providing much needed quality accommodation along with modern community facilities in the heart of Clapham's town centre.

49. Battersea Power Station Village: Circus West Village, Prospect Place and Battersea Roof Gardens, SW11

The regeneration of Battersea Power Station was not simply a repurposing of the station itself, but was part of an enormous project to create an entirely new village around the building, thus revitalising the land immediately beside it and along the river front. The project, masterminded by Rafael Viñoly Architects, was to be carried out in phases, and designs for the buildings delivered by some of the world's most highly acclaimed architects. The first phase constructed was Circus West Village which opened in 2017, five years before the power station's launch. Its architects, SimpsonHaugh and Partners, and dRMM combined talents to produce two striking glazed residential buildings that have an undulating façade and sit at the western edge of the power station site. These contain more than 850 homes in addition to office and retail space. Underneath the apartments at ground level Circus West Village offers residents, office workers and visitors a wide array of restaurants, cafés, and bars, and cultural activities some of which are housed in the railway arches nearby.

The next stage in the process, referred to as the High Street phase, owes its design to the renowned architectural practices of Frank Gehry and Norman Foster.

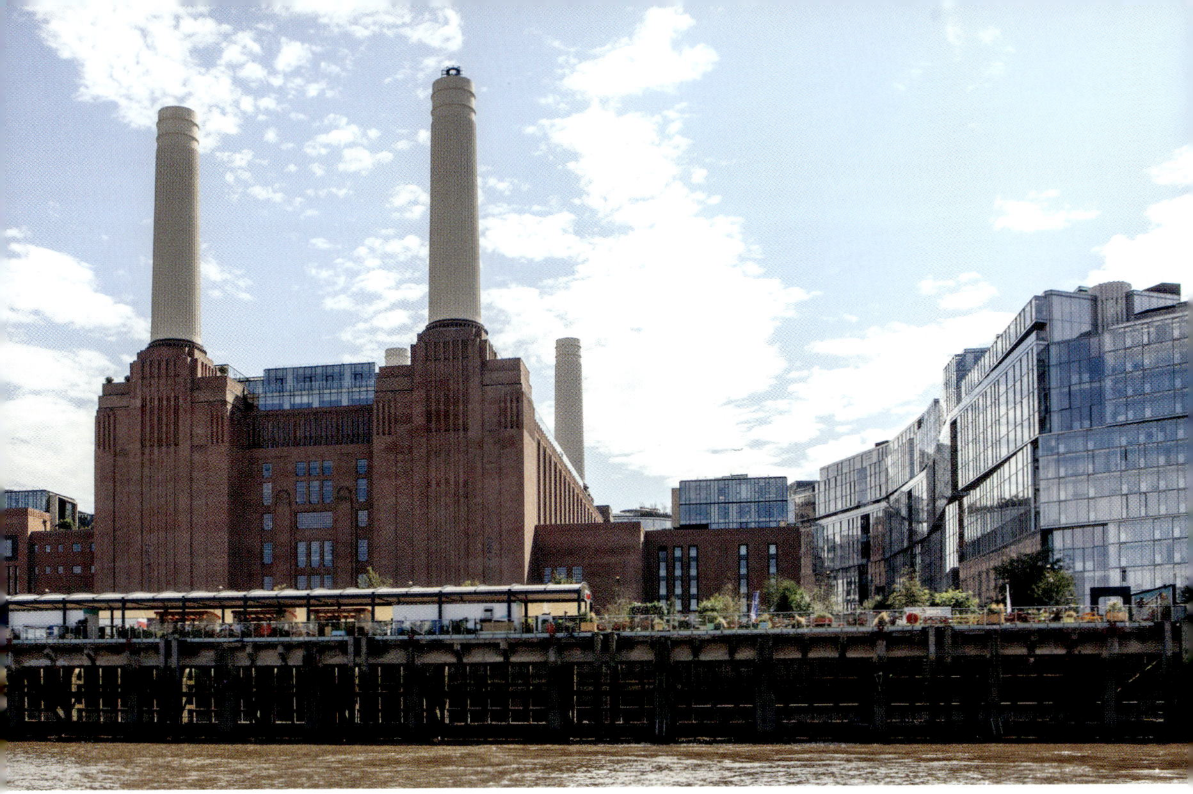

Above: Circus West Village at Battersea Power Station.

Right: Electric Boulevard.

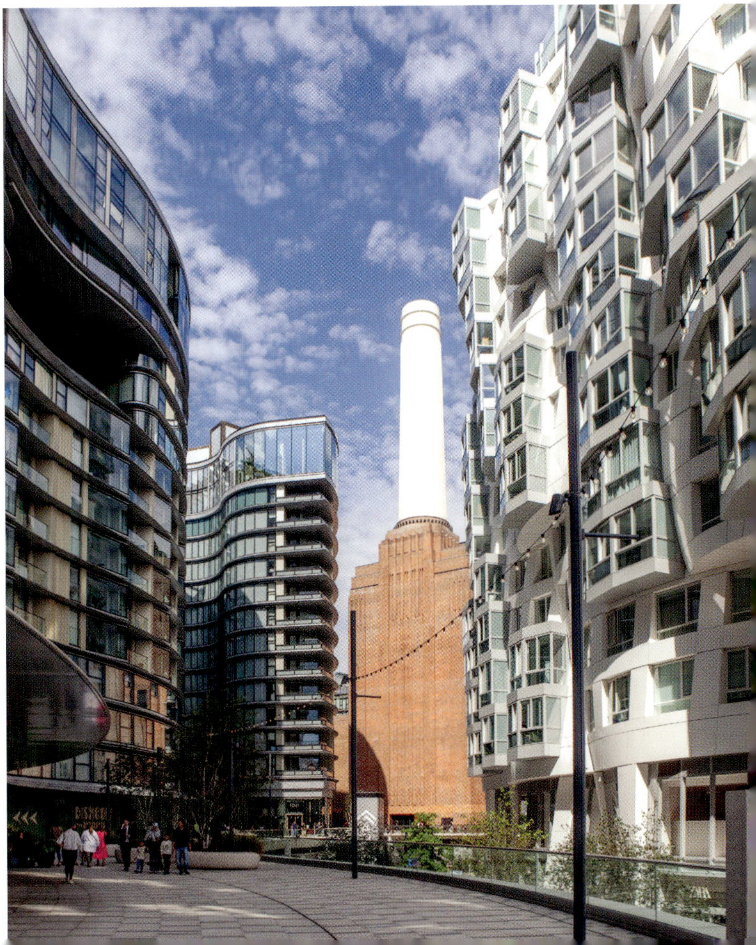

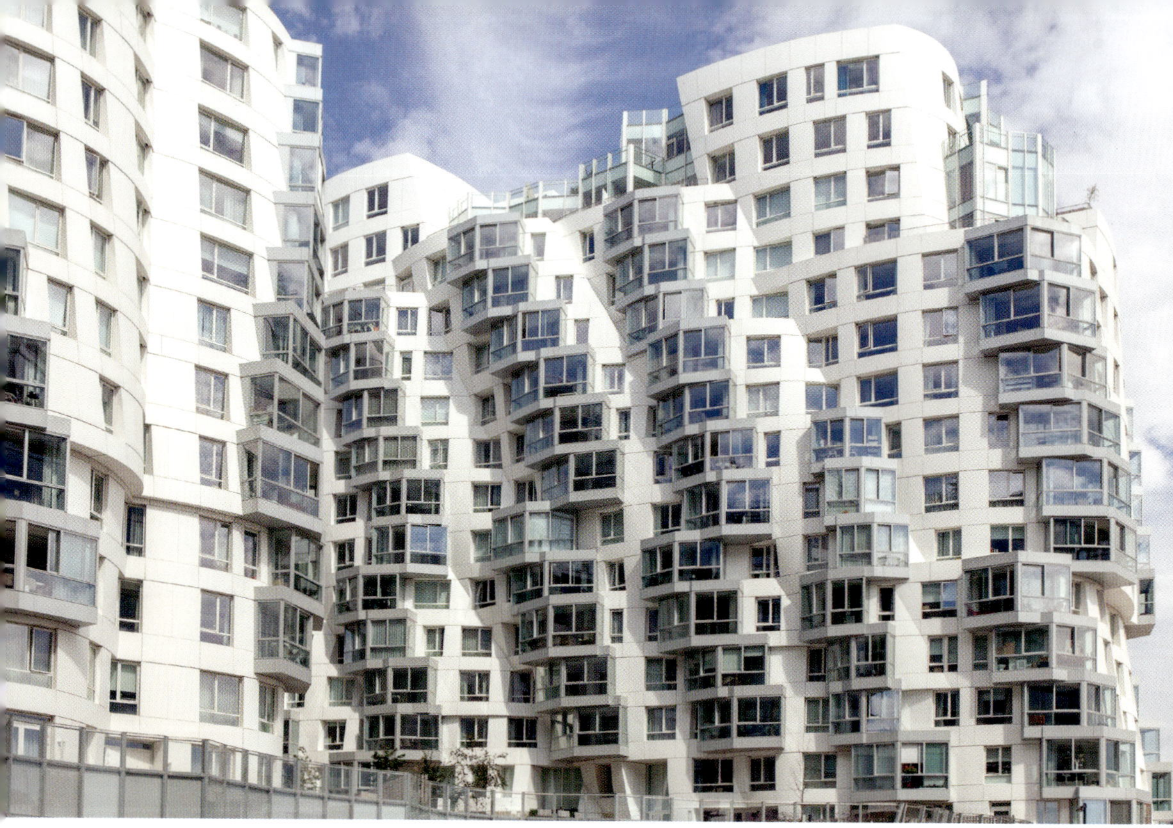

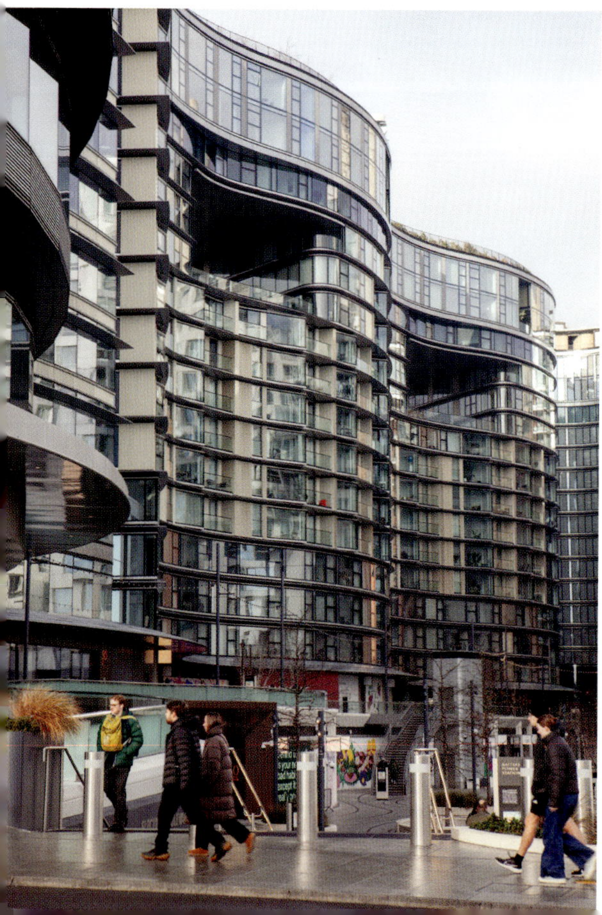

Above: Prospect Place.

Left: Battersea Roof Gardens.

These two phenomenally successful and innovative practices have collaborated to create Electric Boulevard, the power station complex's new main shopping street. The architects have also designed housing and retail space on either side of it – Gehry Partners to the east and Foster + Partners to the west. The former, known as Prospect Place, is Gehry's first residential project in the UK and, in keeping with many of his buildings, is immediately eye-catching. The practice has produced two stunning buildings with rippled white façades and large windows in Gehry's hallmark deconstructivist style, which stand out markedly against the industrial appearance of the power station nearby.

Foster's Battersea Roof Gardens development complements neighbouring Prospect Place with its own rolling shape that hugs the length of Electric Boulevard. In addition to providing more than 400 apartments the building is home to 'art'otel London Battersea Power Station' with its awesome rooftop garden developed by LDA Design along with James Corner, creator of the New York High Line.

50. The Royal College of Arts Campus, No. 1 Hester Road, Battersea, SW11

The Royal College of Art (RCA) has had a major presence in Battersea since 2009 when its Painting School was built in Howie Street. Further expansion took place in 2012 when the Dyson Building opened, and again in 2015 with the addition of the Woo Building. All three buildings were designed by architects Haworth

Dyson Building, the Royal College of Arts.

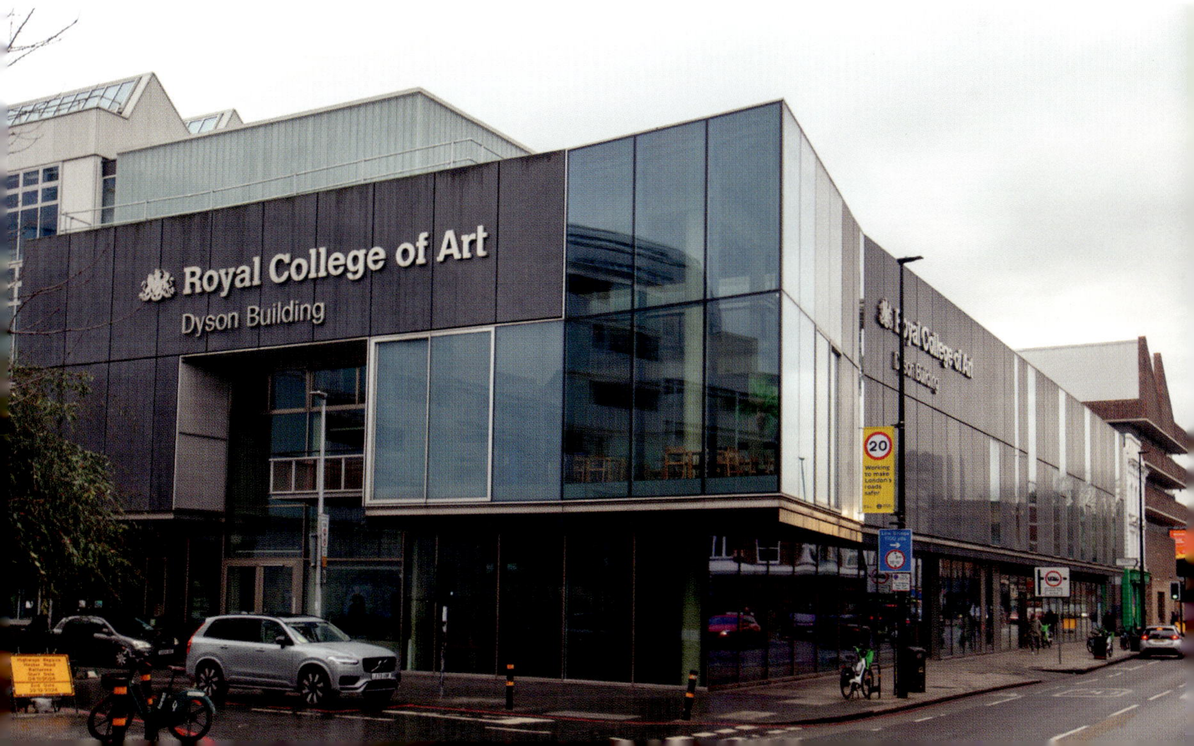

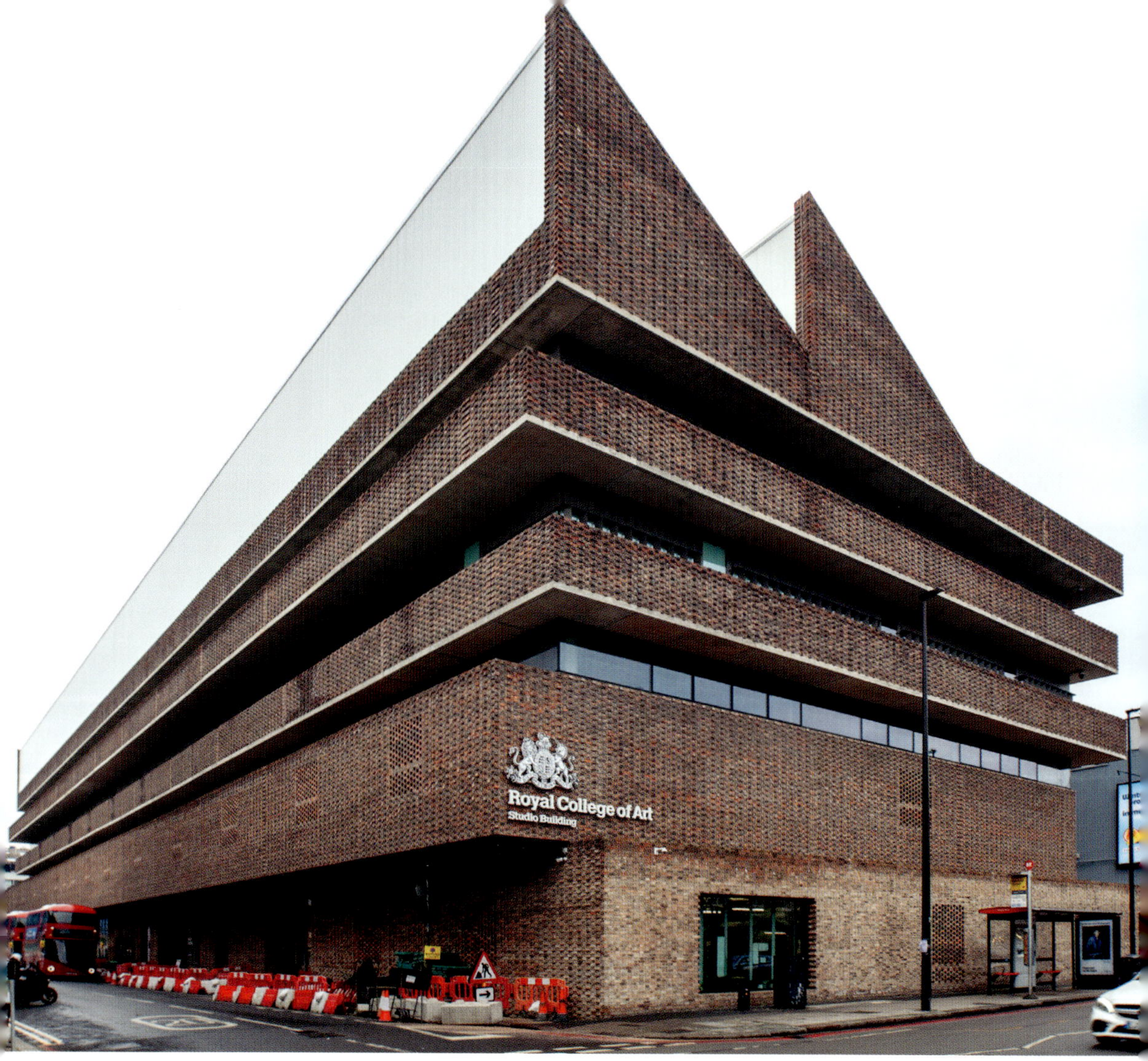

Herzog and de Meuron's Studio Building, the Royal College of Arts.

Tompkins to provide the college with functional, contemporary buildings befitting the world's most influential, postgraduate university of art and design. The Battersea campus that has been created consists of specialist workshops and studios for painting, printing and photography, ceramic and glass, jewellery and metalwork. The Dyson and Woo buildings are linked, with the workshops and studios organised visibly around a long central 'machine hall'.

The RCA, having forged itself a new path into the areas of Science, Technology, Engineering and Maths, was awarded a one-off government grant of £54 million in 2016. This resulted in the commissioning of architects Herzog and de Meuron (known for their work at Tate Modern and its extension) to design a new Design and Innovation campus on Battersea Bridge Road. The building, with its perforated brick exterior, is instantly identifiable while its interior has been designed specifically to promote flexibility of use.

Acknowledgements

The author would like to thank all the people and organisations that have facilitated the production of this book. In particular to acknowledge the help and assistance given by Apple Europe, Battersea Arts Centre, Battersea Power Station, Bolingbroke Academy, St Luke's Church Battersea, St Mark's Church Battersea, St Mary's RC Church Clapham, St Paul's Church Clapham, the Alexandra Hotel, the Clapham Grand, the Falcon Pub, and the Windmill Inn and Hotel.

I cannot emphasise enough the enormous role played by my husband, Alex McMurdo, whose many images are displayed within the book. He has been a continual support whilst the book was being written and has accompanied me on numerous walks along the streets of Battersea and Clapham. I am further indebted to him, Jo and Emily for taking the time to proofread the text, for their feedback and constructive criticism.

I would also like to take this opportunity to thank Amberley Publishing for commissioning the book, and to acknowledge the excellent support and hard work of Jenny Bennett, Nick Grant, Becky Cadenhead and the team.

About the Author

Lucy McMurdo is a modern history graduate and native Londoner who has lived in the capital all her life. In 2003 when she qualified as a London Blue Badge Tourist Guide, she combined two of her major loves, history and London, and has been sharing her knowledge of the city with local and foreign visitors ever since. Always keen to explore and learn about London's secrets, she spends many hours 'walking the streets' looking out for hidden corners, unusual curiosities as well as architecturally significant buildings and ones that have a story to tell.

Lucy's tour-guiding career began over forty years ago when she first guided overseas visitors around the UK. Since then, in addition to tour guiding, she has been greatly involved in training and examining the next generation of tour guides. She has created, taught and run courses in London's University of Westminster and City University and also developed guide-training programmes for the warders and site guides at Hampton Court Palace.

Most recently Lucy has been writing about the city she is so passionate about and is the author of twelve London guidebooks: *Chelsea in 50 Buildings*, *Shoreditch and Hoxton in 50 Buildings*, *Secret Islington and Clerkenwell*, *Southwark and Blackfriars in 50 Buildings*, *City of London in 50 Buildings*, *Hampstead and Highgate in 50 Buildings*, *Islington and Clerkenwell in 50 Buildings*, *Chiswick in 50 Buildings*, *Bloomsbury in 50 Buildings*, *Explore London's Square Mile*, *Streets of London* and *London in 7 Days*.